Reiki FOR DUMMIES®

by Nina L. Paul, PhD

WILEY

Wiley Publishing, Inc.

Reiki For Dummies®

Published by
Wiley Publishing, Inc.
111 River St.
Hoboken, NJ 07030-5774
www.wiley.com

Copyright © 2006 by Wiley Publishing, Inc., Indianapolis, Indiana

Published by Wiley Publishing, Inc., Indianapolis, Indiana

Published simultaneously in Canada

For general information on our other products and services, please contact our Customer Care Department within the U.S. at 877-762-2974, outside the U.S. at 317-572-3993, or fax 317-572-4002.

For technical support, please visit www.wiley.com/techsupport.

Wiley also publishes its books in a variety of electronic formats and by print-on-demand. Some content that appears in standard print versions of this book may not be available in other formats. For more information about Wiley products, visit us at www.wiley.com.

Library of Congress Control Number: 2005932584

ISBN-13: 978-0-7645-9907-1

ISBN 978-0-7645-9907-1 (pbk); ISBN 978-0-470-22175-4 (ebk); ISBN 978-0-471-78583-5 (ebk); ISBN 978-1-118-05474-1 (ebk)

Manufactured in the United States of America

10 9 8

1B/RV/RR/QY/IN

WILEY

About the Author

Nina L. Paul, PhD, has worked in the field of science and health communication for over 20 years. She started down this path at SUNY Purchase, where she received her bachelor's degree in biology and performed research in the field of neuroimmunology. She also published articles for her college newspaper on scientific research topics.

After working in medical publishing at Rockefeller University Press (*Journal of Clinical Investigation*), she received her master's degree and PhD in infectious disease epidemiology (the study of diseases) and immunology from Yale University.

After leaving Yale, Nina pursued postdoctoral research in London and Oxford, England. Nina's research focused on human immunodeficiency virus (HIV) and related viruses and their interaction with the immune system.

Nina also taught science to schoolchildren of different ages and abilities in New Mexico and volunteered at a hospital-based Cancer Information Centre in England. She worked in the field of evidence-based medicine and contributed to the Cochrane Library (a medical database). She is also the author of *Living with Hepatitis C For Dummies*.

Nina believes in a multifaceted approach to health. She became a master of Reiki, which is a universal life-force energy that is transmitted through the hands. She is both a practitioner and a teacher of Reiki and uses Reiki as a way to help herself and others. Check out Nina's Web site at www.ninapaul.info.

Dedication

I dedicate this book to my father, Marvin Paul, the greatest of them all.

Author's Acknowledgments

I thank my teachers:

In England, to Sissel Fowler, my yoga and meditation teacher in Oxford with whom I first studied energy work.

In New Mexico: the amazing Ivan Scheier who ran the Stillpoint Healing Center in Truth or Consequences (T or C), New Mexico and still provides Reiki training and healing to many; Rose Kennedy and Jane Alderson who were my first Reiki teachers.

In Oregon: Kathleen McKevitt on the Oregon coast taught me about mastering Reiki.

In New York: Kathie Lipinski, with whom I learned to teach Reiki and pass attunements to others.

My friends and Reiki pals who, as Reiki teachers, practitioners, masters, students, or recipients, have taught me so much and whose wisdom has landed in these pages:

Anna Maria Soto; Anita D'Onofrio; Barbara Baudouin; Barbara Cali; Barbara Leete; Barbara Lynch; Barry Goodman; Bonnie Caponi; Caroline Aldiss; Laura Maglio; Donna and Al Maldonado; Jada Prane; Joan Schwart; Joseph Cassles; Joseph Natoli; Katie McGowan; Nathan, Noah, and Anna Kasmanoff; Raven Valencia; Rebecca Sularski; Robin and Charlie Liffman; Teri and Sandy Sarin; Vicky Lewis; Wendy Nine, and many others not named here.

I acknowledge the Reiki historians and authors who have sought to keep Reiki alive and healthy for the benefit of all.

I thank the excellent editorial staff at Wiley: Mikal Belicove, acquisitions editor, who got this project started; Natalie Harris, project editor, who calmly kept the ball rolling through thick and thin; and Tina Sims, copy editor, who caught the inconsistencies. I also thank Jill St. Ambrogio for her technical review of the book and Kathryn Born for her wonderful illustrations. I thank my agent June Clark for her guidance and support.

I am particularly grateful for the love and support of my family and close friends, furry and otherwise, who have kept me going in every which way.

Publisher's Acknowledgments

We're proud of this book; please send us your comments through our Dummies online registration form located at www.dummies.com/register/.

Some of the people who helped bring this book to market include the following:

Acquisitions, Editorial, and Media Development

Project Editor: Natalie Faye Harris

Acquisitions Editor: Mikal Belicove

Senior Copy Editor: Tina Sims

Editorial Program Assistant: Courtney Allen

Technical Editor: Jill St. Ambrogio, RMT

Editorial Manager: Michelle Hacker

Editorial Assistants: Hanna Scott, Nadine Bell, David Lutton

Illustrator: Kathryn Born

Cover Photos: © image100/Getty Images

Cartoons: Rich Tennant, www.the5thwave.com

Composition Services

Project Coordinator: Adrienne Martinez

Layout and Graphics: Andrea Dahl, Lauren Goddard, Stephanie D. Jumper, Barbara Moore, Melanee Prendergast, Heather Ryan, Mary Gillot Virgin

Proofreaders: Leeann Harney, Aptara

Indexer: Aptara

Publishing and Editorial for Consumer Dummies

    Kathleen Nebenhaus, Vice President and Executive Publisher

    Kristin Ferguson-Wagstaffe, Product Development Director

    Ensley Eikenburg, Associate Publisher, Travel

    Kelly Regan, Editorial Director, Travel

Publishing for Technology Dummies

    Andy Cummings, Vice President and Publisher

Composition Services

    Debbie Stailey, Director of Composition Services

Contents at a Glance

Table of Contents

Introduction

The touch of a hand is increasingly recognized as being important and also absent in much of modern medicine. Reiki as an alternative and complementary therapy provides the soothing comfort of human touch. This can make a world of difference to someone in pain. Reiki is the energy of love that never ends. You can experience the bliss of Reiki as a recipient and receive healing that is channeled through another. Or you can learn Reiki yourself to boost your personal growth and enlightenment.

Reiki has gained in popularity as more people seek solutions to personal and global problems. You might have tried meditation and yoga or even massage. Reiki is a natural partner to these and other healing practices. The person to thank for the Reiki healing system is a Japanese man named Mikao Usui (1865–1926). He developed the original Reiki system that has blossomed into a multitude of worldwide branches. What is common to all Reiki systems is the channeling of the Reiki life-force energy.

Reiki comes from a higher source — call it God, higher power, creator, or spirit. A series of simple initiations turns on your Reiki "light switch," which gives you the lifelong ability to channel Reiki energy. The benefit you get from Reiki and how much you can help others depend on how often and with what intent you use Reiki. The more you use Reiki, the more you get out of it.

Reiki connects you with the ultimate source of healing at all levels. If you desire peace, consciousness, healing, or enlightenment, then Reiki is for you.

About This Book

Reiki may not seem like a down-to-earth subject, but this is a down-to-earth book about Reiki. The open-access style of the *For Dummies* series makes this comprehensive book on Reiki pleasant to navigate and use.

Reading this book doesn't make you a Reiki practitioner, but you can use this book as a reference and guide as you use Reiki in your own life and to help others.

Offering a worldwide perspective

Reiki is practiced all over the globe, and the Reiki techniques presented in this book include those commonly used from both Western and Japanese lineages. Many classes and sessions today incorporate techniques from both types of Reiki. Japanese Reiki is becoming more popular as previously unknown Japanese practitioners present their version of Reiki in Japan, and in the West. So both Western and Japanese Reiki classes are taught worldwide.

The most well-known Reiki lineage passed from Mikao Usui to Chujiro Hayashi to Hawayo Takata of Hawaii. The students of Takata then taught more students, who became the major source of so-called Western Reiki. My Reiki teachers came from this initial lineage.

I include a discussion of chakra-energy systems even though these weren't part of Usui's original teaching. I think this information helps you to see how the Reiki energy system fits into other energy systems that are used today.

Illustrating symbols and positions

You find the four basic Reiki symbols and some additional nontraditional Reiki symbols illustrated in this book. This information was previously considered secret — to be revealed only after paying a teacher. More and more authors of Reiki material choose to include this information and make the distinction between sacred and secret. The Reiki symbols are sacred. I hope that you take the information on the symbols along with other information in this book in the manner in which it is offered: with deep respect for the people who have come before me, and those who come after me in Reiki.

You find ample illustrations of not only the Reiki symbols but also the Reiki hand positions (for treating yourself or treating another).

If you find a discrepancy between a symbol or illustrations here and what you are taught, I suggest you follow the guidance of your Reiki teacher.

Examining personal stories

Reiki is miraculous in that it can help you transform illness or difficulties in your life. But the exact nature of the miracles that Reiki provides differs from person to person. Reiki may help one person recover from cancer, and another may reach a place of peace and die. One person may find that his marriage is rejuvenated, and another may decide to live apart from his mate.

Because of the individuality of the response to Reiki, I don't include Reiki miracle stories. What may work in one way for you will work in a different way for someone else. I don't want you to read that one woman overcame her infertility with Reiki and think it will work for you that way too. Instead, maybe you're meant to adopt a child who is waiting for you somewhere. You get the picture? Reiki will bring you to *your* highest outcome, whatever that might be.

In terms of my own story, Reiki is a major tool that helps me in every single area. But this book is not about me; like Reiki, this book is coming through me. I add my personal experience where I think it can help the reader in his life. I also include a few other personal stories, in sidebars, to give you a sense of the variety of responses to Reiki.

Conventions Used in This Book

Different Reiki practitioners use different terminology to cover the topics of Reiki, and here are the terms I've chosen to use in this book:

- The person who receives Reiki is called the Reiki *recipient.*
- The person who gives Reiki is called the Reiki *practitioner.*
- Higher power, God, or Universal Energy is called *spirit.*
- Because a Reiki recipient or practitioner can be male or female, I use both the *he* and *she* pronouns throughout the text.

You'll also notice some changes in text font to get your attention:

- The first time I define a term in the chapter, I *italicize* the word.
- I use **boldface** to emphasize action steps.
- When I list Web addresses, I use `monofont`.

What You're Not to Read

Go ahead and read the chapters that interest you. Or, if you're using this book for a Reiki class, read the chapters your teacher recommends. What you do with the other chapters is your own business. What's nice is that you have the information on your bookshelf when you need it.

Also, note that the information presented in sidebars is incidental to the main chapter and you can skip them if you want.

Foolish Assumptions

I assume that you, the reader of this book, fall into at least one of the following categories:

- ✔ You're curious to find out more about Reiki.
- ✔ You're considering trying Reiki for yourself or a family member.
- ✔ You're looking into taking Reiki classes.
- ✔ You want a book to guide you through classes and the beginning of your Reiki practice.

You might be one of the following:

- ✔ **A skeptic who is open minded:** "I'll reserve final judgment until I've read the book or tried it out."
- ✔ **A newbie to Reiki:** "I want to know more about Reiki. Bring it on."
- ✔ **A New-Age aficionado:** "I'm open to just about anything. I want to add Reiki to the techniques I already use."

I'm assuming that you also may be saying, "I'm smart, but I really don't know much about this subject and don't want to spend too much effort getting the information I need to know." In order for you to get this most from this book, I'd like to assume that you're doing the following:

- ✔ Keeping an open mind to the possibility that Reiki can help you
- ✔ Seeing whatever concept you have of God, higher power, universal energy, or spirit as the source of Reiki energy
- ✔ Using Reiki to build upon and supplement your own personal growth and healing practices
- ✔ Being ready to make some changes in your life and let Reiki help you do that
- ✔ Taking what you like from the book (and Reiki) and leaving the rest

Reiki can work for everyone, even someone who doesn't believe in it. The only person for whom Reiki doesn't work is the person who doesn't *want* Reiki. And that's okay, if that's you. Come back if you change your mind.

How This Book Is Organized

Reiki information is separated into the following parts so you can easily find what you need.

Part 1: Discovering Reiki

I provide Reiki basics and background information in this section. The system of Reiki is traced from Mikao Usui's founding of Reiki in Japan to developing Reiki branches all over the world. Though Reiki is an "energy medicine" with similarities to other systems, Reiki has distinctive features that separate it from other energy-healing techniques. The Reiki principles, which were delineated by Usui, are another common feature of all Reiki branches, and they have their own chapter in this part.

Part 11: Experiencing Reiki for Yourself

To experience Reiki is to know a feeling of bliss. Everyone deserves this feeling of absolute harmony, which will keep you coming back for more. Anyone in your family can use Reiki at any age for any cause. Even your pets will appreciate a Reiki treatment to help them with an illness or just as a general energy boost. In this part, find out what a Reiki session feels like and what you can expect. Hint: Expect the unexpected!

Part 111: Becoming Well-Versed in Reiki

Going farther with Reiki means taking Reiki classes, and I explain the many varieties in this part. I include information about the Reiki symbols (2nd-degree Reiki and beyond), techniques to channel and use the Reiki energy to help others, and methods to give yourself Reiki. As a fun addition to this part, I include information on adding crystals to a Reiki practice.

Part 1V: Sharing Reiki with Others

When you have your Reiki practice under your belt, you'll want to contribute to the well-being of others on either a volunteer or professional basis. This part describes how to structure a Reiki session and start using Reiki professionally. You may want to join or start your own Reiki shares or circles or bring Reiki to your local hospital. Reiki has the ability to pass through time and space, so you find out how to use Reiki to heal events all over the world, and even in the past or future. Reiki is a natural companion to many therapeutic treatments, including surgery, chemotherapy, radiation, massage, psychotherapy, and chiropractic work, so practitioners from these other therapies can find ways to use Reiki to help their patients and clients.

Part V: The Part of Tens

This traditional part of the Dummies series lists information in accessible lists of ten. You find uses for Reiki in everyday life, tips to apply Reiki for personal growth, a list of Reiki myths, and ten extra nontraditional Reiki-inspired symbols.

After the Part of Tens, I provide an appendix of Web sites, books, and other contact information to help you go farther with Reiki. That same appendix includes the International Association of Reiki Professionals Code of Ethics. After the appendix is a glossary of Reiki terms in one convenient place.

Icons Used in This Book

Icons are the little drawings in the margins of the book that are designed to draw your attention to certain topics. They serve as guides to the type of information being provided.

I use this icon to accentuate information that is most important to a particular topic. The remember icon highlights the take-home information.

I don't use this icon often, but if you see it, you know that I'm giving you some nonessential information. You don't have to read it, but of course, if you're hungry for everything there is to know about Reiki, feel free to savor every word.

The Tip icon flags especially useful, practical information that can enhance your Reiki experience or practice.

Reiki doesn't involve any danger, so warnings are very few in this book. But if you see this icon, you should pay particular attention to the instructions to avoid harming yourself or others.

Where to Go from Here

The beauty of this book, like all *For Dummies* books, is that you can start reading any place you like. You can flip through the pages and see what page opens up first, or you can scan the Table of Contents for chapters of interest.

You can always read from Chapter 1 and continue onward, though I don't assume you'll read every single chapter or that you'll read the chapters in order. If you're totally new to Reiki, I suggest Chapter 1 for an overview of Reiki. Then you may want to jump to Chapters 5 and 6 to see what Reiki can do for you. I wish you a bountiful healing journey with Reiki!

Part I
Discovering Reiki

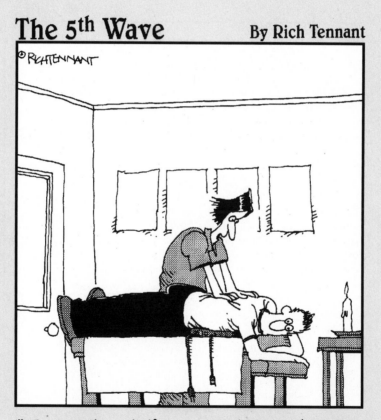

"You can lie on it if you want, but my channeling energy through your body's chakras isn't going to increase your laptop's battery life."

In this part . . .

Reiki is a natural and simple way to achieve healing at all levels: physical, emotional, mental, and spiritual. Reiki is a Japanese word for "spiritual energy," and the system of Reiki has evolved since it was founded by Mikao Usui in Japan. As Reiki has evolved through changes made by different Reiki masters, it still retains its essence: to provide healing to all who seek it.

This part includes basic information on what Reiki is and what it is not. You also find out about the founders of Reiki. In addition, I explain the five underlying principles of Reiki and how this energy system compares and contrasts with other types of energy healing.

Chapter 1

Reiki: The Art of Channeling Life-Force Energy

· ·

In This Chapter

▶ Getting a basic idea of what Reiki is — and isn't

▶ Finding out about Reiki's spiritual foundations

▶ Looking at Reiki as energy

▶ Discovering the origins of Reiki

▶ Seeing ways to experience Reiki

▶ Selecting a practitioner or teacher

▶ Listing the benefits of Reiki

▶ Revealing the symbols

▶ Merging New Age with Reiki

· ·

*Y*ou are deeply relaxed while lying on the Reiki table, as the practitioner lays her hands on different parts of your body. Impressed that this gentle laying on of hands can bring you such peace and joy, you want to know more about it. You've come to the right place, because this book is a guide to the basic practice of Reiki.

In this book, I describe how to use Reiki to heal yourself and your family members, and even treat people who are far away. Reiki techniques can also be used for your pets, your food, and the earth. The more you use Reiki, the more uses you'll find for it. In this chapter, you'll find out how Reiki works, where Reiki comes from, and what help Reiki can give you. You can even discover how to channel the Reiki energy yourself so that you have a lifelong tool to use for yourself and others.

In this chapter you get a taste of what Reiki is all about!

Discovering What Reiki Is and Isn't

Reiki is popping up all over the place, but lots of folks are still confused about what Reiki is exactly. In the context used in this book, Reiki is both:

- ✔ **A healing system that channels universal life-force energy:** This system was originally developed by Mikao Usui in the early 1900s in Japan. For more on Reiki's beginning, see "Exploring the History of Reiki," later in this chapter, and also Chapter 3.

- ✔ **The name of the energy itself:** *Rei* means spiritual wisdom, and *ki* means energy, so *Reiki* means spiritual energy. See Figure 1-1, which illustrates the word Reiki in Japanese characters.

Some people use the word Reiki as a verb, as in "I will Reiki him." What they are saying is, "I will give Reiki to him."

Reiki is available to everyone. Anyone of any age or illness level can receive Reiki. Even newborn babies or people at the end of life can benefit from the relaxation that Reiki provides. See Chapter 6 to find out how every member of your family, including your pets, can use and benefit from Reiki.

What Reiki is

In short, Reiki gives you what you need, whether it's a release of tension or an energy boost, or both. To help you more fully understand what Reiki gives you, here are some terms used to describe Reiki:

- ✔ **Gentle:** Reiki's touch is soft and light.

- ✔ **Harmless:** Reiki can have only positive results.

- ✔ **Natural:** You don't need any equipment or tools.

- ✔ **Healing:** The highest level of healing is the goal of Reiki.

- ✔ **Balancing:** Reiki will balance your energy levels.

- ✔ **Relaxing:** The top reason to try Reiki is to feel the bliss of deep relaxation.

- ✔ **Energizing:** If you're drained of energy, Reiki will revive you.

Figure 1-1:
The
Japanese
characters
for Reiki.

What Reiki isn't

Knowing what Reiki isn't is as important as knowing what it is:

✔ **Reiki is not religious.** Reiki is totally nondenominational. You can practice any religion (or none) and still use and benefit from Reiki. Founder Mikao Usui was influenced by the religions of his country, Shintoism and

Buddhism. But Reiki isn't associated with any religion, and people of all faiths and beliefs are Reiki practitioners. Reiki isn't New Age either (see the section "Combining New Age and Reiki," later in this chapter).

✔ **Reiki is not massage or reflexology.** Reiki is an energy-healing system and not a manipulative system (hands moving the body). Reiki is distinct from reflexology and massage. But Reiki is sometimes confused with other hands-on healing arts, especially reflexology. I'm not sure why; maybe it's because they both begin with the letter *r*.

Understanding the Spiritual Foundation of Reiki

Okay, I know in the previous section I say that Reiki isn't a religion, but it *is* spiritual. The distinction between spirituality and religion has caused a lot of confusion with regard to Reiki. These concepts are overlapping but separate. Here's what I mean:

Spirituality is the belief in your connection with the divine, no matter whether you call it a higher power, God, spirit, soul, or even the stars. The purpose of spiritual development is to improve this connection and see the divinity within yourself and all around you.

Religion provides guidance on how to develop yourself spiritually. It tells you what the divine looks like and gives you frameworks of texts, places of worship, and guides to support you.

You can be part of a religion and not have a spiritual connection. You can have a spiritual connection and not belong to a religion.

Reiki provides a means for spiritual growth. No matter what your religious background, you'll find that the principles are relevant and don't conflict with your religious practice. In fact, Reiki should enhance your personal religious connection. The spiritual aspects of Reiki enable you to do the following:

✔ **Connect to a higher source:** You use prayer and meditation to connect to God or the higher power of your own beliefs. Spiritual connection provides the never-ending supply of Reiki energy.

✔ **Channel the higher energy:** Reiki healing energy is not from the practitioner but comes *through* the practitioner from God or another higher power.

✔ **Keep spiritually healthy:** Just as you maintain your physical health with nutritious food, fresh air, and exercise, you also need to maintain your spiritual health. Prayer, meditation, quiet times, and spiritual exercise (doing kind acts) can help in this regard. Reiki uses the following spiritual tools: Reiki principles, meditation (see Chapter 9), and symbols and chanting (see Chapter 8).

Examining the Energy of Reiki

Reiki is a system of energy healing. You don't actually need to understand *how* the energy of the body works in order to use or benefit from Reiki, but it helps to know the basis for the way that Reiki works, which is examined in the following sections.

Defining universal energy

As a child, did you ever gaze at the stars with wonder and awe? The sun, the moon, the stars, and all the different life forms on our planet radiate an energy that is called a *universal energy*. Because this is the energy that animates humans and other living beings, it's called the *universal life-force energy*. This energy is known by different names. You can call it universal life-force energy, love, God, or spirit. For consistency throughout the book, I use the term *spirit*.

Reiki is a system that allows you to tap into and benefit from this universal energy.

Detecting subtle energy

When I talk about *subtle energy*, I am referring to the energy of Reiki and also the energy fields that are associated with your body. When something is subtle, it doesn't necessarily scream its presence, so you must get quiet to feel its presence. (In Chapter 2, I describe other types of subtle energy systems.)

Meditation is frequently used during Reiki training and before giving Reiki so you can get quiet enough to sense the presence of the Reiki energy (see Chapter 9).

Universal Reiki — with humor and humanity

One of my Reiki teachers wanted me to emphasize here that Reiki is practiced all the world over and that he thought there should be more humor with Reiki. On that note, he provided the following stories:

"My Italian barber wanted me to give him Reiki for his sore shoulder, which fortunately hadn't led to lopsided haircuts but, on the other hand, wasn't helping his singing any. Appreciative of Reiki help, he nevertheless wondered why we didn't do it like his grandmother (a contemporary of Mikao Usui; see Chapter 3), who had learned it from her grandmother. On invited demonstration, he moved his hands faster than most Reiki practitioners usually do, but the same good feeling was there, with a flavor of Italian sunshine."

"Charlie, a Native American Reiki student, gently advised me one day that in his tribe what we called Reiki was a way of life and part of the culture he grew up with — no special training or certificates needed. Soon after, sorrowfully, we gave Charlie a farewell Reiki session, his courageous fight against terminal illness having run its course. Yet, he appeared two weeks later at Reiki circle, barely standing, and without prearrangement, we all bowed to him as he entered, much as we would have done to Mikao Usui. Charlie then showed us one final, powerful 'Reiki' treatment, Native American-style, hands moving above the body, accompanied by a high-voiced Indian chanting that made my hair stand on end and my heart leap. Charlie died two weeks later, but his special message will not be forgotten. With Reiki, we are all connected; the world is one."

The energy field surrounding the human body is also called an *aura,* and it can be sensed with the hands, visualized with the eyes (with some practice), and photographed with special techniques (see Chapter 2).

Scientific instruments have been developed that can detect these subtle energies, which are also called biomagnetic forces. Some studies can even detect the subtle energy coming off an energy practitioner's hands (see Chapter 2).

When you receive a Reiki session, the energy may not feel subtle at all as you feel the heat from the Reiki practitioner's hands and perhaps waves rushing through your body. Each person senses the Reiki energy differently, and with time, your sensations will change. After you're attuned (initiated) into Reiki energy yourself, you may feel Reiki more keenly. And the Reiki practitioner might sense the emanations of life-force energy from the Reiki recipient. Certain Reiki techniques utilize the ability to sense energy (see Chapter 10). But don't worry; you can still practice Reiki with the standard hand positions even if you don't sense anything.

Even if you don't feel Reiki energy, it still works.

Understanding how Reiki works

As an energy-healing system, Reiki works to heal you at the level of your energy to the root of any disease, imbalance, or disharmony.

Though looking at the energy fields emitted by the body is becoming more popular now with the advent of alternative medicine and New Age philosophies, energy healing is actually quite ancient. Traditional Chinese medicine, Ayurvedic medicine, and other cultures have identified and classified this energy that runs throughout the body (see Chapter 2 for a discussion of chakras and meridians).

As a healing energy, Reiki is considered to be positive (no harm can come from Reiki) and intelligent (the energy heals what is needed even if you don't consciously know what you need). The recipient draws the right amount of energy to just the place where it's needed. Frequently a practitioner will feel her hands "drawn" like a magnet to a certain place. In this way, the practitioner is the channel of the universal life-force energy.

Distinguishing Reiki from other forms of energy healing

Energy healing is part of many different cultures. Whether it be acupuncture or the laying on of hands, the use of energy to treat illness is part of human history. See the sidebar "Universal Reiki — with humor and humanity," in this chapter.

Reiki offers a way to achieve spiritual and personal growth and also to heal others. But Reiki is not the only system with these goals. Two systems that are commonly confused with Reiki are:

✔ Johrei: The founder of Johrei, Mokichi Okada, was a contemporary of Mikao Usui (founder of Reiki) in Japan. The Johrei spiritual movement encompasses more than hands-on spiritual healing and advocates individual spiritual development so that everyone can reach "paradise on earth." Visit the Web site www.johrei.com for more information.

✔ Therapeutic touch: In 1972, Dr. Dolores Krieger, RN, and Dora Kunz developed the healing system called therapeutic touch. This energy-healing system involves similar features to Reiki and is taught as a 12-hour workshop. Therapeutic touch requires compassion and desire to develop experience through practice and focus. Therapeutic touch is commonly practiced within the nursing profession. See www.therapeutic-touch.org/ for more information.

Here are other types of energy healing:

✔ Acupuncture

✔ Polarity therapy

✔ Pranic healing

✔ Prayer

✔ Qigong

Reiki is distinct from these other practices through its use of symbols (see Chapter 8) and the attunement process (see Chapter 7).

Exploring the History of Reiki

I want to clarify some misconceptions about the history of Reiki. Even though other hands-on, spiritual, and energy-healing methods have ancient origins, the practice of Reiki is from 20th century Japan. Mikao Usui was born in 1865, and he taught Reiki in the early 1900s onward. He claimed that his system was unique.

Beware of old or false information, which is still present in older books or Web sites. New information has come in the last few years from Reiki historians who have visited Japan and interviewed Japanese Reiki practitioners and found Mikao Usui's memorial stone (see Chapter 3 for details about Reiki history and Chapter 20, which deals with Reiki myths).

When Mikao Usui first developed his system for spiritual healing, he called it *Usui Reiki Ryoho*, which means the Usui method for spiritual healing. As this system was passed on and taught in the West, the name of the system was called simply Reiki. Reiki has exploded into different branches, with variations on Usui's original system. I cover the background of Reiki in Japan and the evolution into Western forms in Chapter 3. I also describe different Reiki branches (Western and Japanese) and the concept of lineage in Reiki.

When you study Reiki, you can trace your lineage back to Mikao Usui through the listing of teachers. Lineage is discussed in more depth in Chapter 3.

The common element of all schools or branches of Reiki is the ability to channel universal life-force energy.

Getting Connected with Reiki

Reiki allows you to feel deeply relaxed, calm, and peaceful. The gentle touch of the practitioner's hands serves to transmit the higher-level healing energy to you. Anyone of any age, religion, or health status can benefit from Reiki.

You can experience Reiki from the perspective of a recipient or receiver of Reiki by booking Reiki sessions with a qualified practitioner. Or you can decide to become initiated into Reiki and begin your Reiki studies. This section briefly discusses both experiences.

Where Reiki can take you

If you're really ready to grow, really ready to change, and really ready to heal, Reiki can aid your progress toward wholeness. Reiki opens you up to receive the blessings of the universal life-force energy.

You may find yourself growing in ways you never imagined. Or rather, you may find yourself returning to a place of peace, feeling of love, sense of calm, and purpose of being that you forgot you ever had.

You will make some changes in your life. They may be small subtle changes, like being nice to a co-worker or letting a car pass you on the highway. You may change how you eat or what you wear.

You'll notice coincidences popping up. People show up to help you, or situations change just when you need them. You're more in the flow of the universe (from receiving the universal life-force energy) or at least more aware of the flow. You trust that life will be okay, that you will be okay, and that Reiki can help you. As you continue your life's journey, you know that you can always use Reiki, on a daily basis, especially as life takes its twists and turns.

Reiki takes you to a safe place, Reiki takes you to your truth, and Reiki takes you home.

Trying a Reiki session

Experiencing a first Reiki session is the point of entry for most folks to either deciding to use Reiki regularly or to go farther and find out how to give a Reiki session.

I list the ways that Reiki can help your entire family in Chapter 6. To find out exactly what you can expect from a Reiki session, look at Chapter 5.

Becoming initiated into Reiki's uses

Utilizing Reiki is as simple to learn as 1-2-3 — the three different levels of Reiki training.

- **First-degree Reiki:** This 1st-level class starts your Reiki flow. You find out about Reiki history and how to use Reiki to heal yourself. I cover self-healing with Reiki in Chapter 11.

- **Second-degree Reiki:** One step up from the 1st degree you find out how to use three Reiki symbols and send Reiki long distance. After this degree, you can become a Reiki practitioner. Chapter 13 describes how to give a Reiki session, and Chapter 15 covers long-distance Reiki.

- **Third-degree Reiki:** This level is frequently divided into two parts, with the first focusing on the fourth Reiki symbol and learning Master's level techniques. The last level covers how to teach Reiki to others.

Chapter 7 gives you the lowdown on Reiki training: which classes you should take, what you will learn, and how to prepare for your attunements.

When you study Reiki, you find out the following:

- The history of Reiki
- The basics of energy healing
- How to use Reiki to heal yourself and others
- How to use a set of symbols that connect to the Reiki energy (see Chapter 8)
- How to teach Reiki to others

You also receive one or more attunements. An *attunement* is an initiation process whereby your ability to channel the Reiki energy is activated.

Choosing a Reiki Practitioner or Master

You may be looking for someone to give you a treatment or someone to teach you Reiki. Here are two ways Reiki professionals identify themselves:

- ✔ **A *Reiki practitioner* (RP) is someone who practices Reiki.** This means the person has studied at least the 2nd level of Reiki and has learned to give Reiki treatments to others.
- ✔ **A *Reiki Master* (RM) is a person who has completed the Master level of Reiki.** The Reiki Master may also be a Reiki Master Teacher (RMT), in which case the person can also teach Reiki.

Note that a Reiki Master is also a Reiki practitioner.

To receive a Reiki session, you may be treated by someone who is either a Reiki practitioner or a Reiki Master. If you want to find out how to use Reiki (see the section "Becoming initiated into Reiki's uses," earlier in this chapter), you need to find a Reiki Master Teacher.

To find a practitioner or teacher who is a good match for you, consider the questions I pose in Chapters 5 and 7. Because this person will be transmitting Reiki energy to you, which is a sacred process, you want to find someone you can trust. You can often find such a person through a friend's recommendation or through following your own instincts about someone you have a good feeling about.

Experiencing the Benefits of Reiki

Each of you has different reasons for wanting to learn about Reiki right now. What you might need from Reiki today may change next week or next year. But whatever your reasons for needing Reiki, know that Reiki always provides help in a safe and natural way.

Healing a physical illness

If you or a family member is suffering with a physical illness, Reiki can help you by providing deep relaxation. Reiki helps you in the following ways when you're in pain or dealing with illness:

- Gives you a break from the pain
- Enhances the healing effects (and reduces the side effects) of any medications (conventional or alternative) you are taking
- Reduces the time you need to heal after surgery
- Promotes your body's own internal healing system

More and more doctors, nurses, and hospitals are providing Reiki services (and other energy-healing systems like therapeutic touch) for their patients. Read more about how Reiki combines with different healing therapies in Chapter 16.

Healing the emotions

Reiki has a special symbol just to heal the emotions and promote harmony (I cover the symbols in Chapter 8). The gentle healing that Reiki provides works well with psychotherapy, massage, medication, and any other treatments you use for emotional problems. Reiki specifically helps on the emotional level in the following ways:

- **Helps you release stuck or buried emotions:** You may cry or have memories come up during a Reiki session. The release helps you feel cleansed, and when memories come up, this may be an indication of something that needs further healing.
- **Gives you a pure sense of love:** Reiki energy is the energy of love. Love contains the power of the universe and brings forth a sense of wholeness and connection.

Relaxation is probably the primary reason that people try Reiki. I find that when I have a Reiki session, I sigh deeply as the tension that I have been carrying around is released. The more you relax, the more your body accepts the Reiki energy.

If you need to relax, Reiki is a healthier choice than using alcohol, drugs, sugar, or other substances.

Getting insights or inspiration

If you're feeling stuck or looking for resolution of a specific issue, Reiki can help. While you're having a Reiki session, you may experience an Aha! moment. You have a realization or insight that answers a question or solves a problem. Even if you don't get inspiration during the session, your practitioner may give you some feedback that she coincidentally picked up during the session. Or you may find that the solution comes to you in your dreams or unexpectedly in the next few days.

Going farther in spiritual development

When you know you need to evolve in your spiritual growth or you want to feel closer to spirit or act from the level of your soul, a Reiki session can definitely help. Reiki training will take you even farther and give you the tools to grow spiritually. The attunement or initiation process removes energy blocks that keep you stuck.

Reiki helps you evolve as a person and also helps you grow in consciousness. Some people say not to study Reiki unless you are ready to change. The way I see it, change is less painful than being stuck in old patterns that keep repeating and repeating and repeating. Reiki can be like the kick in the pants that moves you to the next level spiritually.

Looking at the Reiki Symbols

The symbols are a distinctive and empowering feature of the Reiki system of healing. Four symbols are taught in the 2nd and 3rd degree Reiki training classes. These symbols act as keys to connect the student with the Reiki energy for life. When you are initiated into the Reiki system, the symbols and Reiki energy are transmitted together during the attunement process. Forever after, if you think of, draw out, or say the name of the symbol, the associated aspect of the Reiki energy is called forth.

In past years, some Reiki teachers sought to keep the symbols secret as a way to protect their value and keep them "pure." However, an increasing number of authors of books and Web sites revealed the symbols to the public. I too have decided to provide clear information about the symbols in Chapter 8 so that you have all the information you need for a beginning practice of Reiki right at your fingertips.

Drawing the symbols correctly can be one of the more stressful aspects for a new Reiki student. Two of the Reiki symbols are actually Japanese characters, which for the Westerner can be a little tricky to memorize how to draw. Memorizing how to draw the symbols may be required during Reiki training. Use the illustrations in Chapter 8 to help you practice drawing the symbols. In Chapter 21, I show you some additional symbols that are not part of traditional Reiki but may be taught in nontraditional classes.

When you're using the symbols, your intention is more important than an exact replication of a symbol.

Combining New Age and Reiki

Reiki combines very well with New Age practices and beliefs. Reiki was used in Japan before the New Age began in the West. People who use Reiki today may or may not also embrace New Age ideology.

Manifesting with Reiki

A definition of manifesting is "to bring into form." You may have an idea of what you want (lose weight, finish college, or run a marathon, for example), but you may feel it will never happen. Here are some tips on manifesting in general and how Reiki can be used along with manifesting:

- Think positively about the subject. That means letting go of your fear or belief it won't happen. Believe it will happen. Believe in miracles. A prayer I like on that note is "This or something better."

- Picture or visualize the event happening.

- Put light, sparkles, or Reiki symbols around the picture of the event.

- Imagine that all parties involved experience happiness and joy. What this means is that you don't try to manifest something that will cause pain to anyone.

You can use any Reiki symbols or just imagine the Reiki energy penetrating and surrounding the situation. Do this manifestation work as part of your meditation, write it in your journal, write it out and post it on your wall, or carry it in your wallet. Send Reiki to the situation as often as possible.

The double Cho Ku Rei symbol (see Chapter 21) is frequently used for manifestation purposes.

Some branches of Reiki combine certain New Age practices with Reiki. If you investigate Reiki on the Internet or elsewhere, you might read about Reiki and aliens or Reiki and dolphins. I don't include that material in this book, but that doesn't mean it isn't true or valuable!

I do include information on Reiki and crystals (see Chapter 12) and other Western techniques that some people may consider New Age. As with all things, take what you like and leave the rest. You'll find that Reiki is compatible with all religions, practices, or beliefs.

Chapter 2

Navigating Your Body's Subtle Energy Systems

In This Chapter

▶ Looking at the meaning of subtle energy

▶ Considering your body's aura, meridians, and chakras

▶ Finding out how to detect subtle energy

*T*his chapter is about energy: the energy of Reiki and the energy of your own body. The Japanese word Reiki actually means spiritual energy or universal life-force energy. The way that Reiki works is to energize and harmonize your body's own energy. Modern science is catching up with ancient traditions in seeing the human body as a wondrous interweaving of energy.

This chapter provides you with a road map of some of the ways to describe and find the energy systems in the body. I also discuss the nature of Reiki energy healing.

Describing Subtle Energy

The classical definition of energy is from Physics 101: the ability to perform work. Energy comes in different forms, including chemical, electrical, light, magnetic, mechanical, and nuclear energy.

The energy that is discussed in terms of Reiki or the body's energy fields is called *subtle energy*. The word *subtle* on its own means faint or difficult to grasp, as in a subtle aroma. The energy field that surrounds the human body is also called a *biomagnetic* or *electromagnetic* energy.

Even though the subtle energies may be faint, you still notice them. Here are a few ways you may be aware of your subtle energy:

✔ If you've ever felt that someone was staring at you

✔ If you've ever walked into a room and sensed that something was not quite right

✔ If you've ever felt that someone was standing too close to you, even though you weren't touching

Here's an exercise to help you feel the subtle energy of your body:

1. **Hold your hands out from your body, palms facing each other.**

2. **Try putting your hands together — slowly.**

   As they get closer but not touching, can you feel different sensations?

3. **Try moving your hands closer together and then apart.**

   As you move back and forth, you can feel the energy sensations.

Subtle energy has been measured by scientists with an instrument called a SQUID. Now don't worry about animal rights here. SQUID stands for superconducting quantum interference devices. This device can measure extremely small magnetic fields.

Different cultures have different names for subtle life-force energy in the body, as described in Table 2-1.

Table 2-1	Naming the Subtle Energy in Different Cultures
Healing Culture	*Subtle Energy Name*
Traditional Chinese Medicine (TCM)	Chi or Qi
Japanese Kampo system	Ki
Ayurvedic medicine	Dosha
Homeopathy	Homeopathic resonance
Yoga	Prana

Discovering Your Body's Energy Anatomy

Modern-day science and medicine focus on the body as a complex machine composed of interacting parts. The old childhood song you might have sung with the lyrics "The thighbone is connected to the hipbone and the hipbone is connected to the. . . ." tells one piece of the story of our bodies.

You can see your body with your eyes, but imagine that there is an energy in and around your body that you can't see with your eyes. Some of you are quite comfortable believing and talking about energy you can't see with your eyes. Perhaps you can sense (with your sixth sense) or just "know" with your intuition that this energy exists.

Others of you are more skeptical or suspicious of anything you can't see. Admittedly, even though I am scientifically trained, I am one of those people who just "senses" that the body is really made of and is surrounded by energy. I don't need scientific proof to know about energy. But it's good to know that scientific research backs up the theory that the body is made of energy.

Einstein's famous equation, $E=MC^2$, expresses perfectly that matter (the body) is equal to energy. All you have to do to convert matter to energy (in Einstein's equation) is multiply a fixed number (the constant, c) and square that number to get the numerical representation of the matter in energy form.

I'll leave the details of Einstein's equation to physicists, but what this profound equation says is that matter and energy are the same thing. So, your body, which you can touch and feel, is matter, and it is also energy.

Knowing the body's physical and energetic anatomy

Because Reiki is concerned with treating the energy of the body, it helps to know both the physical anatomy (see Figure 2-1) and the energy anatomy of the body. Even without the information present in Figure 2-1, you're probably already familiar with the location and workings of your body's organs, so this section focuses mainly on your body's energy fields. But do make sure to have a basic familiarity with the organs of the body. That way, if you have a Reiki recipient who tells you he is healing from hepatitis C, you'll know that you should spend some time treating the person's right abdomen just below the ribs.

The energy system of the body has its own organization and so-called energy anatomy, just like the physical system. The anatomy of the body's energy fields (see Figure 2-2) has been described as follows:

✔ Energetic layers of the body:

- **Physical:** What you can see and dissect of the human body
- **Etheric:** The energy field associated with the physical body
- **Emotional:** The energy field in charge of emotions and feelings
- **Mental:** Your thoughts and intellect
- **Spiritual:** Your connection with spirit and the divine

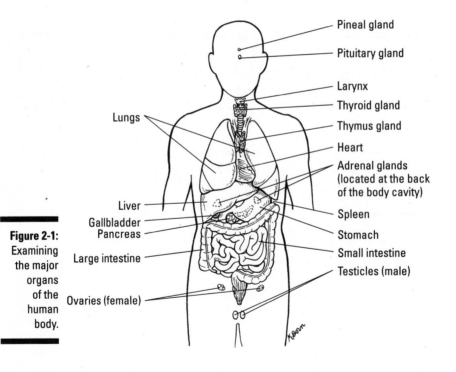

Figure 2-1:
Examining the major organs of the human body.

Pineal gland

Pituitary gland

Larynx

Thyroid gland

Thymus gland

Heart

Adrenal glands (located at the back of the body cavity)

Spleen

Stomach

Small intestine

Testicles (male)

Lungs

Liver

Gallbladder

Pancreas

Large intestine

Ovaries (female)

> These descriptions of the body's layers are simplified for the purposes of this book. The spiritual body, for example, can extend far out in many layers, especially for people who have developed this part of themselves through meditation and other spiritual practice. But I want to give the general idea that the body exists at multiple interacting levels.
>
> ✔ Aura, which contains all these energy layers.
>
> ✔ Meridians, which serve as an energy highway system throughout the body.
>
> ✔ Chakras, which act as energy centers in the body. A central column of energy runs through the body and connects the chakras.

If you view the body this way, you can look at the chakras as organs and the meridians as blood vessels or lymphatic vessels that transport information. These parts of your body's energy anatomy are described in more detail later in this chapter.

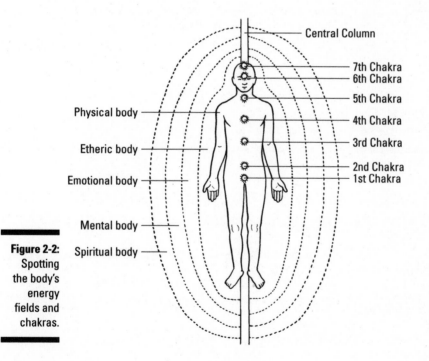

Figure 2-2: Spotting the body's energy fields and chakras.

Reiki is an energy medicine

The basic premise of energy medicine is that disease is a function of some imbalance in any of the energy bodies that translates down (through the chakras and meridians) into illness in the physical body.

The National Center for Complementary and Alternative Medicine (NCCAM) defines energy medicine as a domain in complementary and alternative medicine (CAM). The concepts behind energy medicine are that energy fields can be used to improve your health by directly treating or diagnosing imbalances in the body and its energy fields.

NCCAM separates forms of energy medicine into two parts:

✔ **Veritable:** Able to be measured. Magnetic resonance imaging (MRI) therapy, sound therapy, and light therapy (lasers) are examples.

✔ **Putative:** Not able to be measured. Reiki, acupuncture, Qigong, Ayurvedic medicine, homeopathy, and therapeutic touch are examples.

Just because the energy that is given off by the putative forms of energy healing can't be measured doesn't mean that these techniques don't have value. When studying a form of energy medicine, scientists carry out two types of studies:

✔ Measuring the energy

✔ Determining the effectiveness of the treatment

Acupuncture is proven to effectively treat certain medical conditions, but scientists are still unsure about its subtle energy.

Reiki is well documented to help many people in anecdotal (individual) stories, and further studies are needed to prove its effectiveness in groups of people (see Chapter 16).

Sensing your body's electromagnetic field: The aura

Aura is the term for the overall energy structure associated with an object in addition to the physical body of the object. Aura is the energy field that surrounds, penetrates, and extends outward from your body. The aura is illustrated in Figure 2-2 and it contains all the energy bodies. All objects, living or otherwise, have an aura.

Much has been written about auras in terms of colors and changes that occur.

- Some people can see auras. Psychics and clairvoyants can see color, shapes, and sizes of auras. You can learn to see auras too (check out the next section, "Seeing your aura").

- Changes in the aura precede physical illness in the physical body.

- Healing of the physical body must also include healing of the aura, or the disease will recur.

- A type of photography called Kirlian photography captures the aura on film so that you can visualize it.

If you want to see a picture of the aura of fingertips before and after a Reiki session, check out www.kirlian.org/kirlian/session.htm.

Seeing your aura

If you can see the aura, you'll be more likely to believe in it. Your Reiki teacher may take you through some exercises to sense auras. One exercise you can do is as follows:

1. **Hold your hand in front of you.**

   If possible, use a blank or white background.

2. **Look softly at your fingers; try to close your eyes half way.**

3. **Take your attention to the space surrounding each finger.**

   Move your eyes out a little until you see a color or line. Close to your body, the aura may appear purplish grey or yellow.

It takes a little practice, but keep focusing on the space surrounding your hand. After you get the hang of it, you'll want to keep practicing.

Remember this is a subtle energy. When you think you see something, you have! Trust your impression! Now you can practice seeing auras on yourself in the mirror or on other people. Remember to look softly.

Have you ever looked at old religious paintings? The saint's gold halo in religious paintings is actually a golden colored aura.

Reiki and the aura

When you get a Reiki treatment, the energy treats your entire system, including your aura. For that reason, Reiki can be beamed from across the room or performed with hands above your body (see Chapter 10). The aura is frequently treated before and/or after a Reiki session (see Chapter 13).

Because the aura holds energy of all sorts, a Reiki practitioner might want to do an aura cleansing both before and after the Reiki session. I see it in terms of being like a car wash, where the Reiki session is like a car wash. The aura cleansing before the session is like performing a prewash to remove the heavy dirt before performing the regular Reiki session. The aura cleansing after the session is like performing a waxing to keep in and protect the "good" energy that you now have.

Pinpointing the acupuncture system: The meridians

Mikao Usui, the founder of Reiki, was aware of the acupuncture system, which has been used in China for thousands of years. Acupuncture uses needles to stimulate tiny points of energy in the body. Acupuncture points are like traffic signals that light the way of main thoroughfares for energy movement throughout the body, which are called *meridians*.

Listing the meridians

The body has 12 main meridians that transport energy to the organs and systems of the body. The meridians crisscross through the body from head to toe and exchange information with one another. Imagine that these meridians are running all through the body: front, back, side, head, feet, and hands.

To give you an idea of the different meridians, consider that each is associated with different organ systems. Remember, though, that each organ system is "fed" by more than one meridian and that each meridian is associated with more than one organ. Here is a list of the major meridians:

- Bladder
- Circulation-sex/pericardium
- Gallbladder
- Heart
- Kidney
- Large intestine
- Liver
- Lung

✔ Small intestine

✔ Spleen

✔ Stomach

✔ Triple warmer (endocrine glands)

There are also two systems called central meridian and governing meridian that are used in the Hui Yin breath or microcosmic orbit described in Chapter 9. By holding your tongue at the roof of your mouth and squeezing the muscles of your perineum, you can enhance the energy flow coming out of your hands or breath for use during Reiki procedures (attunements or treatments).

Treating the meridians

Treatment of the meridians, whether by acupuncture, acupressure, or Reiki, seeks to remove energy blocks so that the energy may flow smoothly. Because the meridians are interconnected, balance and harmony between the meridians are essential. An acupuncture or acupressure practitioner plans which acupuncture points he will treat. When you have Reiki treatments, the healing energy will facilitate healing, but the practitioner doesn't necessarily know much about meridians because this information isn't part of standard Reiki training (see Chapter 7).

Any practitioners of energy healing, including Reiki healers, will find it worthwhile to study the meridians and even consider professional study if they feel called to do so.

Locating your energy centers: The chakras

Chakra is an Indian Sanskrit word that means spinning wheel of energy, vortex, or energy center. The human body has multiple chakras that transform information between the different levels of the body, including the spiritual, mental, emotional, and physical. For example, if you have emotional issues involving your heart chakra, the issues could be transformed into heart disease by way of the heart chakra. Similarly, if you're in a state of feeling unconditional love and forgiveness, your heart chakra transforms that energy to a healthy heart and circulation. Table 2-2 describes the chakras and the parts of the body and issues that they govern.

Table 2-2   Chakra Locations, Descriptions, and Governages

Chakra Number	Chakra Name	Organs and Systems	Associated Glands	Issues	Affirmation
1st	Base	Excretory systems and spine	Adrenal glands	Survival and grounding	I have
2nd	Sacral	Reproductive system	Testes and ovaries	Sexuality and creativity	I feel
3rd	Solar plexus	Digestive system	Pancreas	Personal power	I can
4th	Heart	Circulatory system	Thymus gland	Love	I love
5th	Throat	Lungs, vocal apparatus	Thyroid and parathyroid glands	Communication	I speak
6th	Third eye	Lower brain, nervous system, ears, nose, eyes	Pituitary gland	Vision	I see
7th	Crown	Upper brain	Pineal gland	Connection to spirit	I know

Seven major chakras have been identified. If you refer to Figure 2-2, you can see the placement of these chakras in the body:

- ✔ The first chakra is located at the base of your spine going down through the perineum, which is the region between the anus and the genitals.
- ✔ The second chakra is located between the navel and pubic bone.
- ✔ The third chakra is between your diaphragm (the bottom of your rib cage) and navel.
- ✔ The fourth chakra is in the center of the chest.
- ✔ The fifth chakra is at the base of the throat.
- ✔ The sixth chakra is in the center of the forehead.
- ✔ The seventh chakra is just above the top of the head.

Each chakra manages a flow of energy between the physical, etheric, emotional, mental, and spiritual bodies. When your body is healthy, energy flows along the meridians and chakras. But when there is an energy block, the nearby meridians and chakras don't get the energy flow. If this energy block is not cleared, disease of nearby organs can occur.

The good news is that Reiki healing can open blocked chakras. When you perform a Reiki session, you can sense the energy of the chakra on both the front and back of the body (except for the crown chakra).

Ultimately, the source of energy flow comes from outside of the body and extends upward to the heavens for higher spiritual energy and below the body for earth energy. The chakras serve to bring in energy from outside the body, and when the chakras are open and flowing, this energy comes in and supplies the body with energy.

The association of any chakra with a particular organ, system, or gland is not a hard-and-fast rule. For example, the lungs could be associated with the throat chakra or the heart chakra. Use your intuition to determine which chakra is affected if you're working on a particular problem.

Detecting Your Subtle Energy System with Reiki

You may be wondering how it's possible to sense your subtle energy system if conventional equipment can't see or measure it.

Whether you are the provider or recipient of Reiki energy, you'll probably sense the Reiki energy during the session. The recipient should relax and not worry about trying to sense anything during the treatment (see Chapter 5). If you're giving Reiki, you can train yourself to detect this energy by using the following techniques:

✔ **With your hands:** During a Reiki session, the practitioner's hands not only transmit spiritual energy but also receive certain information from the recipient. This information may be tingles, heat, visualizations, or other signs that give the practitioner feedback on where to treat and when to stop. The more you use your hands in treating others, the more sensitive you'll be to this information.

✔ **With your intuition:** Even without touching someone, you can sense the person's energy.

- You can gaze gently and see the person's aura, which may provide information on the person's energy systems.

- The connection made during distant Reiki (see Chapter 15) or by scanning Reiki (see Chapter 10) may enable you to pick up on certain energy information.

- Meditation and visualization also enable you to sense where any energy disruptions are occurring.

✔ **With a pendulum:** You can use a pendulum as a diagnostic tool to see whether a chakra is open or closed (or somewhere in between). When a chakra's energy is flowing, the pendulum is open; when energy is not flowing, it is closed. You can find pendulums in stores that sell crystals (see Chapter 12). I suggest that you find out about pendulum use from your Reiki teacher. You predetermine the signs for "yes" (or open) and "no" (or closed) by "asking" the pendulum what a yes looks like and then what a no looks like. With practice, you can obtain repeatable results.

When you use a pendulum and find that a chakra is closed, do some Reiki on that chakra and then check it again.

If you're working with anyone's energy system in any way, you must have the person's permission first. You then have the responsibility to treat the work and any information you obtain with the highest degree of integrity and compassion for that person. See Chapter 13 for a discussion of the ethics of doing healing work with Reiki.

Chapter 3

Exploring Reiki's Roots and Branches

*T*he main character in the history of Reiki is Mikao Usui, a Japanese Buddhist who founded a healing system later called Reiki. After Usui, various Japanese and Western Reiki practitioners have interpreted and modified the system. Like the growth of any healthy tree, Reiki has developed many branches.

What unites the branches of Reiki is that the main trunk is from Mikao Usui. After that, all Reiki branches diverge from the original to a greater or lesser extent.

Every Western branch of Reiki, which means most of the Reiki taught around the world, comes from Hawayo Takata, who learned from Chujiro Hayashi, who learned from Mikao Usui. In this chapter, I give an overview of Reiki history by describing the contributions of Mikao Usui, Chujiro Hayashi, and Hawayo Takata and how branches of Reiki have evolved. Knowing the history and branches of Reiki helps you determine which Reiki systems are best for you.

If you studied Reiki more than a few years ago, read this chapter to brush up on your knowledge of Reiki history. Much of what used to be taught just a few years ago is now considered myth. Knowledge about Reiki history continues to grow as more information becomes available from Japanese sources.

The essence of Reiki is the same, no matter who teaches it or how they do it. Reiki is a system of healing that is easy to learn. The availability of so many types of Reiki today means that Reiki is available to all who seek it.

Mikao Usui: Founder of Reiki

The history of Reiki (see Table 3-1) begins with Mikao Usui, who was born in 1865 in Japan. During his lifetime, he practiced Tendai Buddhism and studied Japanese martial arts. He is also known to have studied history, medicine, and spiritual practices from other cultures, including Christianity.

What makes Usui's story truly extraordinary is that his drive to pursue his spiritual truth led him to discover Reiki, which has in turn helped so many people around the world.

Usui himself was a great healer and was reported to have helped many victims of the 1923 earthquake in Japan, which hit the cities of Tokyo and Yokohama.

Table 3-1		100 Years of Reiki History
Year	*Location*	*Reiki Fact*
1865	Japan	Mikao Usui is born.
1880	Japan	Chujiro Hayashi is born.
1900	Hawaii	Hawayo Takata is born.
1922	Japan	Mikao Usui spends 21 days at Mount Kurama.
1926	Japan	Mikao Usui dies of a stroke.
1935	Japan	Hawayo Takata is a client of Chujiro Hayashi.

Year	Location	Reiki Fact
1937	Hawaii	Hawayo Takata brings Reiki to Hawaii.
1938	Hawaii	Chujiro Hayashi gives Hawayo Takata a Master Certificate.
1940	Japan	Chujiro Hayashi commits suicide (to avoid WW II).
1976	United States	Hawayo Takata trains her first Master student, Virginia Samdahl.
1980	United States	Hawayo Takata dies.
1985	Japan	Mieko Mitsui teaches the Western (Hawayo Takata/Barbara Weber Ray) version of Reiki in Japan.

Finding Reiki on the mountaintop

In 1922 Mikao Usui went on a spiritual pilgrimage to Mount Kurama, which is near Kyoto, Japan. He fasted and meditated for 21 days while on the mountaintop. This was his own retreat from the world during which time he sought spiritual enlightenment. During this time of meditation and retreat, Usui had a profound experience, during which he "received" enlightenment and the system of Reiki.

Clearly Usui had a significant spiritual experience that influenced his personal life and his teaching of Reiki. His experience on Mount Kurama is included on his memorial stone. Hawayo Takata also talked about Usui's experience on Mount Kurama, although she embellished it with stories of him receiving "bubbles" containing the Reiki symbols.

Teaching Reiki to others

Mikao Usui began imparting his spiritual experiences to others in the early 1900s. Hands-on healing and spiritual healing were popular in Japan at this time. After his enlightenment on Mount Kurama, Usui refined his teachings to a system that more closely resembles the Reiki that is taught today.

The aim of Usui's teaching was to provide students with tools for their own spiritual enlightenment and healing. Usui's system of healing included the following:

✔ Reiki Principles (see Chapter 4)

✔ Reiki hand positions (see Chapter 10)

✔ Meditation (see Chapter 9)

✔ Symbols and mantras (see Chapter 8)

✔ Attunement (initiation) process (see Chapter 7)

Because Usui's system of healing has changed with each successive teacher, I can provide the information on Usui's method only as it is commonly practiced today rather than as Usui once taught it. Some seek the holy grail of Reiki: the original teachings of Mikao Usui. The problem is that no *one* system of teaching will ever be found because Mikao Usui is known to have varied his teachings depending on the student (see the section "Letting Reiki Branches Differ," later in this chapter).

Some of Usui's teachings (or derivations of his teachings) are found in a Japanese teaching manual called *Usui Reiki Hikkei,* which has been translated from the Japanese (see Frank Arjava Petter's books in the Appendix). Despite the historic detail of whether this manual was written by Usui himself or someone else soon after his death, this manual does provide insight into early Reiki teaching. It contains the following:

✔ Reiki Principles (see Chapter 4), which were called "the secret method to invite happiness."

✔ "Usui's Message about Reiki," in which he introduces the concept of his teachings to the general public (see the sidebar "Introducing Reiki to the public").

✔ Healing Guide, a series of hand positions that was probably developed by Chujiro Hayashi (see the section "Exploring the Medical Approach: Chujiro Hayashi," later in this chapter); for a Western derivation of these positions, see Chapter 10.

✔ Meiji Emperor's Poems (called gyosi in Japanese), short poems on topics such as nature that were recited as a way to focus the mind.

✔ Usui's answers to students' questions.

Introducing Reiki to the public

From the Usui Reiki Hikkei, a Japanese Reiki manual attributed to Mikao Usui.

"From ancient times whenever someone develops a secret method the one would teach this to the people among family, as a legacy for the later generations of the family living. That idea, not to open to the public and keep that sacred method in the family, is really the past century's bad custom.

"In modern days we have to live together. That's going to be the basis of happiness, earnestly wanting social progress.

"That's why I definitely won't allow to keep this for myself. Our Reiki Ryoho is a creative idea, which no one has developed before and there is nothing like this in this world. Therefore I am going to open this idea to anybody for the people's benefit and welfare.

"And everyone will receive the blessing from God. With this, expect everyone to have soul and oneness.

"Our Reiki Ryoho is an original therapy method using the power based on Reiki, which is a universal power in the universe.

"With this, first for human beings themselves to be strong and healthy. Then to improve the thoughts, to be mild and healthy, and human life to be pleasant.

"Nowadays inside and outside of living we need improvement and restructuring away from illness and suffering, many fellows have worrying mind out of illness and accident.

"I dare to openly teach this method."

This is a translation of part of the Usui Reiki Hikkei from Andy Bowling's Web site, `www.usuireiki.fsnet.co.uk/UsuiManual.html`. You can also find a translation by Frank Arjeva Petter in his books listed in the Appendix.

Remember that Mikao Usui taught more than 75 years ago — before the age of the course syllabus or computers. He taught individually to each student, which makes it impossible to re-create his teachings exactly. What can be done is to follow the essence of Reiki as best as possible.

Mikao Usui's legacy

Mikao Usui died in 1926. By the time of his death, he is thought to have trained around 2,000 students overall, including 21 who achieved the Master Teacher level. Some well-known teacher students of Mikao Usui include the following:

✔ **Toshishiro Eguchi:** A friend of Mikao Usui who learned Usui's system and also taught his own palm healing (tenohira) system at Usui's center. Eguchi continued to teach and was a famous healer in Japan with his center, Tenohira Ryoji Kenkyo Kai. Eguchi published two books: in 1930, *Tenohira Ryoji Nyumon (An Introduction to Healing with the Palms)* and *Tenohira Ryoji Wo Kataru (A Tale of Healing with the Palms of the Hands)* in 1954.

✔ **Chujiro Hayashi:** Created the system Hayashi Reiki Kenkyu Kai (see the later section "Exploring the Medical Approach: Chujiro Hayashi").

✔ **Kaji Tomita:** Became a famous healer and author in Japan. He called his hand-healing system Tomita Teate Ryoho. His book was called *Reiki To Jinjutsu – Tomita Ryu Teate Ryoho (Reiki and Humanitarian Work – Tomita Ryu Hand Healing)*.

✔ **Juzaburo Ushida and Kanichi Taketomi:** Both past presidents of the Usui Reiki Ryoho Gakkai, a Japanese Reiki society that has been active since the time of Mikao Usui (or just after his death). It started as a group of naval officers who had studied with Mikao Usui and continues to be active. However, the Gakkai has remained a secretive society that is closed to foreigners and has not revealed the methods it uses.

Note that even among Usui's original students, creation of individually modified Reiki branches took place!

Reiki before Mikao Usui

Some Reiki teachers have suggested that Mikao Usui is not so much the founder of Reiki but that he refound Reiki, which is an ancient form of healing. Here are two versions of these theories:

✔ Reiki is an ancient healing energy that had become lost, and Usui channeled this lost ancient energy while meditating on Mount Kurama.

Some groups also feel justified to channel their own versions of Reiki healing, symbols, and attunement methods.

✔ Reiki came from Buddhist texts, and Mikao Usui found these texts in his research.

Certainly Buddhism influenced Mikao Usui's system. Usui himself was a lay Buddhist priest (which meant he could live with his family) and lived in a country that practiced Buddhism and Shintoism. Development of the symbols was certainly influenced by Buddhism (see Chapter 8 for more about the symbols).

Mikao Usui called his system unique, and thus far no researcher has been able to prove that Usui's system of natural healing comes from any particular Buddhist text or ancient civilization. Mikao Usui found a way to a universal truth: that healing and enlightenment are possible and that everyone is capable of this healing and enlightenment. Usui developed his system of Reiki precisely because he wanted to share with others what he had found.

Exploring the Medical Approach: Chujiro Hayashi

Chujiro Hayashi was one of Mikao Usui's students who had a huge influence on the further development of Reiki. When Chujiro Hayashi studied with Mikao Usui, he was a retired naval medical officer. Hayashi was able to spend ten months learning Reiki from Mikao Usui before Usui died in 1926.

Dr. Hayashi, a surgeon, brought a medical approach to the practice of Reiki with his knowledge of anatomy and medicine. He prepared a manual of hand positions that treated different illnesses. He set up the first Reiki clinic, which brought Reiki healing into a medical model of treatments. His clinic was able to treat at least eight people simultaneously on separate mats or futons, with two practitioners working on each recipient.

In his system of teaching Reiki, Dr. Hayashi developed the process of passing on Reiki to students by using symbols and mantras during the attunement process (see Chapter 7), the modern attunement process used by branches of Western Reiki.

Chujiro Hayashi, though a retired naval officer, was a man of peace. As World War II approached, he knew that Japan would go to war and that he would be called back to duty. So at the age of 40, he decided to end his life rather than be forced to kill people in military action. The branch of Reiki that he developed was called Hayashi Reiki Kenkyu Kai; his wife Chie Hayashi continued this branch after he died. As far as I know, this branch has not survived, but his teachings continued through his two most well-known Reiki Master students:

- **Hawayo Takata:** Dr. Hayashi took the important step to train the Hawaiian woman Hawayo Takata (see the following section). Dr. Hayashi was thus pivotal in the spread of Reiki to the West.

- **Chiyoko Yamaguchi:** Chiyoko Yamaguchi, who died in 2003, and her son taught Jikiden Reiki, and one of her former students teaches Komyo Reiki Kai (see the Appendix for contact information about these two Reiki branches.)

Bringing Reiki from East to West: Hawayo Takata

Hawayo Takata plays a critical role in Reiki history because she single-handedly transferred Reiki from Japan to the West. Though Hawayo Takata was an American citizen born in the then territory of Hawaii, she was of Japanese heritage, so she was able to walk in both Eastern and Western worlds.

Hawayo Takata was born on Christmas Eve 1900 and named for her birthplace of Hawaii. Her parents emigrated from Japan and worked hard to make a modest living in Hawaii. To take care of personal business and health matters, Hawayo Takata traveled to Japan in 1935.

Passing Reiki on

For decades, Hawayo Takata practiced Reiki in Hawaii and the mainland United States. In 1976 she trained her first Reiki Master and ended up training 22 Reiki Masters before she died in 1980.

Here are Takata's Reiki Masters:

George Araki

Dorothy Baba

Ursula Baylow

Rick Bockner

Patricia Bowling Ewing

Barbara Brown

Fran Brown

Phyllis Lei Furumoto

Beth Gray

John Harvey Gray

Iris Ishikuro

Harry Kuboi

Ethel Lombardi

Barbara McCullough

Mary McFadyen

Paul Mitchell

Bethel Phaigh

Barbara Weber Ray

Shinobu Saito

Virginia Samdahl

Wanja Twan

Kay Yamashita

Hawayo Takata's students, and their succession of students, brought Reiki to the United States, the Western world, and other countries, including Japan. Some of Hawayo Takata's students are still living, and I provide their Web sites in the Appendix.

Learning Reiki for herself

Just before Hawayo Takata was about to have surgery, she had a premonition that a nonsurgical solution for her health was possible. It turns out that the receptionist at the clinic was Chie Hayashi, who directed Hawayo Takata to her husband's Reiki clinic.

After six months of treatments, Hawayo Takata was cured. She was so impressed with the Reiki method that she was able to persuade Chujiro Hayashi to teach it to her. She studied with Chujiro Hayashi and then brought the system back to her native Hawaii. Chujiro Hayashi and his daughter followed her to Hawaii to help Hawayo Takata set up a Reiki practice.

Takata's tall tales

Many of the stories about Reiki history told by Hawayo Takata (a natural story-teller) and her students and subsequently repeated in many books are now known to be untrue. I mention some of these myths in Chapter 20.

A generation of Reiki students learned old versions of Reiki history told by Takata, with compelling twists and turns involving Jesus and his healing abilities, Christianity, Buddhist sutras, beggars, life-saving events, college presidents, and bubbles of Reiki symbols appearing on Mount Kurama.

In today's world, the old story of Reiki is no longer necessary to keep Reiki alive (see the sidebar "The true role of Hawayo Takata").

The true role of Hawayo Takata

Despite her role in creating Reiki myths (see Chapter 20), Hawayo Takata wanted Reiki to survive in the Western world. When the dust settles, I believe that time will show Hawayo Takata to be the Reiki heroine that she truly was. Imagine that Hawayo Takata managed to preserve a Japanese healing method in Hawaii, the very state that was bombed by the Japanese at Pearl Harbor!

Hawayo Takata had to fight discrimination on both sides. The Japanese saw her as an American. Even today, the Usui Reiki Ryoho Gakkai doesn't train foreigners or admit them as members of their organization. It's a miracle that Chujiro Hayashi (see the section "Exploring the Medical Approach: Chujiro Hayashi" in this chapter) even trained her and helped her with her Reiki practice!

Her work brought Reiki to the West, and students of her system even brought Reiki back to Japan.

Reiki in Japan and the West

When Hawayo Takata (see the section "Bringing Reiki from East to West: Hawayo Takata," earlier in this chapter) died, none of her students were aware that Reiki existed in Japan. Her Masters students tried to put together their notes from the different teachings that Takata had given each of them. Some of her students wrote books or created new Reiki branches.

Reiki in Japan

After Mikao Usui died in 1926, followers of his system in Japan went on quietly without much public notice.

People in the West who studied Reiki weren't even aware that Reiki had survived in Japan. It appears that Japanese Reiki was lying in wait like a dormant seed. In 1985, Mieko Mitsui, a student of Barbara Weber Ray, returned to Japan and began to teach some levels of Reiki (see Table 3-1 and Figure 3-1). Japanese people were eager to study Reiki, and other Reiki teachers from the West also came to Japan to teach Reiki.

Eventually, the increased interest in Reiki stimulated some Japanese-trained Reiki practitioners and teachers to come out of hiding and begin teaching their methods!

Japanese and Western Reiki today

Today a distinction is made between Japanese Reiki, in some branches possibly more faithful to Mikao Usui's original style, and Western Reiki, which has been altered by changes made by Chujiro Hayashi, Hawayo Takata, and even further by successive Reiki teachers.

Japanese Reiki is now being studied in the West as Reiki students yearn to discover the roots of Reiki. As information on Japanese Reiki techniques becomes available, Western branches of Reiki are incorporating this information into their teachings.

In Japan, students of Reiki are also studying both Japanese and Western styles of Reiki. Teachers of Western-style Reiki continue to go to Japan and teach.

In the rest of this book, I present methods from both Japanese and Western branches (see Figure 3-1). In this figure, note that each branch derives from Mikao Usui and one of his students. Each branch is represented by a circle.

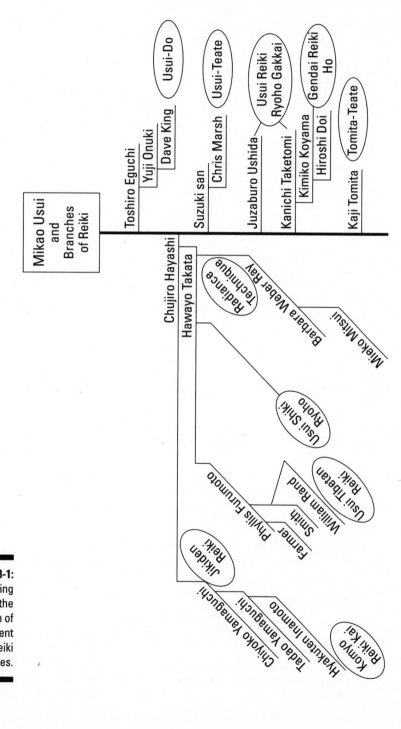

Figure 3-1:
Mapping the evolution of different Reiki branches.

Listing the Reiki techniques

There are so many Reiki techniques from the various Reiki disciplines that it's often difficult to keep track of them all. Here is a list of the most common techniques, what they're used for, and where you can find more information about them in this book:

Name of Reiki Technique	Description	More Information in Chapter:
Byosen Reikan Ho	Sensing imbalance in the body	10
Chakra Balancing	Complementary method to Reiki treatment	10
Crystal Healing	Complementary method to Reiki treatment	12
Distant Healing	Remote healing	15
Enkaku Chiryo Ho	A form of remote healing	15
Gassho Meditation	Prayerful hands meditation method	9
Group distant healing	Sending healing as a group	14
Gyosi Ho	Healing by staring	10
Hand positions	Placement of hands for Reiki treatment	10
Hatsurei Ho- meditation	Generating spiritual energy	9
Healing the past and future	Sending Reiki across time	15
Hui Yin Contraction	Keeping energy in body	9
Jakikiri Joka Ho	Cleaning inanimate objects	12
Joshin Kokyo Ho	Focusing the mind with your breath	9

Name of Reiki Technique	Description	More Information in Chapter:
Kenyoku Ho	Dry energy bathing	13
Koki Ho	Healing with the breath	10
Nentatsu Ho	Mental technique to treat habitual thought	16
Reiji Ho	Being guided by spirit	9
Reiki box	Form of distant healing	15
Reiki Mawashi	Sending energy around a group circle	14
Seishin Toitsu	Attaining a unified mind	9
Self-Reiki	Placement of hands on self for Reiki treatment	11
Shuchu Reiki	Treatment by many practitioners	14

Looking at Reiki Branch Lineage

As I mention throughout this chapter, there are many Reiki branches, which each teach a form of Reiki. My focus in this book is on branches that show a direct lineage back to Mikao Usui. Refer to Figure 3-1 to get an idea of the way that different branches have diverged.

The concept of lineage in Reiki just means who taught whom. All Reiki students, practitioners, or teachers of the Usui Reiki are linked to one another because all are connected to Mikao Usui.

Tracing your Reiki lineage means looking back from teacher to teacher, going all the way back to Mikao Usui.

Not everyone is concerned with lineage. If you want to know how your branch of Reiki or your teacher links back to Mikao Usui, ask your teacher to provide this information.

Each Reiki branch has a founder. Technically, Mikao Usui is the ultimate founder. When a Reiki Master changes the teachings, he usually renames the teachings, calls it a Reiki branch, and calls himself the founder.

In the Appendix, I give contact information on 25 different Reiki branches, which represent most but not all Reiki branches that exist. Of these, 16 are more directly derived from Mikao Usui, and I list the lineage that connects each of these branches to Mikao Usui.

You can also find those branches that aren't directly derived from Mikao Usui, but are related, in the Appendix. These branches are actually more like off-shoots of the original Reiki tree rather than branches.

Japanese Usui Reiki branches

Here are the major branches of Reiki in Japan that I am aware of. You can find Web site information for these branches in the Appendix. The lineage for each branch starts with Mikao Usui and continues to the current founder or teacher of that branch.

- ✔ **Gendai Reiki Ho:** Lineage: Mikao Usui, Kanichi Taketomi, Kimiko Koyama, Hiroshi Doi. Founder: Hiroshi Doi

- ✔ **Jikiden Reiki:** Lineage: Mikao Usui, Chujiro Hayashi, Chiyoko Yamaguchi, Tadao Yamaguchi. Founders: Chiyoko Yamaguchi and Tadao Yamaguchi

- ✔ **Komyo Reiki Kai:** Lineage: Mikao Usui, Chujiro Hayashi, Chiyoko Yamaguchi, Hyakuten Inamoto. Founder: Hyakuten Inamoto

- ✔ **Usui Reiki Ryoho Gakkai:** Lineage: Mikao Usui, Juzaburo Ushida, Kanichi Taketomi, Yoshiharu Watanabe, Toyoichi Wanami, Kimiko Koyama, Masataki Kondo. Founder: Mikao Usui. This organization seeks to preserve Mikao Usui's teachings, but unfortunately is restrictive in terms of both its membership and the information it gives out.

- ✔ **Usui Reiki Ryoho:** Lineage: Mikao Usui, Kanichi Taketomi, Kimiko Koyama, Hiroshi Doi. Founder: Hiroshi Doi

Japanese-style Usui Reiki

The following two branches were taught by Japanese Reiki practitioners to Western students, who are the founders of these branches:

✔ **Usui-Teate:** Lineage: Mikao Usui, Suzuki san, Chris Marsh. Founder: Chris Marsh. Also called "Method to Achieve Personal Perfection."

✔ **Usui-Do:** Lineage: Mikao Usui, Toshishiro Eguchi, Yuji Onuki, Dave King. Founders: Dave King (Canada) and Melissa Riggall (deceased), who presented this system based on Eguchi's work.

Western Usui Reiki branches

The main branches of Western Reiki all derive from Hawayo Takata:

✔ **The Radiance Technique (Authentic Reiki):** Lineage: Mikao Usui Chujiro Hayashi, Hawayo Takata, Barbara Weber Ray. Founder: Barbara Weber Ray, who claims that she is the sole successor to Hawayo Takata.

✔ **Usui Shiki Ryoho:** Lineage: Mikao Usui, Chujiro Hayashi, Hawayo Takata. The Reiki Alliance is a group that formed after Hawayo Takata died. Both the Reiki Alliance and Phyllis Lei Furamoto (who is Hawayo Takata's granddaughter) claim that Furamoto is the true successor to Hawayo Takata. Many independent Reiki Masters (including myself) have studied under this system but are not necessarily part of the Reiki Alliance.

✔ **Usui/Tibetan Reiki:** Lineage: Mikao Usui, Chujiro Hayashi, Hawayo Takata, Phyllis Lei Furumoto, Carrell Ann Farmer, Leah Smith, William Lee Rand. Founder: William Lee Rand (United States). This is my lineage for my Reiki Master training with one of William Rand's students, Kathie Lipinski.

Additional information on other branches of Reiki as well as other non-Usui (post-Usui) forms of Reiki is listed in the Appendix.

Choosing a Reiki Branch for Yourself

No one school or branch of Reiki is the best or truly speaks for all of Reiki. I suggest that you take the following steps before choosing a Reiki branch:

✔ Check out what types of Reiki classes are available in your location.

✔ Speak to Reiki practitioners whom you know. Ask them what they liked and disliked about their classes or teachers.

✔ Try out a Reiki session with a teacher you're considering (either a private session or a Reiki circle).

✔ Go to a Reiki circle or share in your community and get exposed to many teachers at once.

✔ Speak to potential Reiki teachers and ask them the questions I suggest in Chapter 7.

Letting Reiki Branches Differ

Despite questions and even some differences of opinion among branches on aspects of Reiki practice, the system of Reiki not only survives but thrives! The intrinsic power of Reiki goes beyond any disagreements over different interpretations. The differences between Reiki branches are similar to differences in branches of religions, where each has different practices but ultimately has the same goal.

Variety of practice is almost built in to the way that Reiki was taught and passed on by Mikao Usui, Chujiro Hayashi, and Hawayo Takata. Refer to Figure 3-1 to note the evolution of different branches of Reiki. Here, I examine the similarities and differences between Usui and Takata:

✔ Both Usui and Takata trained each student differently:

  • Usui based his teachings on what he felt would be best for each student and the student's particular spiritual level. For example, some students got symbols and some did not.

  • Takata didn't allow students to take notes. When they got together after she died, the students were shocked to find they had each been given different variations of the teachings.

✔ Neither Usui nor Takata clearly appointed a successor:

  • Controversy apparently exists among Japanese Master students of Mikao Usui. The Usui Reiki Ryoho Gakkai claims to be the official society started by Mikao Usui. Other students of Mikao Usui who have been interviewed by Western Reiki historians dispute this claim.

  • When Hawayo Takata died, she didn't have a clear successor. Eventually Barbara Weber Ray (the Radiance technique) and Phyllis Lei Furumoto (Hawayo Takata's granddaughter) each claimed to be the successor. Furumoto was called the "lineage bearer" and "grandmaster" by the Reiki Alliance.

The lack of either a consistent and universal teaching or creation of one official school to carry on each of their Reiki systems led the successors of Mikao Usui, Chujiro Hayashi, and Hawayo Takata to each create their own versions or branches of Reiki practice. Because of these differences, different branches have some differences of interpretation of the Reiki system and practice.

The benefit of no obvious successor to Reiki is that there are many varieties from which to choose and learn!

Reiki belongs to everyone. No one person or branch is the sole lineage bearer.

Picturing the Future of Reiki

Like a carpet of wildflowers, Reiki has spread to different countries with different branches and different versions. Like any new natural form, some versions will thrive, and some will die out. Mikao Usui, Chujiro Hayashi, and Hawayo Takata have left the world with so many different Reiki seeds, they ensure that some will germinate fruitfully.

The way for Reiki to survive is to practice the Reiki Principles (see Chapter 4). The future of Reiki will take care of itself.

Chapter 4

Looking at the Reiki Principles

An important feature of Reiki, which is sometimes overlooked, is that Reiki was designed as a potent tool for personal and spiritual growth, and to this end, it's important to know the five Reiki Principles.

The five Reiki Principles form the cornerstone of what is essentially a Reiki spiritual practice. All branches of Reiki derived from Mikao Usui's teachings (see Chapter 3 for information about Reiki branches) use some version of the Reiki Principles. Whether they're called Reiki Principles, Reiki Precepts, or Reiki Ideals, these five statements are used as guidelines to right living and spiritual development. When you use the Reiki Principles, you're following directly in the footsteps of Mikao Usui. In this chapter, I describe the Reiki principles: what they are and how to use them.

It's not enough to just read the Reiki Principles and just turn the page. To get the full benefit and value of Reiki, you must aim to live by the Reiki Principles. Don't worry — they express universal truths that would be approved by any religion!

Describing the Reiki Principles

The Reiki Principles are so important and so intrinsic to the practice of Reiki that they are engraved on Mikao Usui's tombstone (see the sidebar "Reiki principles from Mikao Usui's memorial stone"). Before Usui's memorial stone was discovered and available in English, the Reiki Principles were taught in different versions by different teachers. Hawayo Takata taught the Reiki Principles, and her students continue to pass these on.

Reiki Principles from Mikao Usui's memorial stone

Hawayo Takata (see Chapter 3) and also her students taught the Reiki Principles. When Reiki historian Frank Arjava Petter located the memorial to Reiki founder Mikao Usui in Tokyo, he translated and published this information. The following excerpt was taken from the full Usui Memorial written by Juzaburo Ushido and Masayuki Okada in February 1927. The translation was by Masano Kobayashi, Chetna Kobayashi, and Frank Arjava Petter (Source: *Reiki Fire* by Frank Arjava Petter, 1997, Lotus Light, Twin Lakes, Wisconsin).

"Reiki not only heals diseases, but also amplifies innate abilities, balances the spirit, makes the body healthy, and thus helps achieve happiness. To teach this to others you should follow the five principles of the Meiji Emperor and contemplate them in your heart.

They should be spoken daily, once in the morning and once in the evening.

1. Don't get angry today.

2. Don't worry today.

3. Be grateful today.

4. Work hard today (meditative practice).

5. Be kind to others today.

The ultimate goal is to understand the ancient secret method for gaining happiness (Reiki) and thereby discover an all-purpose cure for many ailments. If these principles are followed, you will achieve the great tranquil mind of the ancient sages. To begin spreading the Reiki system, it is important to start from a place close to you (yourself), don't start from something distant such as philosophy or logic.

Sit still and in silence every morning and every evening with your hands folded in the Gassho or Namaste. Follow the great principles, and be clean and quiet. Work on your heart and do things from the quiet space inside of you. Anyone can access Reiki, because it begins within yourself!"

It is believed that Usui knew of the five principles from the Meiji Emperor of Japan or from a book of his time that listed similar principles: *Kenzon no Gebri* by Bizan Suzuki, published in Japan in 1914.

Don't worry if you have different forms of the Reiki Principles. Teachers from varying Reiki lineages (see Chapter 3) may present the principles in slightly different versions or translations (from the Japanese original). But the meaning of all versions is essentially the same.

The Reiki Principles are five simple statements describing how to live — just for today:

- ✔ Just for today, don't get angry.

- ✔ Just for today, don't worry.

- ✔ Just for today, be grateful.

- ✔ Just for today, be honest in your work.

- ✔ Just for today, be kind to yourself and others.

Staying in the present: Just for today

The most important part of the Reiki Principles is the beginning statement: just for today.

Today is really where it's at. Yesterday is over, and tomorrow hasn't happened yet. If your thoughts and energy are in the past or future, there's little time left to experience the present. When you're not in today, that's when you feel that life is passing you by.

Spending too much time reminiscing, looking at old photos, and wondering "what if?" is living in the past. Sitting with your daily planner, fixing for your future, worrying about next year, next month, or even tomorrow is living in the future.

Staying in today is like balancing a seesaw. Spending too much time wandering in the past or in the future will take you away from today.

Here are some tips to help stay in the present moment:

- Take note of your senses: Ask yourself what you see, feel, hear, smell, and taste.
- Be with someone you love or an object of beauty like a sunset or a flower. Just focus on your love and merge with that.
- Spend time with young children!
- Try breathing exercises or meditation (see Chapter 9) to help focus on the present moment.

Seeing the *present* moment as a gift (or a *present*) makes every experience a joy to unwrap!

When receiving or giving Reiki, being fully present also allows the Reiki energy to be at its brightest and highest intensity.

Going through the five Reiki Principles

In this section I list the five Reiki Principles and give you some ways to think about how to use these principles.

Don't get angry

Everyone feels anger at one time or another. Triggers for anger occur when someone does you wrong, hurts your feelings, or challenges your security.

The goal of this Reiki Principle is to express your anger in a way that doesn't hurt anyone (including yourself). Anger that isn't properly channeled leads to violence, war, crime, stress, and disease.

Anger that is properly channeled can be used to further your personal growth. The anger is a signal that you have an imbalance or conflict that needs to be addressed (see the steps later in this section). You can transform your anger by making changes in your thinking or actions.

Not getting angry doesn't mean to push away your anger. Suppressed anger can come back to bite you (and others). Like a smoldering flame, anger that is submerged will arise again, perhaps even stronger and more destructive.

Here are steps you can take to help you transform your anger:

1. **See the anger.**

   You can't do anything about your anger if you don't first recognize that you are angry.

2. **Take a timeout.**

   Count to ten, breathe deeply, and think about the situation before reacting. Avoid knee-jerk reactions. Don't send angry e-mails or shout angry words.

   If the anger dissipates on its own; then let it go! If you still feel angry, you must go deeper to see what's going on.

3. **Decide what the anger means.**

   Anger frequently masks other emotions, such as fear. For example, you might be angry with your husband for quitting his job because you fear being poor. Your fear about financial insecurity is what's underneath the anger.

4. **Take action.**

   If you fear financial insecurity, maybe you need to spend less or find ways to bring in more money. If someone in your life is making you angry on a regular basis, maybe you need to spend less time with that person.

Feeling angry isn't pleasant. Sometimes, you may be tempted to drown the anger in food, alcohol, or other addictive substances. You can't run from the anger. Use it instead to lead you farther in your spiritual journey. If you take your anger and meditate on it, you'll find a message for you. Your anger is actually a great teacher to lead you to your truth.

Learning to recognize and transform your anger from a knee-jerk reaction to calm action takes dedicated practice. You probably can't change from Ms. Angry Lady to Ms. Calm Lady overnight. But you can follow the "just for today" idea to change your thinking and behavior. Slowly but surely, your anger will diminish.

If you find that you can't resolve your anger on your own, find a therapist, counselor, or spiritual advisor who can help you.

Don't worry

A worrier is a person who worries about bad things that *may* happen. The irony is that worry drains the body and mind of the energy it actually needs to deal with any crisis! The best way to prepare for life's situations — and life always thrusts some sort of challenge — is to be in optimum condition in mind, body, and spirit.

Here are some tips to reduce worry:

- **Live in the present.** Worry is always about how past events might catch up with you and how future events might hurt you. What about right now?

- **Distract yourself from the worry.** Talk to a friend, laugh at a movie, or get involved with your life. You can wash your kitchen floor, pet your dog, or go for a walk.

- **Take action.** If you're worried about a person or situation, take any action that can help. For example, if you're worried about your son's health, perhaps you can find a new doctor or make him healthy food to eat.

- **Pray.** Constant worry denotes a lack of trust. Work to strengthen your connection with spirit. Pray about or send distant Reiki (see Chapter 15) to whatever worries you have.

- **Let go of the worry.** After you've taken any necessary action and prayed or sent distant Reiki, it's time to let go! To help yourself let go, try living in the present and distracting yourself.

Most of the time what you worry about never happens! Practicing the Reiki Principles regularly will keep you in better shape to handle what problems do arise in your life.

Be grateful

Appreciating what you have, no matter what it is, is essential for happiness. Here are some tips to help you keep an attitude of gratitude:

- **Keep a gratitude list or journal.** Write down everything from the smallest things (like your teeth or a hot bath) on up to the larger things, such as the love of your life.

- **Give thanks before or after each meal.** Thank the animals or plants that give their life energy, the farmers and suppliers, and the people who prepare your food.

- **Make gratitude a habit.** When you go to bed at night, take mental note of what you're thankful for in the day that has just ended.

Cultivating an attitude of gratitude helps develop humility because you're acknowledging that you're dependent on help from other people and spirit.

Be honest in your work

Work is how you connect with the world around you and provide for the exchange of resources (money) that allows you to stay warm and well fed. Sometimes this Reiki Principle is stated as "work hard."

Here are some questions to ask yourself about this Reiki Principle:

- **Am I honest in my dealings with my employers and clients?** Am I working with integrity, or am I trying to cheat my employer?

- **Am I following my true calling?** Many people are searching to know what their best job is. The best job is to do the utmost with what you're doing right now. If and when it's time to change, your inner voice will let you know. Following the nudging of your inner voice can be scary because many people fear change. (You can practice self-Reiki to help with these fears; see Chapter 11.)

- **Am I honoring myself in my work?** Working hard doesn't mean abusing yourself. Knowing when to work late and when to take a rest is part of the art of living.

- **Am I using my gifts and talents?** Work is more than paid 9-to-5 employment. You might also volunteer, raise children, and keep a home. You may have many different skills and abilities and use different ones at different times and situations. For example, you might be a gifted musician and play music with friends on weekends.

The type of work you do is not as important as your attitude and dedication to the project. And remember: just for today.

Be kind to yourself and others

The ultimate test when practicing a spiritual life is acceptance of and love for yourself and others. Being kind acknowledges that spirit is present in every living being. I had the opportunity to visit Japan for a scientific conference before I studied Reiki. One thing that impressed me was that people whom I passed in the street bowed to me, and I bowed to them. I was told that the concept behind this practice is that "the spirit in me sees the spirit in you." As a starting point for having more compassion in your life, you can try these suggestions:

- **Practice random acts of kindness.** This great concept couples the act of compassion with humility. You need not tell anyone what you have done, but it helps you anyway. An act of kindness can range from letting someone go ahead of you in the supermarket line to giving an anonymous financial gift. You can deposit coins in expired parking meters!

  ✔ **Listen to people.** Showing love for others is to give them what they want, not what you think they want.

  ✔ **Start by being kind to yourself.** You can't really love others if you don't love yourself. By loving yourself, you also demonstrate to others how you expect to be treated.

By practicing this and the other Reiki Principles, you begin to see all beings as manifestations of spirit. Even if you have petty disagreements with someone else, being kind means practicing from the deeper knowledge that love is behind all people, even if they're not aware of it. The funny thing about cultivating loving thoughts is that they have a way of growing and making the world a place filled with love and light.

Love is the essence of Reiki.

Incorporating the Reiki Principles into Your Daily Life

After you read about the Reiki Principles, you may think, "Okay, I've read them, now what?" The principles are deceptively simple, but it actually takes effort to consistently live by these principles day in and day out. Spiritual growth is a lifelong process.

Some teachers may ask you to make a promise to uphold the Reiki Principles before or after receiving an attunement (which open you to the Reiki energy; see Chapter 7 for more about attunements). It's up to you to decide how and when you will use the Reiki Principles in your life.

The most important part of the Reiki Principles states "just for today." Do the best you can to practice these principles today. Tomorrow will be another today, and you can start over again.

Saying it in Japanese

The Reiki Principles were originally intended to be chanted (in Japanese, of course) in the morning and in the evening. This practice was not included in Hawayo Takata's teachings, or Western Reiki.

For the purists out there who want to hear or say the Reiki Principles in Japanese, check out one of these Web sites:

  ✔ www.Reiki.org/Japanese Techniques/5Principles.html

  ✔ www.reikidharma.com/en/Reiki/en_ Reiki_pri_low.html

Soon, you'll be able to say the Reiki Principles in Japanese by yourself!

Reiki Principles from Hawayo Takata

Here is a variation on the Reiki Principles that was taught by Hawayo Takata to her students:

Just for today, do not anger
Just for today, do not worry
Honor your teachers, your father and mother, and your neighbors; count your blessings; and show appreciation for your food
Earn your living honestly
Be kind to everything that has life

From *Reiki: Hawayo Takata's Story* by Helen Haberly, 1990, Archedigm.

Here are some ways to use the Reiki Principles on a daily basis:

- Remind yourself of the principles by reading them silently or aloud and thinking or writing about each of the five Reiki Principles at least once a day. (Learn to recite them in Japanese by consulting the sidebar "Saying it in Japanese.")

- Put up a copy of the Reiki Principles in a prominent place in your home or office.

- Some Reiki people use the Gassho meditation (see Chapter 9), putting the hands in a prayer position in front of the heart, when reciting the Reiki Principles.

The more time and effort you put into the Reiki Principles, the more peace and serenity you will find.

Additional Versions of Reiki Principles

Here are two other Reiki Principles from other versions that I feel deserve some mention.

Just for today, be humble

The principle "be grateful" is sometimes interpreted as "be humble." I like this version because it reminds me to release my ego, which can prevent Reiki from flowing.

To be humble is to have *humility,* which is an absence of pride or arrogance. I see humility as recognizing your place in the universe: not too small and not too big. Here are a few other ways to look at this principle:

- ✔ To be humble is to understand that any gift or power that you possess comes from a higher source.
- ✔ To be humble is to know that you're not better or worse than any other human being or Reiki practitioner.

Having humility gives you a safe place to rest. You don't need to be better than anyone, and you don't need to compete. Realizing that you're a channel for a higher power takes the need to control out of your hands. If you are a Reiki practitioner, you have no control of how your energy work will help others. You do the work and leave the outcome to a higher power.

I like this principle. It puts me right in the place I need to be!

Honor your parents, teachers, elders

Hawayo Takata and her students added these versions to the Reiki Principles. One of my Reiki teachers gave me "Honor your parents, teachers, elders." In the sidebar version ("Reiki Principles from Hawayo Takata"), it is "Honor your teachers, your father and mother, and your neighbors; count your blessings; and show appreciation for your food."

This principle brings in the biblical commandment to honor your parents and adds teachers and others to the statement.

Perhaps Hawayo Takata adapted this principle to fit the story of Reiki she devised to enable Reiki to fit into the Christian Western culture during World War II, when anti-Japanese sentiments ran high.

Use the version of the Reiki Principles that feels right to *you.*

Part II
Experiencing Reiki for Yourself

The 5th Wave   By Rich Tennant

"I think my body's energy centers ARE well balanced. I keep my pager on my belt, my cellphone in my right pocket, and my palmtop computer in my inside left breast pocket."

In this part . . .

The best way to find out about Reiki is to try it! Go to your local healing center, beauty salon, or complementary health practitioner and ask about Reiki. Once you find a Reiki practitioner or a Reiki circle, you begin the journey of healing. The chapters in Part II tell you what you need to do to begin exploring the benefits of Reiki.

The noise and distraction of the outside world stop when you're receiving Reiki. As the Reiki practitioner channels the beautiful healing energy of Reiki, you might feel yourself floating as you enter a deeper and deeper state of relaxation. You might even fall asleep! The benefits of Reiki continue after the session as the relaxation continues.

The Reiki benefits don't stop with you. Your entire family can use Reiki to relax and to enhance the healing of medical, emotional, or stress-related problems. Even your pets can enjoy the benefits of Reiki.

Whether or not you go on to become a Reiki practitioner, you'll always come back to the essence of Reiki: receiving the healing energy yourself.

Chapter 5

Getting the Reiki Treatment

*R*eceiving Reiki is a delightful experience. The more you relax and let yourself absorb the Reiki energy, the more you'll get out of it. You might experience Reiki in a professional, one-on-one session, or you might attend a Reiki circle and receive shorter treatments there. You might find out about Reiki from a friend or relative who then extends an informal offer to give you a Reiki treatment in your home.

In this chapter, I go through the Reiki session from the point of view of the recipient, describing what to expect while receiving Reiki, what to look for in a practitioner, and what you can do to most benefit from Reiki. If you want to know more about what the practitioner is doing, you can ask her or read Chapter 13, which describes the session from the point of view of the practitioner.

A first Reiki experience

A young man who came to a Reiki circle that I attended wrote this of his first experience lying on the Reiki table:

"I was a bit nervous, as I didn't know what was going on. However, within the first five minutes, I was able to detach from reality, let go, and not only enjoy but feel, truly feel, the energy, magic, and life that was transpiring around me, through me, and around me. Magic, truly magic. I have not felt that safe, free, good, and pure in a long time, like five years at least."

Finding the Right Reiki Practitioner for You

Reiki practitioners come in all ages, shapes, and sizes. You can even give Reiki to yourself if you have studied Reiki (see Chapters 7 and 11). Here are two types of Reiki practitioners you'll encounter:

- ✔ **A friend or family member who practices Reiki:** You might find out about Reiki from a friend or relative who then extends an informal offer to give you a Reiki treatment in your home.

- ✔ **A professional Reiki practitioner:** You generally pay for these services, which are provided in a specially designated location. Professionalism in Reiki is growing as more practitioners establish businesses where they provide Reiki (see Chapter 17).

The difference between a professional Reiki session and a freebie session from a friend is like the difference between a chef's meal cooked at home or cooked in his restaurant. Both are exquisite but are prepared in different environments.

A Reiki practitioner is a professional just like a massage therapist, chiropractor, or even a doctor. The Reiki practitioner has spent time learning his trade and polishing his skills. In the future, health insurers may cover Reiki services.

Locating a professional practitioner

If you're ready to try a private Reiki session, how can you find a good practitioner? You can find Reiki in a beauty salon, a chiropractor's office, a village hall, or a private office. Try these suggestions:

✔ **Get personal recommendations.** Nothing beats a positive reference from someone who's actually been to a Reiki practitioner. Ask your friends and family and your health care practitioners, including massage therapists, chiropractors, and psychologists, if they can recommend a Reiki practitioner.

✔ **Go to your local Reiki circles that are open to the public.** Individual Reiki practitioners or groups of Reiki practitioners may run regular Reiki circles or host special Reiki events in your neighborhood. These public events give you the opportunity to try out Reiki and ask about Reiki practitioners in your area. The sessions are usually shorter than the usual private session, and you may have more than one person working on you. Read more about Reiki circles in Chapter 14.

✔ **Look in your local newspaper.** They may have ads or news stories about Reiki practitioners.

✔ **Call your local hospital.** Some hospitals run Reiki programs or have Reiki practitioners on staff.

Interviewing your potential practitioner

After you have the names of some professional Reiki practitioners, you can contact them by phone or in person to see which one appears to best meet your needs. Ask them the following questions:

✔ **What level of Reiki are you?** A professional Reiki practitioner should have studied 2nd-degree Reiki or beyond. Read more about degrees of Reiki in Chapter 7. Although people with 1st-degree Reiki training may treat family members or within the setting of a Reiki circle, they don't have the experience to treat professionally.

✔ **What healing systems do you use alongside Reiki, if any?** Find out whether they use other systems of healing, such as reflexology or polarity therapy. Some massage therapists or other healers combine Reiki with other healing arts. Let the practitioner know if you want a combined session (which sometimes costs more) or want to receive only Reiki.

✔ **What do you see as the value of Reiki, especially for me?** This question is important because it gives insight into the practitioner's view on how Reiki can help you. See whether the answer meshes with how you feel about receiving Reiki.

✔ **How many sessions do they think I will need?** This answer gives you further insight into the practitioner's perspective on how Reiki works. Some practitioners recommend a series of appointments, especially for dealing with long-term illness or stress. Others take a more laid-back approach and leave it to you to decide.

✔ **How long have you have practiced Reiki?** It helps if the practitioner has been working on her own healing with Reiki or another healing modality for at least a year if not decades! However, I'm a firm believer in quality over quantity when it comes to practicing Reiki, as some people work on healing for years to get to the same place as another person can get in a year.

On a practical note, consider these questions for yourself:

✔ **Is the location of Reiki convenient for you?** The closer to home, the easier it will be for you to get there.

✔ **Can you afford the price of the Reiki?** You'll be more likely to repeat your Reiki experience if you can pay the fee. If the cost is too high, speak to the practitioner. Some Reiki professionals use a sliding fee scale.

✔ **Can the practitioner travel to your home or office?** Some Reiki practitioners, like their massage therapist counterparts, take traveling Reiki tables and travel to a location of your choice. Doing so frequently involves a greater cost, as the price of the session includes travel expenditures. However, this service is useful if you are homebound.

✔ **Do you feel comfortable with this person?** This, for me, is the most important thing. For you to be able to relax, you need to have some basic trust that the person knows what she is doing and treats you with respect.

Trust your gut (your intuition) when choosing a Reiki practitioner. If someone "feels" right to you, then she is, no matter what the answers to any questions might be. On the same note, if someone "feels" wrong, then that person isn't the right one for you, no matter how well recommended the person might be.

Preparing Yourself for Your First Reiki Session

Approach Reiki in a light-hearted way in order to relax and enjoy yourself. I think you'll be impressed with how well you feel at the end of the session.

Doing a bit of reflection before the session can help you focus and get in the Reiki frame of mind. If you can, write down all the things you want the Reiki session to accomplish. Your list might read something like:

✔ To get rid of this headache

✔ To make my neck feel better

✔ To improve my relationship with my daughter

✔ To stop worrying about my marriage

By knowing what you want to get out of the session, you set the focus to achieve just that. The practitioner might ask you, "What are your intentions for this session?" By thinking ahead of time, you'll know exactly what it is you need.

I sit in my car for a couple of minutes before going to receive a Reiki session, taking the time to breathe and meditate. Doing so helps me to be more focused and relaxed when I enter the Reiki room.

Try not to have a heavy meal or lots of caffeine just before a session. You are going to relax and receive energy. If your stomach is digesting or your body is speeding, you may not feel so ready to lie down and receive a little bliss.

Exploring a Reiki Session from Beginning to End

Every Reiki session is unique, and the exact steps of each session depend on the practitioner and the recipient. Given that, you'll find a general structure to the Reiki treatment that varies slightly from practitioner to practitioner.

The length of an average full Reiki session performed by one person is one hour, but check with your practitioner to be sure. You might have a shorter session, especially if Reiki is performed at a Reiki circle with more than one practitioner (see Chapter 14).

You might lie on your back for the entire session or start on one side and be given a gentle reminder midway to turn over.

What to expect before the session

Reiki begins when you meet and greet — or connect with — the practitioner. Tell your practitioner if anything is troubling you so that she can address that issue. This is the time to set intention by saying something like "I'm hoping to relieve tension and get rid of this headache."

Entering the Reiki room

Each room is different depending on the personality of the practitioner and whether this room is dedicated to Reiki or used for different purposes.

The room can be dark, with candlelight providing the only light, or bright with sunshine. Music may be softly playing, and you may see crystals and flowering plants sitting on shelves or spiritual artwork hanging on the walls. Or the room may be simple and unadorned.

Take in the relaxing ambience that is present. Breathe in the peace that is the true purpose of your Reiki session.

Filling out forms

Your Reiki practitioner may ask you to fill in some forms before the session, and you may have to sign some forms for legal purposes. These forms usually ask for your name, contact information, and information about any health issues and medications you take. The forms may include disclaimers stating the following:

- The practitioner is not a physician and is not licensed by the state.
- Reiki serves only as a method of relaxation and stress reduction.

Some providers also ask you to commit to your part of the healing process (see the section "Committing Yourself to Healing with Reiki," later in this chapter).

Lying down on the table

Most practitioners use a sturdy table that allows you to feel supported and allows the practitioner to stand or sit while gently putting his hands on you. If you're short like me, you might need to use a stool to climb up on the table!

Staying comfortable

You remain fully clothed during a Reiki session, but you'll want to take off your shoes, tight belts, watches, eyeglasses, or outer clothing that is restrictive to your comfort. At a spa, you may receive a robe to relax in. The practitioner typically offers pillows to place under your neck or legs for comfort, or a blanket to stay warm.

Speak up at any time during the session if you're uncomfortable or too cold, or if you need a tissue or want the music turned off. It's your time to relax, so make sure the environment is right for you!

Undergoing the Reiki session

The Reiki session is a sacred time during which you are receiving the Reiki energy. The practitioner might say some prayers out loud or silently to aid her spiritual connection and good intentions for your session.

Reiki comes through the Reiki practitioner, so she prepares herself to be a clear and open channel for the Reiki to flow to you.

The practitioner will move her hands to different parts of your body as a way to direct the Reiki. At times her hands will lie on your body, and other times they'll hover above your body. You may feel a sensation of heat coming from the practitioner's hands. Don't worry — this feeling is normal, but if it's uncomfortable for you, tell the practitioner.

Relaxing during the session

The Reiki session is a delicious experience during which you can close your eyes and know that you have an hour of freedom. The telephone, traffic, e-mails, or the doorbell won't disturb you.

You may drift off into a dreamlike state or even fall asleep. Don't worry if you do. You're supposed to be relaxing, so whatever you do is right for you. Try not to judge yourself or any thoughts you might have. Just let it all flow.

Experiencing the sensations of Reiki

Each person experiences Reiki in his or her own way. You may feel tingles or shivers during Reiki. Energy waves are passing through your body, and everyone experiences what this feels like in a different way. I list some other sensations you may experience during the Reiki session in Table 5-1.

Table 5-1	Common Sensations during a Reiki Session
Sensations You Might Feel	*Effects of Deep Relaxation*
Cold or hot	Temperature change
Crying or laughing	Emotions
Sighing or coughing	Energy release or lungs clearing out
Stomach gurgling or feet or hands twitching	Involuntary body movement
Dreamlike state or sleep	State of relaxation
Seeing images or colors or hearing music	Extrasensory perceptions

Your intuition is heightened during a Reiki session, which is like being in the state between waking and sleeping, so don't be surprised if you get a dreamy message from beyond! You may get a fleeting image or memory. You may get insights to some long-standing problem, similar to what you might experience during meditation or daydreaming.

There is no right or wrong, or good or bad, in anything you feel during the Reiki session. Please just let yourself be!

Approaching the end of your session

You'll know the session is ending when the practitioner taps you on your shoulder or tells you, "Take your time getting up from the table."

Don't rush off the table. Just as you might take a little time when you wake up in the morning before hopping out of bed, you need a little time now. You may feel lightheaded or woozy, so you want to go slowly to avoid tripping over your feet.

Session accomplished: After the Reiki session

After the session is over, you'll put on your shoes, pay the practitioner, and talk about your experience. The practitioner will probably ask you, "How do you feel?" You may have some questions or comments. Sometimes the practitioner will have feedback for you, such as "You look more relaxed now" or "I sensed that you really took in the Reiki energy." You may decide to book another appointment.

Getting grounded

Don't go off too soon after the session, especially if you're driving. Take the time to get grounded and come back to the world. You may need to sit for a while, breathe deeply, or take a little walk to feel more grounded.

Detoxing

The relaxation process might set off a detoxification process, which is just the removal of stuck toxins in your body. One of the ways that Reiki works is by removing any energy blocks in your body. As stagnant energy makes its way out of the body, unwanted toxins will leave through your urine, phlegm, feces, or sweat. Drinking lots of water helps the process of detoxification. Just as it's recommended to drink water after a massage, you should also drink water after a Reiki session.

Maintaining that good feeling

After a Reiki session, you'll feel good. If you can, try to keep this feeling of relaxation going as long as you can. Take a stroll in nature, sip tea quietly in your garden, or take a relaxing bath.

Capturing the Aha! moment

You may get inspirational messages from your Reiki session that you need to capture on paper so you don't forget them! Try to bring paper and a pen to your sessions so you can write down any thoughts before they slip away. For example, you may get an insight into a long-standing problem or get an idea to help you at work.

What you think are your important issues when you walk into the Reiki session may well change after the session. The insights you gather during the session may lead you to deeper issues to address. Be thankful for the gifts of healing and clarity that Reiki bestows upon you and be gentle on yourself as you travel your healing path.

Probably the most important insight to gather from a Reiki session is love and acceptance of yourself, as the sacred being that you are.

Repeating Your Reiki Experience

For most people, one Reiki session isn't enough to satisfactorily change life-long habits, illnesses, or thought patterns. If you've been a worrier type of person all your life, one Reiki session will certainly help you. But when the next crisis hits, will you have the ability to react in a calm way?

If you have a serious illness, multiple Reiki sessions stand a better chance of helping you in the recovery process. For example, if you have a form of cancer and are receiving chemotherapy, consider scheduling Reiki weekly during this time, or schedule one Reiki session before or after each chemo session. The more often you receive Reiki, the more it can help you cope with the stress of your health problem.

Your Reiki practitioner will suggest how often you should visit him, or you may have an idea of what would feel best for you. Sometimes you can get a discount by booking multiple sessions at one time. During a stressful period of your life, weekly sessions can keep you feeling bright-eyed and bushy-tailed. If things are rolling along nicely, then consider monthly sessions to keep yourself tuned up.

If you're keen on Reiki but can't get to a practitioner regularly, consider learning Reiki yourself to supplement your sessions by giving Reiki to yourself (see Chapter 11).

Try a different Reiki practitioner if you're not sure about the first one. Use the suggestions I provide in the section "Finding the Right Reiki Practitioner for You," earlier in this chapter.

Using Reiki in Tandem with Other Therapies

For many ailments, you may need to use the services of more than one type of practitioner, in addition to your Reiki practitioner. For example, you may want to also see a psychotherapist, a massage therapist, a nutritionist, or a medical doctor. For example, I have been feeling stressed by my father's death and feeling achy while sitting at the computer. A Reiki session beautifully restores my balance and heals at a deep energy level. But I still visit my chiropractor to help my body adjust on a physical level. I find that using different practitioners as needed brings out the best level of healing.

Reiki combines well with all the healing arts, whether they're complementary treatments, such as massage, or conventional medical treatments, such as surgery or chemotherapy. Chapter 16 describes ways of combining Reiki with other types of treatments.

Reiki was love at first sleep

A friend in London had just learned Reiki and offered to give me a session. I traveled to her flat, and she performed Reiki on her sofa. I quickly fell asleep. All that I recalled was that Reiki was relaxing.

A year later, I got the opportunity to learn Reiki myself while living in New Mexico. I was fortunate to be living near an active Reiki community that had Reiki circles twice a week. I experienced Reiki from many people who lived or passed through the area. From these gracious people, I learned so much about Reiki — mostly that I loved it!

I never tire of Reiki, and it helps me come into my self. I can get lost in the everyday world of busyness. Reiki brings me the feeling of awakening from a deep relaxing sleep. I am refreshed and ready for the challenges and joys of life.

Committing Yourself to Healing with Reiki

Healing with Reiki is not a completely passive process. It may seem passive because during the Reiki session you're lying on the table with your eyes closed, receiving the energy transmitted through the practitioner. But you can take action before and after the Reiki session to make the most of what Reiki has to offer on the physical, mental, emotional, and spiritual levels.

The Reiki practitioner, and the Reiki itself, are tools you use as you grow and heal in your life. No matter how gifted the healer or how powerful the Reiki, you participate in the healing process by being open to growth and change. One way that Reiki works is by helping you to be open to such change. You may not want to change at first, but eventually as you truly desire to feel better within yourself, you may see that certain changes will help. You may notice changes in the following areas of your life:

- ✔ **Your thought patterns:** Reiki gives you insight into your underlying thoughts and beliefs that may hold you back from achieving your goals. Constant negative thinking brings about negative results. Positive thinking brings about positive results.

- ✔ **Your physical lifestyle:** Destructive behavior or lifestyle choices conflict with growth and healing. For example, you may want to consider your eating and exercise habits and possible addictive behavior. As you allow more healing through Reiki into your life, your behaviors become healthier. You don't have to force the change; you'll want to change.

- ✔ **Your relationships:** How you interact with others can bring joy or grief to yourself and people around you. Reiki can help you become calmer so that you have more patience and tolerance with others (and yourself).

- ✔ **Your job:** Your paid work and other activities are another place for you to express your true self and contribute to the world. As you become more in touch with your inner self through Reiki, you might change your job or your relationship to your work.

How far you go with Reiki depends on how you follow up on your Reiki sessions. As a result of Reiki, you may get a thought that smoking is hurting you or you have to start singing. To really benefit from Reiki, take the insights you get while on the Reiki table and put them into action.

Chapter 6

Letting Your Entire Family Experience Reiki

*R*eiki is a gentle universal energy and can be used for anyone of any age. Children are particularly open to Reiki energy, and older adults can benefit from the relaxing Reiki touch. Even furry, feathery, or finned family pets can use a little Reiki! In this chapter, I describe the many ways that Reiki can benefit you and your family members.

In this chapter, I also describe how you can be helped by the typical Reiki session, as outlined in Chapter 5. But Reiki is flexible, and there are other ways to give Reiki in situations where a lie-down, one-hour, hands-on session isn't possible. These techniques include using hands above the body (see Chapter 10), beaming the Reiki from the other side of the room (see Chapter 10), or even sending Reiki from another location altogether (see Chapter 15).

Everyone responds to Reiki in his own way. You may be surprised when the person you least expect turns out to love Reiki the most.

Helping Yourself with Reiki

Reiki is a gentle healing energy. Your body can use this energy for just about anything it needs. Here are some common reasons to use Reiki:

- You're stressed out and need some tender loving care.
- You're taking doctor-prescribed medications and want to reduce or eliminate the side effects of these drugs.
- You're low on energy or feel blah or unmotivated and need a pick-me-up.
- You haven't been sleeping well.
- You feel stuck emotionally or mentally and want some insights on how to move forward.
- You just want a delicious treat for your body, mind, and spirit.

You can think of Reiki as a dose of love. When you receive a Reiki session, you'll feel the effects that love can give you. This isn't love from any particular person; it's just the essence of love and how that can heal you.

How can Reiki help you? In oh so many ways. Reiki helps you to do the following:

- **Relax:** The desire to feel more relaxed is the main reason people try Reiki. If you're feeling anxious, stressed, or tense, Reiki can help you feel calmer. When you're feeling relaxed, your body is better able to handle life's ups and downs. Because Reiki aids relaxation, it can help you cope with and heal from any problem or illness.

- **Handle a physical illness:** Another main reason people try Reiki is to help overcome disease or pain. Your body is made of energy (see Chapter 2), and Reiki helps balance your energy and remove any blocks to the flow of energy. Reiki works not only to reduce anxiety, lessen pain, and relax you but also works at the underlying cause of disease. I discuss how Reiki works alongside conventional and alternative medical treatments in Chapter 16.

  In a family situation, Reiki helps to heal everything from minor scrapes and bruises to the flu or even major accidents or long-standing illnesses. At the very least, Reiki relaxes you enough so that you can have a better attitude toward your illness, which helps you get better quicker.

✓ **Handle an emotional upset:** After you suffer a loss, such as the death of a loved one or the end of relationship, you can surely benefit from the boost that Reiki can provide. Here are some examples of times to try Reiki:

- **When you suffer an emotional shock, such as the loss of a relative or friend:** I know of a woman who benefited from Reiki after she lost her fiancé to a sudden tragic death. Reiki was one of the methods she used to help herself cope with this loss and rebuild her life.

- **During life transitions:** Changes in life, even positive changes, can be stressful. Moving home, starting a new job, or having a baby can stir up the emotional pot, and Reiki can help you make sense of your situation and feel ready for change.

- **If you're in emotional burnout:** Perhaps you're taking care of an elderly parent, trying to be supermom to young children, or working two jobs to make ends meet. If you feel like you're at the end of your rope or about to fall apart, Reiki can help.

- **When you're making decisions:** Suppose that you have a major life decision to make and you feel stuck. You may be trying to figure out whether to change a relationship or job or what course of action to take for a business venture. Perhaps you want some clarity about what to do about a physical ailment. Reiki helps you relax, and while you're relaxing, the answer just might come to you!

✓ **Feel spiritually connected:** As you relax with Reiki, you detach from your everyday cares and worries. Now you can hear the still voice inside of you. You can feel peace. You're connecting with your higher self and with spirit. Also, some people find that Reiki helps their intuitive process, so you just might awaken your inner psychic!

Cycling through Life with Reiki

When you use Reiki to deal with life — yours or someone else's — it's like turning up the frequency on a radio a notch. Things are a little lighter and a little brighter. These are the effects of a subtle energy such as Reiki. Any time of life, from beginning to end and everything in between, can blossom from Reiki.

Starting with pregnancy

With pregnancy comes a slew of physical changes in the mother's body as the baby develops and grows. Both mother and child benefit from the gentle energy that Reiki provides. Reiki offers some specific benefits during pregnancy:

- ✔ Reiki doesn't require any physical manipulation of the body. Reiki uses a gentle touch directly on the body or even above the body.

- ✔ Reiki can be performed above blankets and in any position, so mothers-to-be can make themselves comfortable in a sitting or lying position.

- ✔ Reiki can be performed at any time during pregnancy.

- ✔ The baby can also be treated with Reiki with hands directly on the mother's belly or with Reiki hands hovering above. When a baby starts getting Reiki, he may respond, so watch out for moving and kicking!

Reiki at the beginning of life

Here are two people's accounts of how Reiki can be used before and during birth.

Anita tells the story of the birth of a healthy son to her and her husband, aided by Rachel, a Reiki practitioner, and the medical staff: "When I found out that I was pregnant, I was a little concerned because of my age (42). I began to receive Reiki every Friday until the birth of my son. My delivery was difficult and very painful. Although the Reiki could not completely take away the pain, it helped me be sure that my son was 100 percent okay, and I knew he was healthy and safe. I trusted Rachel. I felt very connected to God during this time, and I know that the energy was working for the highest good for all of us. I believe that if I had not received Reiki during the delivery of my son, I would have not made it through the miracle of birth. My son is healthy, bright, and full of energy. He asks me for Reiki all the time. He is really a Reiki baby; he even attends a Reiki circle on Friday nights. Reiki has truly been a gift from above."

Rachel, the Reiki practitioner, shares her story: "Reiki has helped me in many aspects of my life and also has given me such beautiful gifts. I have had the privilege to administer Reiki to several women during their pregnancies and the delivery of two. From the day that Anita knew she was pregnant, I and our circle of practitioners gave her Reiki weekly, and I was present during the delivery of her son. With each of Anita's contractions, I felt the energy even stronger and felt more connected to Anita and her child. Her delivery was quite difficult, and they wanted to do a C-section. Reiki helped her have a regular delivery."

The purpose of Reiki is to bring out the highest good for the people being treated, which means both mother and child!

Cherishing childhood with Reiki

Reiki and children are natural partners. Children intuitively understand the subtle energy of Reiki (see Chapter 2 for info about subtle energy). For mothers, fathers, grandparents, and any guardian or caretaker of children, learning Reiki lets them give energy to their children.

A mother's touch is a particularly powerful healing force for children. If a mother is attuned to Reiki (meaning she has become a channel for Reiki energy; see Chapter 7), she'll transmit Reiki through her touch. The same is true for fathers and all who care for children!

Receiving Reiki

You can give Reiki to newborn infants, toddlers, or school-age children. Reiki can help your child do the following:

- Relax before exams or tryouts
- Relax before starting a new school
- Cope with a loss of a family member
- Fight a cold or flu
- Heal sprains or broken bones
- Relax when a new baby arrives or before or after a move to a new town

Generally, younger children require a shorter Reiki period than adults. (This is true of animals also.) But, if a child is ill, then she might absorb Reiki for a longer period.

Children don't express themselves in the same way as adults, but they also feel stress and emotional turmoil. Reiki can be very helpful for emotional or physical ailments.

Practicing Reiki

Some children express an interest in learning Reiki too. They may be attracted to it after receiving a Reiki session, or they may follow your progress as you learn Reiki and want to learn alongside you.

If you are a Reiki Master teacher, then you can attune children as feels appropriate. Start with 1st-level Reiki and see how the child responds. You should modify any class for children because they don't need to learn all the history or methodology at this point.

When children are attuned to Reiki, they can help give Reiki to a family member, friend, or pet who is sick. Doing so empowers children by letting them contribute to the well-being of others.

Traipsing through the teenage years with Reiki

Reiki has a lot to offer teens going through the trials and tribulations of growing up into adulthood. Some teens show a great deal of interest in Reiki. They may be interested in spiritual or healing pursuits or just may want to join Dad in his Reiki studies.

Receiving Reiki

Teens may benefit from a Reiki session that is as long as that for an adult (see Chapter 5), but always respect their wishes if they want a shorter session. Actually, that advice applies to anyone of any age.

Reiki really works well with teenagers. They need the relief from the stress of all the changes in their bodies and feelings.

Practicing Reiki

Teenagers may express an interest in studying Reiki. Depending on their maturity and level of interest, they can study Reiki alongside adults.

Ask the Reiki teacher to meet the teen to determine the best type of training. See Chapter 7 to read about Reiki training and how to find a Reiki teacher. Some Reiki teachers give special classes for children or teens in addition to classes for adults.

Learning Reiki can be quite empowering for young adults because they can use it to boost their energy and deal with the trials and tribulations of teenage years. Reiki may be just the thing to help them through relationship, school, and family woes. When teens see all that Reiki can do (see Chapters 18 and 19), they'll probably agree that this therapy is pretty cool.

Reiki in the family

When more than one person in the family has some Reiki training, you can share Reiki experiences with each other. You can attend Reiki circles or retreats (see Chapter 14), work on Grandma as a Reiki team, and share your adventures learning about Reiki together.

Don't be disappointed if your child or mate loses interest in Reiki after a while. They may not share the same level of interest in Reiki as you do, but that doesn't mean they don't like Reiki or you!

Let each person in your family use Reiki in the way that's comfortable for her. Not everyone is destined to practice Reiki every single day or even weekly or monthly. Remember that after people are trained, they are "attuned" to Reiki for life. They can always use Reiki — if they want to.

Teenagers enjoy giving Reiki on a volunteer basis. Whether at a Reiki circle (see Chapter 14) or an animal clinic, a Reiki-trained teenager is eager to add her hands alongside others.

Gracing the senior years with Reiki

Reiki can ease the aging process by helping adults stay calm in the face of changing health and lifestyle situations. Because Reiki is so gentle, it can be used no matter what the health situation. In Chapter 16, I describe how Reiki complements different health treatments.

Receiving Reiki

Adults may have more aches and pains or have to deal with increasing numbers of health issues as they age. Reiki can be very useful to help elders stay relaxed and help the body's internal resources work better. Any time is a good time to get a Reiki session, but Reiki may be especially beneficial for people who

- ✔ Are undergoing a life transition such as divorce, the death of a spouse, a move, or retirement. Reiki brings a feeling of calm and of being centered.

- ✔ Are worried and stressed. Reiki brings relaxation.

- ✔ Have an illness. As people age, healing takes longer. Reiki may speed up the healing process (see Chapter 16).

- ✔ Want a pick-me-up. Everyone deserves to experience an energy boost, or even some moments of bliss.

Energy is ageless and forever

Reiki knows no age limitations and is as useful in the last stages of life as it is at the beginning. It's a shame that many people fear the aging process and see it only as a loss of health and opportunity. Many forget the wisdom and depth of perception that is a blessing of age and experience.

As long as you are here on earth, you have the opportunity to experience and share love and joy. It can be a simple act, such as enjoying the smile of a child or the feel of a warm breeze. If you are feeling down, a change in perspective can open you to feel better within yourself. Reiki can provide this type of change by helping you connect to an inner sense of calm, peace, and bliss.

Reiki works with energy, which is the part of you that never dies. Reiki connects you to your soul and spirit. Reiki helps you deal gracefully with whatever challenges come your way by helping you connect with the deeper part of yourself that never dies.

Reiki can be a breather during a difficult time!

Practicing Reiki

In your own senior years, you may have more time on your hands. The children have grown up and moved on, and your work may have slowed down. This is a perfect time to learn Reiki.

You may find that you want to learn Reiki for one of the following reasons:

- ✔ **To help yourself deal with illness:** You can give yourself Reiki treatments (see Chapter 11).

- ✔ **To help your spouse or friend with an illness:** As a caretaker of another, Reiki is a valuable aid (see Chapter 16).

- ✔ **To help yourself grow spiritually:** Reiki opens your energy channels, allowing you to see more clearly. Read about energy systems in the body in Chapter 2 and personal growth with Reiki in Chapter 19.

- ✔ **As a tool for manifestation:** You'll feel empowered by using Reiki to help you achieve your goals. A friend of mine used Reiki to help empower her goal of moving out of her family home that she had lived in for 36 years. She used the manifestations techniques (see a sidebar on the topic in Chapter 1) to pave the way to move into her first home of her own at the age of 66!

Check out Chapter 7 to find out about Reiki classes and teachers. Your wisdom and experience gained over the years will certainly aid you as a Reiki practitioner.

Concluding life with Reiki

Just as Reiki is valuable during entry into life during birth, Reiki is also helpful at the end-of-life transition. Hospitals, hospices, and nursing homes are becoming knowledgeable about Reiki because of the value this treatment has for patients and their families (see Chapter 16). See the sidebar "Reiki at the end of life: A personal journey" for my own Reiki experience with loved ones near death. To read about how hospitals and hospices use Reiki, see Chapter 16.

Reiki at the end of life: A personal journey

I was honored to be able to use Reiki with both of my parents at the end of their lives.

My mother was unconscious after suffering a severe intracerebral hemorrhage and was on life-support systems. When I heard of her situation, I sent distant Reiki (see Chapter 15) while flying on the airplane to get to her. As she lay in the intensive care unit, I was able to use Reiki on areas of her body that were free from machinery, especially her hands and feet. Although the Reiki didn't keep her alive, it helped me feel that I could do something to ease her situation.

My dad died at home, just days after signing on with hospice. He was conscious until moments before his death and requested Reiki from me hours before his death. My dad was a strong, proud man. I don't remember him ever staying home from work, and he enjoyed robust health until he got older and his heart and lungs developed disease. He was interested in the fact that I did Reiki, but he never wanted to try it. As his illness progressed, he talked about trying Reiki but was never ready to do so. When drugs no longer helped him, he finally was ready to try

Reiki. He wanted to start with someone other than me, so we found George, an older gentleman with enthusiasm for Reiki. George brought light and hope to my dad's bedroom. My dad was able to let go of his oxygen for the duration of the session and a short time afterward. After the session, my dad was quiet and looked peaceful and contemplative.

The next day was to be my dad's last. His condition was worsening, and I offered him Reiki, which he accepted two different times. He particularly wanted the peace that Reiki offered.

I was next to my Dad when he moved toward his death. I gently let my hands transmit Reiki as my sister and I spoke words of love.

My sister asked me afterward if Reiki hastened my dad's death. I don't know about that, but I do know it brought him peace. I believe it also aided his transition to the next world.

I was amazed that my dad had finally accepted Reiki, a gentle, beautiful energy. This was a gift not only for him but also for my family and me.

REMEMBER From an energy perspective, energy is never destroyed, but it does change form. Death is a transition from life on earth as we know it to the afterlife. Reiki aids this transition by transmitting the pure energy of love, which gives relief and peace.

Using Reiki for the Family Pet

Animals also benefit from Reiki. Whether you have cats, dogs (see Figure 6-1), birds, fish, or ferrets, you can use Reiki to help your pets. Don't forget your horse or other large animals, who also benefit from Reiki.

Figure 6-1:
Performing
Reiki on
a dog.

TIP Any animal that receives regular grooming from a human is probably receptive to being touched for Reiki. If you want to give Reiki to an animal who is not usually touched, such as fish or wild animals, use techniques where you give Reiki from afar, such as beaming (see Chapter 10) and distant Reiki (see Chapter 15).

Knowing when and where to go for Reiki

Reiki works well with animals for the same reasons it works well on children and people of all ages. Have you ever noticed that when you pet an animal, he rolls over to receive more or looks at you with lovey-dovey eyes or sighs?

Animals respond to your loving touch and intention. Reiki is another way to help your animals feel better.

You can give Reiki to animals in the following situations:

✔ **When they are ill:** Reiki helps the healing process and works with any type of medical intervention.

✔ **When they are young or old:** You can use Reiki on an animal of any age or situation.

✔ **When they have been through a trauma:** Animals can use loving energy after they've experienced any type of abuse, loss, or move, or if they seem to exhibit depression or other behavioral disorder. Even if you don't know what the problem is, you can use Reiki to help.

Finding the right pet practitioner

If your pet can travel, you can take him to a Reiki clinic. You may find that a pet trainer, pet groomer, or breeder also offers Reiki services. Here are some suggestions for finding a Reiki practitioner for your animal friend:

✔ Any Reiki practitioner can give Reiki to your pet, although some practitioners specialize in giving Reiki to animals.

✔ Animal lovers who work as animal handlers or in veterinarian's offices are taking Reiki training so they can use Reiki in their work. Some Reiki practitioners specialize in treating animals or even a particular type of animal.

✔ In some cities, you may find Reiki clinics for pets! Obviously, you need to have an animal who can travel and behave among other animals.

✔ You can learn Reiki yourself (see Chapter 7) so you can help your animals.

Reiki and the horse named Bandit

Bandit was a beloved horse who was instrumental in a therapeutic program to help children and adults with special needs. One day, he had an accident in which he landed on his side and dislocated some of his spine. He was unable to move, and his heartbroken owner didn't know if she would have to have him euthanized. She wanted to know how to help this horse who had helped so many.

A group of Reiki practitioners, including one who specialized in massage and Reiki for horses, gave Reiki three times a day for quite some time in order to get Bandit into the trailer so he could go to the vet for a bone scan to assess the damage. If his damage was severe, humane euthanasia was the only option.

The good news was that Bandit's injuries could be healed, so his Reiki treatments continued. When the treatments stopped, Bandit was reportedly not only healed but was also better than before the treatments! He had a bigger stride after treatment than before.

Nine years later, Bandit did have to be euthanized because of old age and complications of emphysema. But his owner and other friends gave him Reiki at the end of his life, and he reportedly leaned into the Reiki practitioners' hands so as to suck up the Reiki energy.

Bandit's owner is a Reiki practitioner who uses Reiki to help all the horses that she uses in her program.

Listening to animals

Animals differ in their responsiveness to Reiki depending on their illness, personality, and how well they know you. Here's how you can read an animal to determine how to administer Reiki:

- ✔ An animal may screech, fly, growl, hiss, or run away as a way of telling you it doesn't want to be touched. In that case, you can use distant Reiki or beaming techniques.

- ✔ An animal may let you perform hands-on Reiki but then shift positions or look at you funny. Move your hands a few inches above the body and continue Reiki, if you feel that it's still needed.

- ✔ An animal may tell you it wants Reiki by coming near you when you are giving Reiki to yourself or someone else.

- ✔ If you're lucky, an animal will move itself so you can give Reiki exactly where it's needed.

Follow all the suggestions and guidelines for a session with animals just as you would for your most beloved relative. Read Chapters 9, 10, and 13 before treating an animal.

Using different techniques

If you feel comfortable or get an intuitive message to get closer to an animal, you can then try performing Reiki with your hands hovering above the pet (see Chapter 10). You can eventually move into an actual hands-on session.

Adapt the techniques used for humans to animals. Because animals can't give their express permission for you to perform Reiki, make sure you approach any animal in a slow and respectful manner when starting to give Reiki. Doing so gives the animal the opportunity to understand what you are doing and lets the animal make his feelings known.

You may want to start by beaming Reiki to the animal from across the room (see Chapter 10) or sending distant Reiki (see Chapter 15). These techniques may be sufficient for treating an animal.

Intention is the single most important factor in the success of a Reiki treatment. Intend or pray for the highest level of healing for the animal and that you be a pure channel of Reiki energy. Healing is not from you, but through you. Be clear about your role as a Reiki healer and why you are treating the animal. See Chapters 9 and 13 for more information about preparations before and after a Reiki session.

Here are the general techniques to use on animals:

- ✔ **Distant Reiki:** This type of Reiki can be performed from anywhere, so you don't need to be near the animal to do this. See Chapter 15 for tips on performing Reiki from afar. You can use this technique to treat any trauma an animal might have suffered in the past or to help the animal with any event in the future.

- ✔ **Beaming Reiki from across the room:** When you are with the animal, start with beaming to connect with the animal from a safe distance. You and Rover then get a chance to connect with each other before moving closer. See Chapter 10 for more information. I have used this method of healing for animals in zoos or aquariums.

- ✔ **Reiki with hands hovering over the body:** Some pets tolerate this type of Reiki for a longer period of time than hands-on Reiki. See Chapter 10 for more information. My cat tolerates hands-on healing for just so long. When I get "the look," I move my hands off the body.

- ✔ **Hands-on Reiki:** Adapt the standard hand positions for humans (see Chapter 10) to your pet. Some animals are much smaller, but the basic idea of anatomy is the same.

- ✔ **Group Reiki:** For larger animals, especially horses or large dogs, a few people can perform Reiki simultaneously, sending much love and healing at once. See Chapter 14 for more information on group healing.

Giving Reiki to a sick animal helps the human companions of animals as much as it helps the animals themselves.

As is the case for humans, Reiki healing sometimes leads to a curing of an animal's illness, but it may also lead to a peaceful death. Reiki doesn't change the natural order of events, but it enhances the experience by giving a dose of love.

Part III
Becoming Well-Versed in Reiki

The 5th Wave   By Rich Tennant

"Just for today, don't worry. Just play something light and airy until the other musicians show up."

In this part . . .

In Part III, you advance in your knowledge of Reiki so you can start helping yourself and others.

To get attuned to the Reiki energy, start studying with a Reiki Master Teacher. I describe how to find a Reiki class, the different levels of Reiki training, and what you might expect from your classes. This part covers the Reiki symbols, techniques to connect you with the Reiki energy, and techniques (mostly different hand positions) for treating others.

Don't forget to put yourself first! You can best help people with Reiki after you learn to use it on yourself, so this part explains how to give yourself a Reiki treatment.

Many practitioners use crystals as a special add-on to Reiki, so I discuss that topic, too.

Chapter 7

Seeking Reiki Training and Classes

*B*y taking a Reiki class, you'll be initiated to the Reiki spiritual energy and also learn techniques so you can use Reiki to help yourself and others. Consider Reiki training when you're ready to move forward with Reiki.

Reiki training is usually separated into three successive levels, but the classes themselves come in different shapes and sizes. In this chapter, I discuss what to look for in a Reiki teacher and class, how classes are organized, and what to do to maximize your experience before you get to class and after you take the class.

From the 1st-degree Reiki level, you gain the ability to channel Reiki energy and treat yourself and your family members. You can stop there, or you can advance farther so that you can treat other people, use Reiki symbols, and give other people Reiki attunements (initiations).

After you've been initiated with Reiki, your ability to channel Reiki lasts for life, and you'll find that the more you use it, the stronger it gets.

Examining Reasons to Study Reiki

People study Reiki for a variety of reasons. You may simply have a strong personal desire to learn Reiki, or perhaps you want to join your sister or husband in their Reiki adventures. The benefits of Reiki are as endless as the energy supply itself. Here are some of the reasons that you may want to study Reiki:

✔ **To enhance your personal growth:** You may already meditate or practice yoga or T'ai Chi and want to learn the methods of Reiki to supplement your spiritual practice. Or you may be new to conscious spiritual growth. Wherever you are, you'll find help with Reiki. See Chapter 19 to find out about using Reiki for personal growth.

✔ **To heal yourself of a chronic illness:** At the very least, Reiki can help you deal with anxiety or stress and help you calm down or sleep at night. See Chapter 16 for information about combining Reiki with other therapies.

✔ **To help a sick or ailing relative:** Find out how to give a Reiki session in Chapter 13.

✔ **To use Reiki in your healthcare practice as a**

- Nurse

- Doctor

- Psychotherapist

- Massage therapist

- Other healing practitioner

✔ **To use Reiki for your pets:** You can give your beloved pet some Reiki just as you would for a child or friend. Read about using Reiki with animals in Chapter 6.

✔ **To use Reiki in your animal care practice:** You can use Reiki whether you work in a veterinary clinic or at a zoo or aquarium.

✔ **To run your own Reiki business:** If you want to eventually have a Reiki business of your own, start by taking the classes and finding out as much as you can about Reiki and being a Reiki practitioner (see Chapter 13).

For all of you, taking a Reiki class will help you achieve your goals. I wager that it will also help you in other ways that you may not have even imagined. For as you receive the Reiki energy attunement, or initiation (see the section "Answering Questions about Attunements," later in this chapter), your energy levels are heightened, and change and growth are inevitable!

Asking the Right Questions about Reiki Classes and Teachers

You can find Reiki teachers by the same methods you would use to find a Reiki practitioner (see Chapter 5).

To find a Reiki teacher, ask your friends, family, and massage therapist or chiropractor if they have a personal recommendation. Visit a local Reiki circle (see Chapter 14) to meet prospective teachers, and check out the resources in the appendix.

The International Association of Reiki Professionals (IARP) has a Reiki teacher code of ethics that's listed in the appendix. Use this list to give you an idea of an ideal teacher and Reiki learning experience.

In deciding which teacher is for you, start by determining what it is that *you* want to get out of Reiki training.

The types of questions to ask a potential teacher depend on your motive for learning Reiki. If you're on a spiritual quest, you may be looking for different qualities than if you want to use Reiki in your medical practice.

Consider these questions for a prospective teacher:

- **What is your experience practicing and teaching Reiki?**

  Experience is measured not only by years but also by the level of interest and commitment to the practice. For example, a person can teach one class a year or one a month. A teacher can give sessions to family members or have a full-time Reiki practice. Other things may also matter to you. For example, you may want to know whether your Reiki teacher is involved in Reiki circles, shares, or hospital visits or whether your teacher is also a nurse or healthcare practitioner.

- **What is your Reiki branch and lineage?**

  Reiki has many different branches that differ from each other, especially in the way that Reiki is taught and passed on. The lineage is the "genealogy" of your teacher traced back to Mikao Usui (see Chapter 3 for a discussion of lineage). Though all Reiki branches channel the same energy, the way that Reiki is practiced can differ. Your teacher uses the methods in which she has been trained.

- **Can I contact you after the class?**

  A teacher is hopefully willing to answer your burning questions after the class and provides an e-mail address or telephone number.

When the student is ready, the teacher appears

When you're conscious about working with spiritual energy, you'll recognize coincidences more and more. For example, teachers always show up when they're needed. I have found the statement that "when the student is ready, the teacher appears" to be true for me. Sometimes I don't realize that I am ready to learn something until it appears right under my nose!

In some cases, the teacher is a life situation or challenge. In other cases, a person suddenly shows up, just when you need him. If you're ready to learn Reiki, you'll find a teacher.

Ask questions about the class itself:

✔ **Can I get a class outline?**

Look for a class that provides plenty of time for hands-on work where you practice Reiki techniques. You want to get enough practical experience to take away with you. Also make sure the class has a question-and-answer period.

✔ **Are there any prerequisites for this class?**

Some teachers won't let you take 2nd-degree Reiki with them, for example, if your 1st-degree Reiki was with another teacher.

✔ **How long does it take to complete the class?**

Is this a one-day class or a weekend? How many sessions will you attend?

✔ **How many students are in the class?**

You may have a private class in which you're the only student, or you may be in a large class. As long as you're able to ask any questions you might have and get hands-on practice of Reiki techniques, the number of people in the class is not a huge issue. Personally, I prefer smaller classes with between two and eight students.

Consider the costs and benefits to you.

✔ **What can I do with Reiki after this class?**

If you have a specific goal in mind, such as practicing Reiki on others or teaching Reiki, ask the teacher if the class will adequately prepare you.

✔ **What type of certificate will I receive?**

Different branches of Reiki and indeed teachers within branches provide different types of certificates. Generally, you receive separate certificates for the three separate levels of Reiki training. Make sure you'll get a certificate at the successful completion of the class. Find out what you need to do to get the certificate.

✔ **What is the cost of the class?**

Find out the exact cost of the class. Does the teacher only accept cash or also credit cards? Do you have to pay a deposit in advance? Can you get a refund if you can't attend the class?

Add any other questions that are important to you.

Knowing the Reiki Classes and Certification

The first thing to know about Reiki classes and certification is that standards differ among Reiki branches and individual Reiki teachers. Unlike healing therapies such as massage or nursing, there are currently no state-mandated requirements or licensing procedures for Reiki. As a result, Reiki is more freely available, but it also means that comparing courses isn't easy. Still, Table 7-1 gives you an idea of Reiki class levels (or degrees) and what to expect from them.

Certification in Reiki means that the teacher has printed his own certificate, or it is available from a particular branch of Reiki. This is not a state-level certification but simply means that you have a piece of paper saying you finished a class.

Table 7-1	Summarizing Reiki Classes		
	1st Degree	*2nd Degree*	*3rd (and 4th) Degree*
Common names	Reiki I	Reiki II	Reiki III (a and b) or ART and Master Teacher
Japanese Reiki	Shoden	Okuden	Shinpiden
Symbols taught	None	First three symbols	Master's symbol
What is taught (in a nutshell)	Reiki history, giving yourself Reiki, Reiki hand positions	Long-distance techniques, giving a Reiki treatment to others	Giving others attunements, teaching Reiki to others
Other comments	Reiki I and II are sometimes taught together	Reiki I and II are sometimes taught together	May include two levels

Read Chapter 3 to find out about Reiki branches and lineages. Talk to people you know who are Reiki practitioners and see which branch you would like to study under.

Different types of Reiki courses

When you start looking for a Reiki class, you'll find all sorts of possibilities. Here are the types of classes you'll find:

✔ **Traditional in-person classes:** Here you will get the benefit of meeting the teacher and other students and learning in a classroom setting. You can watch the teacher perform Reiki and discuss issues and questions as they come up in person. The classes range in length:

- **Weekend:** Some teachers give all three degrees of Reiki in two- or three-day workshops. This class is geared for the busy person who wants to learn as much as possible as quickly as possible.

- **Longer periods of time:** These classes vary from weeks to months to years to complete all levels of Reiki. The period between levels of Reiki (see the section "Looking at individual Reiki levels," later in this chapter) allows you to incorporate the energy and information of each class before moving to the next.

The cost of these classes varies by teacher, but they are generally in the range of hundreds of dollars rather than thousands of dollars.

✔ **Long-distance classes:** The benefit here is lower cost, or even free attunements. But you miss the benefits of an in-person teacher-student relationship. Here are the types of distance classes:

- **Video:** Some teachers send attunements through a video that you can watch at home. The advantage of a video is that you can watch it repeatedly.

- **Internet or telephone long distance:** You can obtain long-distance attunements over the telephone or Internet. Many attunements obtained this way are free or low cost, which is the major appeal.

The quality for all classes varies. Follow the suggestions in the section "Asking the Right Questions about Reiki Classes and Teachers," earlier in this chapter.

If you can afford it, in-person classes win hands down over long-distance classes because you get to see the teacher perform and discuss Reiki, learn how to draw and pronounce the Reiki symbols, and get experience in giving a Reiki session — all with the guidance of the teacher right beside you! You also get to meet other Reiki students and practice on each other. In addition, you learn the all-important ethics of Reiki practice.

When you want to practice Reiki professionally in any way, in-person classes are the ticket. Reiki may be simple, but using Reiki with integrity means doing your honorable best to have the training and experience to do so.

What you put into your training is what you get out of it.

Preparing for your Reiki class

To get the most out of your Reiki training, follow your teacher's suggestions, which probably include some variation on the following:

- Read any materials you teacher has prepared or suggests. This goes without saying, right?
- Read through this book. The more you prepare, the better able you'll be to understand what is presented in class.
- Meditate or take walks through nature. Connect with your spiritual side.
- Think about what you want to get out of the class. When you know what you want, you can set that intention rolling.
- Avoid alcohol, illegal drugs, and nicotine for at least a day or week before class.
- Try to eat lightly and avoid stimulants such as caffeine or sugar on the day before and day of the class.

You're trying to keep your body somewhat pure to get the most out of the attunement process.

Looking at individual Reiki levels

Here is a rundown of the different levels of Reiki classes and what you can expect in each of the three levels.

Reiki 1st-degree course

This class is your entry to Reiki. You receive one or more attunements to the Reiki energy. I describe attunements in the section "Answering Questions about Attunements," later in this chapter. Now your channel to Reiki energy is open!

You find out the basics about Reiki so you can help yourself (with self-Reiki), help family members, and know enough about the history to explain to others what Reiki is and where it came from.

Topics

Here are the standard topics covered in most 1st-degree courses:

- ✔ **What Reiki is and what Reiki can do:** This class covers the basics of Reiki, including some of the information in Chapters 1 and 2.
- ✔ **The history of Reiki:** You find out about Mikao Usui and other Reiki founders as described in Chapter 3.
- ✔ **The lineage of Reiki:** Your teacher may provide a handout showing how you are now connected by a series of different teachers back to Mikao Usui.

No Reiki symbols are taught in 1st-degree Reiki.

Techniques

You'll find out about the following techniques in 1st-degree Reiki:

- ✔ **Self-Reiki hand positions:** Not only will you learn how to give yourself Reiki, but you'll also be advised to do so on a daily basis after the class. See Chapter 11 for info about self-Reiki.
- ✔ **Reiki hand positions to treat others:** You'll practice the basic hand positions on other students in the class (see Chapter 10 for illustrations of Reiki hand positions and techniques).

First-degree Reiki may be taught on its own or in combination with the 2nd-degree course. In some cases, your teacher will ask you to wait between classes so the attunement can do its work before you move on to the next level.

Reiki 2nd-degree course

You enroll for the second level of Reiki training when you want to know more about Reiki and become a practitioner. This training advances your spiritual growth and trains you to provide Reiki to others in person or at a distance.

Topics

If the following topics weren't covered in your first-level class, they surely will be discussed at the second level of Reiki training:

✔ Designing a Reiki healing session

✔ Understanding the ethics of treating others

✔ Performing distant Reiki

For information about performing a Reiki session and maintaining a code of honor in your work, see Chapter 13.

Reiki symbols

Many people study 2nd-level Reiki because they want to use the Reiki symbols. The following symbols are taught:

✔ Power symbol: Cho Ku Rei

✔ Mental and Emotional symbol: Sei Hei Ki

✔ Distance symbol: Hon Sha Ze Sho Nen

You find out how to draw these symbols and how to use them in Chapter 8.

Techniques

You find out how to use the symbols when you channel Reiki. You use these for two techniques:

✔ Distant Reiki treatments (see Chapter 15)

✔ Self-treatment and treating others

After taking a 2nd-degree Reiki course, you're usually considered to be a Reiki practitioner.

Reiki 3rd-degree course: Master course

The Master level of Reiki is sometimes split into two levels of classes: IIIa and IIIb or Advanced Reiki Techniques (ART) and Master Teacher. Each Reiki branch or school may use different names to denote the two levels.

Some schools of Reiki require waiting six months or more between 2nd-degree Reiki and the Master course or between the ART and Master Teacher courses. The idea behind waiting is that you integrate your experience from the earlier course so you're better prepared for the later course.

Topics

Master's level topics include the following:

- Becoming a Reiki Master
- Mastering yourself
- Finding out how to teach Reiki
- Going farther with Reiki

Reiki symbols

You learn to use the Master's level symbol Dai Ko Myo. In some branches of Reiki, you may also learn the Raku, Tibetan Dai Ko Myo (Dumo), or Tibetan Fire Symbol. I describe these nontraditional Reiki symbols in Chapter 21.

Techniques

You discover how to perform all levels of attunement and how to teach Reiki classes.

In each of the Reiki levels, your teacher will include additional techniques, such as some that I explain throughout the book. As the additional material varies widely, it's best to check with your teacher beforehand.

Defining Reiki Master

A full Reiki Master, which is sometimes called a Reiki Master Teacher, is simply someone who has studied the Master Reiki symbol and has been trained to give attunements to others. Nowadays, training to become a Reiki Master takes anywhere from one day to a few days and in some cases a year or longer.

In the past, becoming a Master took longer, but recent developments in Reiki provide training more quickly. For this reason, what you can expect in a Reiki Master differs widely.

A true Reiki Master understands that the word *Master* is about mastering themselves. A Reiki Master helps other people to follow the path of mastering themselves. Ultimately, each person is responsible for his or her own healing and spiritual growth. You can find a Reiki Master to help you, but your journey is your own. If you become a Reiki Master, you are given the tools to empower yourself, but what you do with them and how you help others is up to you.

In some ways the name *Master* is unfortunate because it implies a mastery that does not always exist and which for many is a lifetime endeavor. The word *teacher* is probably more appropriate.

Some Reiki schools differentiate between Reiki Master and Reiki Master Teacher. In many cases, the term Reiki Master implies that the person is also a teacher. Unfortunately, there is no consistency in these designations among schools of Reiki. Ask your teacher if you have any questions about the titles.

Answering Questions about Attunements

The Reiki *attunements* are a form of initiation that opens you to a higher vibration of energy and gives you the ability to channel Reiki energy. What this means is that your body has been tuned into the high-level Reiki energy. With each successive attunement, you receive a higher or finer level of energy. After you have been attuned, you are open to the Reiki energy for life.

The attunement is the most mysterious and intriguing part of Reiki (after the symbols). In the following sections, I answer some of your questions.

Do I need to receive an attunement to access this high-level energy?

No. But few people are naturally attuned to this energy. Very spiritual people (think monks and saints) through their spiritual practice may already access this energy.

Practitioners of other energy work, such as T'ai Chi or Qigong, may also utilize this type of energy, but it may take years or decades of practice to consistently reach this energy.

What is unique about Reiki is that it opens your energy channels to receive this high-level energy quickly and with no effort on your part.

What about repeating attunements?

By all means, you can repeat the attunement process. In Western Reiki, the attunement process is considered complete and permanent. You are opened to the Reiki energy of each level, and no further attunements are necessary. But repeat attunements can be performed and are helpful, especially if you haven't been using Reiki for a while.

By using Reiki regularly after the attunement, you keep the channels open and growing.

In the traditional Japanese Reiki branches, a different type of attunement called a *reiju* is performed. This more subtle type of attunement is intended to be performed regularly. It can be likened more to osmosis, in which the energy of the recipient is elevated just by being in the presence of the Reiki Master who intends for your channels to open.

What will happen to me during the attunement?

Like a Reiki session, you can experience a number of different sensations during the attunement (see Chapter 5 for more about experiencing a Reiki session).

I am a visually oriented person, and at different attunements, I have "seen" fire and water, symbols, or spiritual masters or just felt blissful. Other people hear things, see colors, or feel different sensations. It is a personal mystical experience.

If you have asked for a message from the attunement, an answer to your question may come during the time of the attunement or just afterward.

What happens after the attunement?

The period after an attunement (especially the first attunement of a particular level) is considered a time of cleansing and change. This is a period when the rest of you (your thoughts, behavior, and so on) will catch up with the higher level of spiritual energy you are now channeling.

For you to be ready to channel high-level energy, any blocks in you are removed or minimized. You can liken an attunement to a bulldozer coming in and removing any blocks to the Reiki energy being channeled through you.

Many teachers suggest that this cleansing period occurs over a period of 21 days. In Reiki, this number derives from the number of days that Mikao Usui meditated and fasted on Mount Kurama (see Chapter 3). You will have your own period of cleansing.

You may find that the period after an attunement feels like a detoxification period, so drink a lot of water and get enough rest.

Chapter 8

Discovering the Reiki Symbols

. . . .

In This Chapter

▶ Seeing the significance of the symbols in Reiki

▶ Discovering how to draw and say the Usui Reiki symbols

▶ Uncovering each Usui Reiki Symbol

▶ Connecting to the symbols

▶ Going beyond the Usui Reiki symbols

. . . .

A distinctive feature of Reiki is the use of a set of symbols to help the practitioner connect with universal healing energy. By *symbol*, I mean an image or word that evokes the Reiki energy. The symbols work as keys that unlock the flow of Reiki energy.

Although you don't absolutely need the symbols to access Reiki energy, they are useful tools, especially if you're new to Reiki or energy healing.

Reiki founder Mikao Usui (see Chapter 3) designated four different symbols; the first three symbols are taught in 2nd-degree Reiki training, and the fourth Master's symbol is taught in 3rd-degree Reiki training (see Chapter 7). Nowadays, you are initiated to the symbols during what is called the attunement process.

In this chapter I discuss the use of symbols in Reiki and present the four Usui Reiki symbols. I hope to answer some of your burning questions about this hot topic.

If you're interested in alternative or nontraditional Reiki symbols, check out Chapter 21.

After you're attuned to Reiki with the symbols, those symbols will forever be linked in your consciousness to Reiki. Reiki flows whether or not you consciously use the symbols. As you develop in your Reiki practice, you can decide for yourself how often and where and when you use the symbol.

Understanding Reiki Symbols

The symbols themselves are listed in Table 8-1 and further described later in this chapter. In this section I describe the significance of the symbols to the Reiki system.

The two most important things to know about the Reiki symbols are

- **Reiki can do no harm.** If someone wants to do harm, he can't do so with the Reiki symbols or energy.

- **Reiki symbols connect you with the Reiki energy.** Each Reiki symbol takes you to the Reiki energy by way of different "entrances" to the "house of Reiki energy."

Symbols are used in two different ways to connect with Reiki energy:

- **During the attunement or initiation process:** The teacher uses symbols to pass the symbols and energy linked together to you. You receive an attunement at every level of Reiki training (see Chapter 7).

- **During a Reiki session:** The practitioner uses the symbols to focus and bring forth the Reiki energy (see the section "Activating the Reiki Symbols," later in this chapter).

Making it easy to connect

Mikao Usui specifically developed this system of using the Reiki symbols to make it easier to access Reiki energy.

Here's a brief explanation of how the symbols work. During your Reiki attunement (see Chapter 7), the symbols are joined with Reiki energy and presented as a linked form. Thus you receive the symbols embedded with the associated Reiki energy. So any time in the future that you call up the Reiki symbol, the attached Reiki energy is also called.

This type of association is used by the subconscious mind all the time. When a taste or smell reminds you of something else, you say it conjures up the idea of something else. Mikao Usui designed the Reiki system to use the symbols to conjure up the Reiki energy.

When you're an advanced student of Reiki, you may find that you don't use the symbols so much because you connect directly to the energy. Whichever way you go, with or without the symbols, you are connected to the energy.

Looking at the background of the symbols

Here's a little Reiki history for you: Mikao Usui originally taught Reiki without the use of symbols, but he added them for some of his students as a way to help them understand and connect to the Reiki energy. The lineages after Usui of Chujiro Hayashi and Hawayo Takata both use symbols in their teachings and branches of Reiki (see Chapter 3), and the symbols are integral to the attunement process. Most Reiki practitioners in the world are from these lineages.

In Japan, some Reiki practitioners use a different type of attunement that doesn't use symbols. This type of initiation is called a *reiju*. I describe attunements and reiju in Chapter 7.

Mikao Usui chose the four Reiki symbols because he was familiar with them. They are either little pictures or true symbols, or characters (words) also used in Japanese, which are called *kanji*.

- The first two symbols (Cho Ku Rei and Sei Hei Ki) are actual symbols (mystical images) from Buddhist or Shinto traditions. They also have assigned Japanese names.

- The last two symbols (Hon Sha Ze Sho Nen and Dai Ko Myo) are Japanese kanji, which are Chinese characters (words) used in Japanese. Each of these symbols has many possible meanings, depending on how you interpret the individual characters.

Using symbols without an attunement

Maybe you haven't taken a Reiki class. You may wonder about the value of symbols without receiving an attunement to them. In most cases, the symbol will just look like an interesting drawing. You probably won't connect with the symbol as Reiki energy because you haven't been through the initiation or attunement process. If you have done lots of meditation or energy work, you may be able to sense the energy of the symbols and somehow connect yourself to Reiki through the symbols.

Yes, it's theoretically possible to attune yourself to the Reiki symbols. But that's almost like saying you could learn medicine by reading a medical book. In both cases, something would be missing, namely the careful passing on of tradition from teacher to student and quality assurance that the information was indeed correct.

Although the symbols are interesting drawings and have historical and possibly mystical significance, you need an attunement from a Reiki teacher for the symbols to be able to truly connect you to Reiki energy (see Chapter 7).

Some of you may prefer to wait until class to see the symbols, saving the excitement for then. If you haven't yet learned the Reiki symbols and want to wait until after you take your Reiki class (see Chapter 7), skip this chapter and Chapter 21, which lists nontraditional symbols.

Looking at symbolology

A *symbol* is a representation of something else. An example of a symbol is the use of the eagle to represent the United States. Road signs and maps use symbols to represent bridges, hills, and roads. Humans have used symbols from the days of cave dwelling. Cave drawings used series of symbols to tell a story.

The Reiki symbols as drawings are two-dimensional squiggles on a page. Because they represent a deeper energy, you may feel a chill or sense of recognition or other sign or response when you first encounter a Reiki symbol.

Symbols tap into the deeper consciousness that is beyond words. When encountering a Reiki or other sacred symbol, the energy you receive transcends the lines on the page. You may sense the energy that is associated with this symbol from the years of its use in metaphysical practices and more recently by thousands of Reiki practitioners, or you may pick up some vibrations when hearing its name. The cross is a great example of a spiritual symbol with a long history of use. Two examples of the transcendence of sound are Hindu and Gregorian chants. When you listen to these chants, the words are less important than the sounds they make.

Removing the secrecy

Symbols were originally kept secret by Hawayo Takata to in an attempt to keep them sacred. Now many people in Reiki speak of keeping the symbols sacred but not secret.

For me it was a breath of fresh air when the symbols were freely published and not confined to secrecy. I was excited to find the symbols clearly drawn and explained in Diane Stein's book, *Essential Reiki* (published by The Crossing Press), as well as material from authors of other books and Web sites, some of which are listed in the appendix.

It is with respect for all Reiki Masters and practitioners past and present as well as the potential for Reiki to help so many that I provide the Reiki symbols, shown in Table 8-1.

Table 8-1	The Reiki Symbols				
Symbol	*Western Name*	*Abbreviated Initials*	*Western Quality of the Symbol*	*Japanese Name*	*Japanese Quality of the Symbol*
	Cho Ku Rei	CKR	Power	Symbol 1	Focus
	Sei Hei Ki	SHK	Mental and emotional	Symbol 2	Harmony and balance
	Hon Sha Ze Sho Nen	HSZSN	Distant healing	Symbol 3	Connection
	Dai Ko Myo	DKM	Master	Symbol 4	Empowerment

Taking a Close Look at the Four Reiki Symbols

In this section I give information on the four different symbols that were used by Mikao Usui. Use this information along with the summary in Table 8-1. The Western description of what the symbols "do" is slightly different than the Japanese description. And in the Western traditions of Reiki, each symbol is called by its name, whereas in Japanese traditions of Reiki, each symbol is called by its number: first, second, and so on.

I believe you will find your own uses for these symbols, which will change over time as you continue to use Reiki.

Cho Ku Rei

This first symbol, Cho Ku Rei (pronounced *cho koo ray*), is called the Power symbol (Figure 8-1). This symbol does the following:

- ✔ Focuses energy
- ✔ Connects you to the earth
- ✔ Purifies physical or visible objects such as parts of the body or inanimate objects
- ✔ Adds power when used alongside other symbols

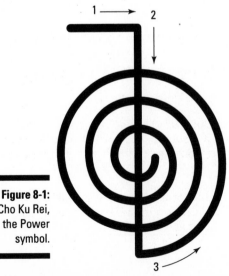

Figure 8-1:
Cho Ku Rei, the Power symbol.

Use this symbol to do the following:

✔ Feel connected to your body, or grounded

✔ Protect yourself or loved ones

✔ Heal physical illness or pain

✔ Purify or cleanse a room, car, or food

Some say that using this symbol is like turning on the light switch to the Reiki energy. It has a grounding or solid feeling as it connects you to the earth. The focusing feature is activated when you use the symbol in a specific location, thereby focusing the energy there. See Chapter 18 for more examples of how to use the Cho Ku Rei to protect yourself in everyday situations.

Cho Ku Rei is an ancient symbol found in Japan and may have Buddhist or Shinto origins. The exact meaning of this phrase as intended by Mikao Usui is not known, but one translation is "put the power here."

Sei Hei Ki

The second Reiki symbol, Sei Hei Ki, is pronounced *say hay key* (see Figure 8-2). The mental or emotional symbol does the following:

✔ Purifies and heals feelings and emotions

✔ Empowers the heart

✔ Promotes a sense of balance

Use this symbol for the following purposes:

✔ To heal emotional or psychological problems such as depression or grief

✔ To bring a feeling of love and forgiveness for self and in relationships

✔ To change your habits or heal addictions

The Sei Hei Ki symbol is the same as a form used for meditation in Tendai Buddhism, which is the form that Mikao Usui practiced. The words Sei Hei Ki can be translated to mean "one's natural disposition" or habit; another translation is "emotional composure."

Sei Hei Ki originated from a "seed syllable" or meditative form called Hrih in Sanskrit or Kiriku in Shinto. The symbol calls upon the Buddhist deity Amida Nyorai, who is the Buddha of Infinite Light and Life.

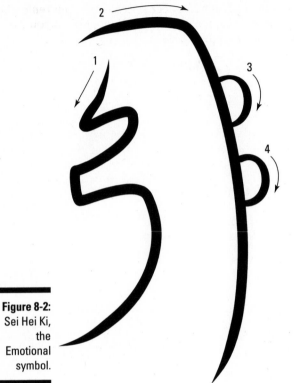

Figure 8-2:
Sei Hei Ki,
the
Emotional
symbol.

The difficulty in knowing the translations of symbols 1 and 2 stems from the fact that the Japanese characters have to be implied from the sounds of the symbol's mantra. Remember that the symbol itself is not a Japanese character, but a squiggly drawing that has been assigned Japanese-sounding words. Just like the sound of the word "to" can also be written "too," each sound can represent more than one character.

Hon Sha Ze Sho Nen

The third Reiki symbol, Hon Sha Ze Sho Nen, is pronounced *hahn shah zey show nen.* This symbol, also known as the Distance symbol, is a set of actual Japanese characters (see Figure 8-3). This symbol is a more complicated symbol and mantra, so some people have to take a bit more time learning to say it or memorizing how to draw it.

Practice drawing this symbol for your 2nd-degree Reiki class, but remember that afterward you can always look at a copy of the symbol when you use it. Also, the more you practice, the easier it gets!

The Distance healing symbol does the following:

- ✔ Removes the illusion of space and time
- ✔ Connects to spirit
- ✔ Brings a unity of all beings

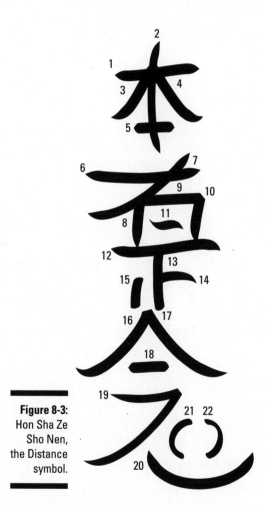

Figure 8-3:
Hon Sha Ze
Sho Nen,
the Distance
symbol.

Use this symbol to do the following:

- ✔ Send Reiki at a distance (see Chapter 15)
- ✔ Connect with God or spirit
- ✔ Connect with the higher self (soul) in yourself or others

Hon Sha Ze Sho Nen is a set of Japanese words, so it can be translated as a Japanese sentence. But each "word" has many meanings, so the sentence can be translated or interpreted in different ways. One way it can be translated is "right consciousness is the basis of everything."

Dai Ko Myo

The Master symbol, Dai Ko Myo (pronounced *die ko mio*), is part of the training to become a Reiki Master.

Note that what is drawn in Figure 8-4 is now considered the most authentic form of the Usui Dai Ko Myo. Some differences are thought to be from brush stroke by calligraphers. Various other versions of this symbol have been published and taught. Remember that the intention behind the symbol is much more important than a difference in a particular stroke of the kanji.

The Dai Ko Myo means the following:

- ✔ Mastership
- ✔ Empowerment

Dai Ko Myo is similar to Cho Ku Rei with perhaps a more subtle energy that is connected to the higher self. You use the Master symbol for the following:

- ✔ To pass Reiki attunements
- ✔ During Reiki treatments
- ✔ During meditation

Like the Hon Sha Ze Sho Nen, Usui Dai Ko Myo is a form of Japanese words that can be translated in a few ways, one of which is "great bright light."

In Chapter 21, you find two alternative Master symbols.

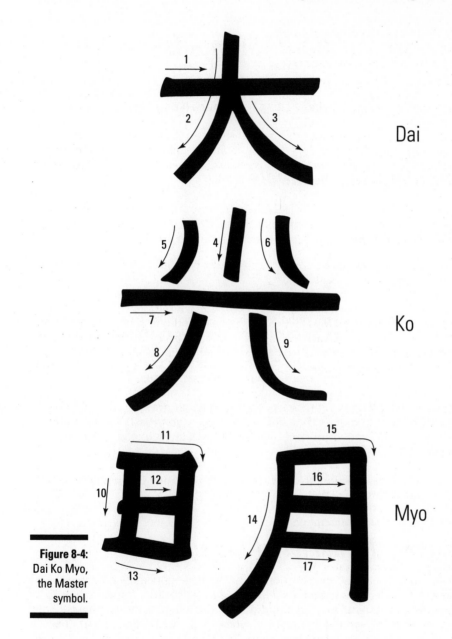

Dai

Ko

Myo

Figure 8-4:
Dai Ko Myo,
the Master
symbol.

Memorizing the Reiki Symbols

When you first find out how to use the Reiki symbols, you'll refer to this book or your teacher's handouts regularly. But one goal of Reiki training is for you to be able to remember the image and name of each symbol so that you can use it as needed.

Drawing the symbols

When you study the symbols (see Chapter 7), your teacher might emphasize *how* to draw the symbol. This emphasis has evolved from the fact that Japanese characters (kanji) are written in a certain order:

- From top to bottom
- From left to right

The Distance and Master symbols are Japanese kanji, and a certain order is taught for drawing them. An order is also taught for the Power and Emotional symbols. When you look at Figures 8-1 through 8-4 for the symbols, note that arrows are used to guide you in the direction of your pen. Start with the first stroke at number 1 on the figure and proceed from there.

My personal feeling is not to worry too much about drawing the symbol exactly right or in exactly the right order. Just try your best. Watch out for variations: Different books have slightly different instructions for drawing the symbols.

You can have fun learning to draw the symbols by using colored pencils, felt-tip markers, or watercolors.

Saying the names of the symbols

In addition to learning to draw the symbol, you need to know how to say its name. I provide a pronunciation guide for each of the four Usui symbols in their respective sections, earlier in this chapter. Whereas the Japanese system of Reiki calls the symbol by number (symbol 1, symbol 2, and so on), the Western system uses a Japanese name. This Japanese name is called a *jumon* or *kotodama,* which are two different Japanese words for chanted words or syllables, which you might call a *mantra.* The mantra, like the image of the symbol, carries the Reiki energy.

What is more important about saying these names is not the dictionary definition of what they mean, but the actual sound or vibrations made when pronouncing them.

If you want further explanation, consider the Sanskrit word *om* as an example. Just as the sound of the mantra *om* is also the name of a symbol (see Chapter 21), *om* is also an evocative sound on its own without even visualizing the graphic symbol. Likewise, the mantra associated with each Reiki symbol can also evoke the Reiki energy. Both the image *and* the sound of the image's name are linked to Reiki energy.

Activating the Reiki Symbols

In the preceding sections, I suggest some specific ways to use each of the Reiki symbols. But you may use any symbol in any situation. After you're attuned to a particular symbol, maintain your connection to this symbol by using it during meditation and self-Reiki treatments and when treating others with Reiki. The more you try different symbols in different situations, the more you realize what works best for you.

To activate the symbol, all you need to do is think of it. It will be in the form of "seeing" or drawing the image of the symbol and saying its name.

Visualizing the symbols

Here are some ways you can visualize the symbols in Reiki:

- Draw the symbol in your palm before performing Reiki. Some practitioners draw each symbol in their palm and say its name three times while clapping their hands three times to seal in the energy.
- Draw the symbol in the air.
- See the symbol in your mind's eye (visualize the symbol on your closed eyelids).
- Draw the symbol on the roof of your mouth with your tongue.
- Imagine the symbol in your eyes or on your breath as you send the Reiki energy with that symbol along with your eye vision or your breath.

You can imagine a symbol entering a body part and enveloping the cells with its energy. Visualize a Reiki symbol (Cho Ku Rei, for example) inside a tumor, symbolically replacing disease with health.

Get creative with the symbols and put yourself inside of the symbol. Imagine the symbol expanding and holding you. The symbols are happy to expand and bend to help you out!

Using the sounds of symbols

A symbol's name can be chanted aloud, but most practitioners say the names silently to themselves while using the symbol.

Say the name of the symbol three times. There is a power to saying something three times. What comes to my Western mind is Dorothy in *The Wizard of Oz,* clicking her shoes together three times and saying three times, "There's no place like home." Frank Baum, the author of *The Wizard of Oz,* presumably understood the power of three.

When you say the symbol's name, for example, Cho Ku Rei, that is like a mantra bringing forth the associated energy.

Looking at More Symbols, Reiki and Otherwise

Besides the four Usui Reiki symbols described in this chapter, a number of additional symbols are used in different Reiki branches. I list some nontraditional symbols in Chapter 21.

You may encounter additional symbols from the following sources:

- ✔ **Other Reiki branches:** Karuna Reiki, Tera Mai Reiki, Seichim, and other branches of Reiki use additional symbols.

- ✔ **Your own religious or spiritual practice:** You may want to use the cross, the star of David, or other religious symbols.

- ✔ **Your own psychic or intuitive processes:** You may "see" new symbols while dreaming, meditating, or getting a Reiki attunement. In Chapter 21, I provide an example of a personal symbol that I received.

A favorite Reiki symbol

Reiki Master Theresa Sarin considers the Tibetan Dai Ko Myo her favorite symbol and has shared the following story about how she uses this symbol:

"Each morning I stand in front of my Sacred Space, a table with crystals, angels and some statues of saints, as I face the rising sun. I allow the morning sun to bathe and enfold me as I breathe in the sun's newly risen energy. I then sign the Tibetan Master Reiki symbol over myself, becoming the symbol itself. I let it fill me and surround me as I silently chant the symbol's name three times. I then recite this poem:

Great Being of Light,
 Shine your Light here all day and night,
Great Being of Light,
 Shine your Light here all day and night,
Great Being of Light,
 Shine your Love here all day and night.

I stay open to receive all the Light this Master symbol brings, allowing it to fill and charge me so that I may begin my day full of Light and Love. I then ask that Reiki continually express itself through me throughout the day, helping me to accomplish my divine purpose and presence on earth. Finally, I end my morning prayer giving thanks for my many blessings."

Don't get caught up in a frenzy to obtain more and better symbols. The Usui Reiki symbols work! Follow your intuition and see if it's right for you to keep studying and acquiring more symbols through new attunements and Reiki classes.

Chapter 9

Getting Ready to Channel Reiki Energy

eiki works kind of like electricity, so think of yourself as the electrical cord through which the Reiki flows. When you get initiated (attuned) during a Reiki class (see Chapter 7), it's like being plugged in to the Reiki source. Now when you put your hands on yourself or someone else, Reiki just flows. You have the ability to increase how much Reiki light shines through you by clearing and opening yourself to channel even greater amounts of Reiki energy.

This chapter is about connecting with the Reiki energy. Most people use some form of meditation, prayer, or intention to power up and focus the Reiki flow. I describe techniques you can use to connect to and focus the Reiki energy. You can use these methods to increase the levels of Reiki energy you can channel. Use this chapter to help yourself prepare before giving Reiki to yourself and especially before treating others.

The Reiki energy comes through you, but it's not your energy. This is a subtle but important distinction. If you try to use your own energy to heal another, you'll find yourself feeling depleted. The value of using Reiki is that you're accessing an infinite source of power that not only goes through you to heal others but also renews you along the way!

Stepping out of the way

You become a better channel of the Reiki energy when you can put away all of your own preconceptions, issues, judgments, and needs and just focus on the energy itself.

So if you *need* to make someone better, you'll be less likely to help them. This is because your focus is on you and your need to help, instead of focusing on being a Reiki channel.

Try to let go of your needs and just work on letting the energy flow; then both you and the recipient of Reiki will probably feel better!

Connecting with the Reiki Energy

Your spiritual connection is always there, but it may be drowned out by the noise of the world. Like a buried treasure, you can get to the Reiki energy if you set your intention to do so!

To connect with the Reiki energy, it helps to do the following:

- ✔ **Take time to connect.** Just as being busy, doing errands, or reading the newspaper can keep you from communicating with your family, they can also keep you from connecting spiritually. A quick way to connect with higher energy is to make some time to do one of the following:

  - **Get quiet.** Just turn off the noise of radio, television, and cell phones and sit quietly.

  - **Listen to music.** Sacred sounds can get right to the heart of the matter and let your spirit soar. But use whatever music moves you.

  - **Be with nature.** Plants and animals communicate through stillness. Take a walk through the park or spend time with your cat.

- ✔ **Pay attention.** The more attention that you pay to your spiritual connection, the stronger it becomes. During meditation in particular, you are paying attention to the spiritual union, sensing connection in the silence.

Many religions use prayer and meditation for spiritual connection. The system of Reiki healing doesn't have specific prayers, but you can create your own (see the next section, "Combining Prayer and Intention with Reiki"). Meditation goes hand in hand with Reiki and is covered in the section "Meditating to Connect with Reiki Energy," later in this chapter.

Some people explain prayer as taking time to talk to spirit and meditation as taking the time to listen. In both cases, you're stoking the fires of your spiritual connection, which is directly linked to channeling Reiki energy. The more connected you are spiritually, the easier it is to connect with Reiki energy.

Reiki is the energy of light and love, and being spiritually connected in terms of Reiki means recognizing that you are connected to this powerful source of light and love.

Combining Prayer and Intention with Reiki

Whether you call it "asking in prayer" or "stating in intention," both are great ways to start a Reiki session. The most important thing is that the prayer feels right to you. You can devise a prayer that you use all the time or create a different one for each situation.

Here are some examples of prayers to use before giving Reiki:

Thank you [name for God, saints, angels, or spirit guides that you work with] for your presence today at this Reiki healing session for [name of Reiki recipient].

I pray that [name of Reiki recipient] receives the highest good from today's Reiki session.

I pray that I may be a clear and open Reiki channel for the pure flow of Reiki.

I pray that I give and receive Reiki with love, acceptance, and compassion.

I pray that I am guided to bring the highest level of healing possible for [name of Reiki recipient].

I pray that [Reiki recipient] and I are surrounded and protected by the light and love of Reiki.

You can use this as a prayer or remove the "I pray that" wording and use the statements as positive affirmations.

Any prayer you use before a Reiki session demonstrates that you're doing the following:

- ✔ **Clarifying the goals of treatment:** Before the start of the session, formally state what the goal of the treatment is. This clarifies the focus (sets the intention) for the Reiki session. See Chapter 19 to read more about setting intention.

- ✔ **Letting go of control:** Out go judgment or expectations of what the session will be. You're giving that power over to the Reiki energy.

- ✔ **Asking for guidance:** You will receive guidance during the session. It's up to you to trust this guidance and follow your intuition.

- ✔ **Asking for protection:** I like to ask for protection for myself and the Reiki recipient. Doing so sets the intention for a safe working environment and keeps away any energy that is less than positive. I describe techniques for energy clearing and protection in Chapter 13.

Meditating to Connect with Reiki Energy

While meditating, you're creating the space and time for detachment from the distractions of the world so that you may become conscious of your spiritual connection. During meditation, you receive peace and inspiration. Meditating has so many benefits, including providing stress release and creating balance and harmony.

You can use meditation as part of your personal spiritual practice or just before performing Reiki. Because Reiki practice is about receiving this spiritual energy and passing it through you, meditation has a close relationship to Reiki.

Meditation to meet your Reiki guides

Some Western Reiki teachers take you on a meditation to meet your Reiki guides. It's believed that everyone has spirit guides watching over and helping out. You might envision these figures as saints, gods, angels, or masters from your own religion. After you become attuned to the Reiki energy, you might sense or request the help of other guides such as Mikao Usui, Chujiro Hayashi, or Hawayo Takata (for info about them, see Chapter 3).

You may experience that certain guides come to you specifically to aid you in Reiki. The purpose of a meditation to meet your Reiki guides is to introduce yourself to these beings.

Two important features of meditation are sitting and breathing. Make sure you're comfortable in your sitting position. Take a few deep breaths to release tension and then let your natural in-and-out breathing take place.

Many spiritual practices, including Reiki, recommend daily meditation. You can use any form of meditation that is comfortable for you. Mikao Usui recommended meditating on the Reiki Principles (see Chapter 4). See Chapter 19 for more about meditation and Reiki.

Prayerful hands: Gassho

Gassho is a Japanese term that represents a hand position and can also be used as the basis of a meditation. The Gassho (with or without bowing) is used in Zen and other forms of Buddhism. People of all religions in Japan and other Eastern countries use the Gassho hand position as a sign of greeting, gratitude, or respect or even to make a request. The hand position may be combined with bowing. Gassho is similar to the Indian Namaste hand position (which you may know if you practice Yoga).

Gassho hand position

Put your palms together in prayer position, and you have performed the Gassho! During Gassho, your hands may be placed in front of your chest (see Figure 9-1), your lips and nose, or your forehead (see Figure 9-2).

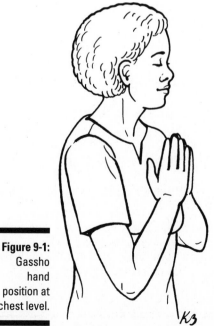

Figure 9-1:
Gassho
hand
position at
chest level.

K3

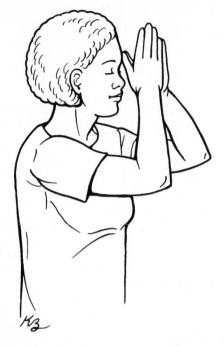

Figure 9-2:
Gassho
hand
position
resting on
forehead.

Use the Gassho hand position before and after a Reiki meditation or session.

Gassho meditation

Sit with your eyes closed and hands in the Gassho position. Focus on the point where your middle fingers are touching.

Breathing meditation: Joshin Kokyu Ho

Joshin Kokyu Ho is the Japanese method (Ho) of breathing (Kokyu) to focus or cleanse the mind (Joshin). This method brings breath down to the belly, which is called the hara in Japanese. (See the sidebar "Breathing to the belly," in this chapter.) To use this technique, follow these steps:

1. Sit or stand comfortably.

2. Use the Gassho position to start and then close your eyes.

3. Move your hands to your thighs with palms upward to receive the energy as you breathe in.

4. Breathe in through your nose.

   Imagine the energy entering your body from the top of your head (seventh chakra, the crown) and traveling down to your belly (second chakra, the hara). You might visualize the energy as white light coming through your body.

5. Hold the energy in your belly and then let the breath out through your mouth.

   Imagine the energy (white light) within your body leaving through every pore on your skin.

6. Continue the cycle of breathing in and out (Steps 4 and 5) until you feel you're an open channel for the Reiki energy.

7. End the exercise with a simple Gassho (see the earlier sections on Gassho).

Be careful with breathing exercises if you have any medical issues like high blood pressure. Follow the wisdom of your body (intuition) to know when a technique is right (or not) for you.

Gassho architecture

In Japan, Gassho means more than a hand position in Reiki. It's also the name for a type of large farmhouse built in the 17th century. These delightful houses have steep thatched roofs that mimic the shape of the hands in Gassho, with palms touching each other. The Gassho house is large and has many levels, allowing extended families to live in one home. Frequently, the top floor was used to grow silkworms or make *washi paper* (traditional Japanese paper made from the bark of mountain trees).

The Gassho farmhouses are located in geographic areas with lots of winter snow. The steeply sloping roof helps the snow to fall off, thus saving the house from snow damage.

Focusing technique: Seishin Toitsu

A variation or addition to Joshin Kokyu Ho, Seishin Toitsu ("creating a unified mind") takes the energy of the breath and brings it to the hands. Seishin Toitsu has many meanings in Japanese, but the simplest is "concentration." This technique helps to concentrate the Reiki energy and is thus useful to perform before a Reiki session. To perform Seishin Toitsu, follow these steps:

1. **Sit or stand comfortably.**

2. **Use the Gassho position to start and then close your eyes.**

3. **Move your hands to your thighs with palms upward to receive the energy as you breathe in.**

4. **Breathe in through your nose.**

   Imagine the energy entering your hands. Bring the breath energy up your arms to your shoulders and down to your belly (hara).

5. **Breathe out, through your mouth.**

   Imagine the energy within your body going from your hara, up your body to your shoulders and out your hands.

6. **Continue the cycle of breathing in and out (Steps 4 and 5), feeling the pulse of energy through your hands until you feel the energy is flowing freely.**

7. **End the exercise with a simple Gassho (see the earlier sections on Gassho).**

This technique helps to sensitize your hands, which is very helpful before starting a Reiki session. Your hands will be flowing with Reiki energy and "aching" to get started!

Hatsurei Ho is an advanced Japanese Reiki technique that combines Kenyoku Ho (see Chapter 13), Joshin Kokyu Ho, and Seishin Toitsu.

Chakra meditation

In Western Reiki, incorporating chakras into Reiki work is common. The body has seven major chakras, from the root (perineum) up to the crown (the top of the head). To review the individual chakras and their relationship to the body's energy, see Chapter 2.

Working with your chakras helps you to sense energy in yourself and others. The more you work with chakras, the easier it is to activate them and keep them in balance.

Meditating on chakras is usually performed as a group during a Reiki circle (see Chapter 14) or in Reiki classes (see Chapter 7), but you can also try it on your own. By meditating on your chakras, you become familiar with the energies of each chakra and help to keep your energy flowing.

1. **Get comfortable in your seat.**

2. **Take a few deep breaths to let go of tension.**

   Focus on your breath — in and out.

3. **Take your attention to your root chakra (perineum).**

   Visualize the color red and stay at your root chakra for a few minutes. Feel yourself connected to the inside of the earth.

4. **Move to your sacral chakra (between your navel and your genitals).**

   Visualize the color orange. Stay at your sacral chakra for a few minutes. Feel yourself bathed in creative juices.

5. **Move to your solar plexus chakra (above your navel and below your chest).**

   Visualize the color yellow. Stay at your solar plexus for a few minutes. Feel the power of your inner fire.

6. **Move to your heart chakra (the center of your chest).**

   Visualize the color green. Stay at your heart chakra for a few minutes. Experience love and compassion.

7. **Go to your throat chakra.**

   Visualize the color bright blue. Stay with your throat chakra for a few minutes. Let your expressive vibrations flow.

8. **Go to your third eye chakra (at the center of your forehead).**

   Visualize the color indigo (purple). Keep your focus on your third eye for a few minutes. See your vision expanding.

9. **Go to your crown chakra (the top of your head).**

   Visualize the color violet (purple-red). Stay at your crown chakra for a few minutes. Connect with spirit.

10. **Let the energy flow out from your crown and down over your body.**

    As the energy comes down from your crown, it surrounds you in a shimmering protective light.

11. **Take your attention back to the root chakra and feel the energy flow up through the chakras to the crown of your head.**

12. **Repeat Steps 10 and 11, feeling the energy flow up through your chakras and down and around you.**

    When the energy is flowing, you can let go of thought and enjoy the sensations of peace and light.

While you meditate, you can touch each chakra or let one or both hands hover near the chakra.

Contracting the Hui Yin

The Hui Yin technique helps to concentrate the Reiki energy in the body before giving or even during a Reiki session. It is used during some meditations given in advanced Reiki classes.

At your perineum (the space between the genitals and anus) is a Chinese energy point called the Hui Yin. Reiki Masters from some Western branches use advanced exercises (Violet Breath) and meditations (Hui Yin meditation) involving this Chinese energy point. And some Japanese exercises also contract this point (see the information on Koki Ho in Chapter 10).

The idea here is that the Reiki energy can escape through the Hui Yin point. When you contract it (squeeze the muscles in your perineum), the energy flow in your body is stronger. Contracting the Hui Yin is the same feeling as performing Kegel exercises (recommended for women).

To preserve more energy in your body and thus increase the level of Reiki energy that flows through your hands, follow these tips:

- Keep your tongue at the tip of your mouth.
- Squeeze your Hui Yin (perineum, first chakra between your anus and sex organs).

Feel the sensations of Reiki energy in your hands. When you squeeze the perineum, you probably feel a stronger sense of energy in your palms.

Breathing to the belly

Reiki meditation or focusing exercises bring the energy of the breath down to the belly, which is considered to be the seat of energy in Japanese and Chinese traditions.

The breath

You breathe all the time (I hope). But you may not be aware of your breath. Meditation helps you focus on breathing. As you pay attention to each breath, in and out, in and out, everything else fades away. In this quiet space, you can focus on bringing the universal life-force energy through each breath.

Though your breath enters through your nose, you might imagine the energy of the breath entering through the top of your head, at the crown chakra. You can visualize the energy as white or gold light coming through your crown.

The belly

Lurking within your belly is a seat of many treasures. In Japanese and Chinese traditions, the belly is considered the center of energy, or *ki* in Japanese and *qi* or *chi* in Chinese. This is the area below your navel and above the pubic bone, about 2 inches below the navel. Two Japanese terms are used to denote the belly: hara and tanden. *Hara* just means belly. *Tanden* is called *dantien* or *tantien* in Chinese and means ball of energy, or energy field.

The belly is also the seat of the second chakra in the Indian tradition.

The Reiki breathing techniques, Joshin Kokyu Ho and Seishin Toitsu, help to focus the energy by bringing it down to the hara and out through the pores of the skin.

If you practice karate, Qigong, or T'ai Chi, you will also hear of these terms for this energetic center in the belly.

You can perform a circuit of energy going down the down the front of your body and up the back of your body. This is part of the microcosmic orbit that helps to increase the levels of energy in your body.

Receiving Guidance through Intuition

You are being guided during a Reiki session, and you receive that guidance through your intuition. You may experience intuition as a gut feeling, instinct, or insight. You may not even realize what's happening, but you get a thought to "move to the next position" or "put your hands over the heart." This is the type of intuition I am talking about here.

As you develop confidence in using intuition, it becomes your most important tool in knowing exactly how to format the Reiki session for each person to cater to their individual needs. Two Reiki techniques rely on intuition: Reiji Ho and Byosen Reikan Ho (see Chapter 10). For Reiji Ho, you are guided where to put your hands next. For Byosen Reikan Ho, your hands are guided to parts of the body that have "disease" or need Reiki. Both of these techniques require that you follow your inner knowing or intuition to know where to place your hands during a Reiki session.

Guided by spirit: Reiji Ho

This Japanese method (Ho) prepares you to be guided (ji) by spirit (Rei). Use this method to increase your awareness of Reiki guidance (intuition).

1. **Stand and put your hands in the Gassho position (refer to Figure 9-1).**

   Set your intention: to connect with Reiki.

2. **When you feel that you've connected with the Reiki energy, bring your hands (still folded) up to your forehead and rest there for a moment (refer to Figure 9-2).**

   You and your hands are now ready to start a Reiki session! Trust that your hands are guided to go to the right positions.

3. **At the end of the Reiki session, when you no longer feel guided to put your hands on any part of the recipient's body or aura, conclude with a Gassho.**

This simple exercise powerfully sets the stage for intuition to flow.

Developing your intuition

Intuition isn't one of those subjects taught in high school, or college for that matter. The word itself suggests you get tuition, or instruction, from inside yourself: in-tuition. You can develop your intuition the way you develop any skill: practice and more practice.

Here is a great way to develop your intuition for use during Reiki. Find an open-minded Reiki partner (perhaps one of your classmates from Reiki training) who is open to this exercise. You're going to practice using intuition on this friend.

1. **Start by meditating, praying, and connecting with spirit.**

   Everything written about in this chapter helps you to open the "space in your mind" so an inspiration can come through. State something like "My intuition tells me exactly what to do during this Reiki session. I receive and trust my guidance."

2. **Perform Reiki with an intuitive approach.**

   Use the Reiji Ho technique or Byosen Reikan Ho (see Chapter 10). Don't move your hands until you get a message telling you where to go next. If you don't know, then use your

   - **Inner vision:** Close your eyes and see if an image comes to mind. You might see a picture of a right shoulder.

   - **Sensations:** See if you feel in your own body a tingling sensation. If you feel a new sensation (that is, not your own long-term knee problem) that seems to have just arisen, then put your hands on the recipient's body in that place.

   - **Thoughts:** You might get a thought, such as this: "Put your hands on the jawbone."

   - **Sound:** You might hear or sense the word "breathing," in which case you can focus Reiki on the nose and lungs.

   If nothing comes to you, then just pick the next position out of a hat. Imagine you are reaching into a hat with pieces of paper with different body parts listed. Pick out a piece of paper. What does it say? Go there.

3. **Ask the recipient for feedback.**

   You might say, "I don't know why, but I got the signal to put my hands on your left elbow." And the person might tell you, "I banged my elbow on the car door this morning!"

The more you're open to intuition and follow it, the better you'll become at using and interpreting your intuition.

When you're able to trust yourself and follow your intuition, Reiki sessions may not be what you were expecting, but they'll help the recipients. They may even ask you how you knew to put your hands in just the right place. ·

Integrity goes hand in hand with intuition. Read Chapters 10 and 13 so you know how to give a Reiki session before you put your hands on anyone. If you feel confused about intuition, then just use the standard hand positions listed in Chapter 10. In particular, read the section about ethics and boundaries in Chapter 13.

To read about using intuition in your personal life, see Chapter 19. Messages come every day all the time. The real measure of growth is being able to hear those messages and then follow them.

Chapter 10

Healing Others with Reiki Positions and Techniques

. . . .

In This Chapter

▶ Positioning your hands for a Reiki session

▶ Using intuitive and sensing techniques

▶ Performing Reiki with your hands off the body

▶ Opening the chakras with Reiki

. . . .

After you have the Reiki energy flowing (see Chapter 9), you're probably eager to share this energy with others. Start by practicing to use the hand positions on yourself (see Chapter 11). Then you're most of the way toward being ready to treat others because the hand positions you use on yourself are very similar to those used on others.

This chapter provides you with Reiki techniques to use when you give Reiki to another person. The main course of the session is the set of standard hand positions, and 19 positions are illustrated and described. You can also use Japanese intuitive techniques and methods to give Reiki without even touching the body.

The techniques provided here are starting points or suggestions. Learning to use Reiki techniques is like learning how to draw. After you master the techniques, you can develop your own unique style. In Chapter 13, I explain how to develop your own Reiki style and put together the Reiki session.

Examining Full-Body Hand Positions

The hand positions described in this section derive from Hawayo Takata and her successors (all of whom you can read about in Chapter 3). Your teacher may provide a shorter or longer version of this set of hand positions.

Other hand positions, which were used by Mikao Usui and Chujiro Hayashi, are now available in published translations from the Japanese originals (see the resources in the appendix). In many cases, these positions are similar to or overlap the Western hand positions that are more commonly used. The treatment manuals from Usui and Hayashi have specific recommendations for problems with different organs.

Ultimately, the best way to perform Reiki is to use any set of hand positions or techniques as the starting point for an intuitive session in which your hands are guided by spirit to go exactly where they are needed (see the section "Knowing Where to Go and When to Leave," later in this chapter).

Here's a set of guidelines to consider before delving into the positions:

- ✔ Start with the recipient on her back on a massage table. If you need to work on a chair or on the stomach, modify instructions as needed.

- ✔ Stand or sit while performing Reiki; do whatever is most comfortable for you.

- ✔ Make sure you have access to walk around (or sit next to) the massage table.

- ✔ Modify the instructions in this chapter as needed if you are working on someone who is smaller than average, such as a child, or larger than average, such as a professional basketball player.

- ✔ Try to keep your fingers together for all Reiki positions.

- ✔ Move gently from one position to another.

- ✔ Study up on human anatomy and chakra locations; you can consult the illustrations of the human body and chakras in Chapter 2.

- ✔ Follow all ethical considerations when working with your hands on someone, as mentioned in Chapter 13.

Disease, problems, and pain usually have multiple causes and multiple effects. The full-body Reiki treatment is valuable because it covers the range of different meridian pathways, chakras, and parts of the body.

In the descriptions of the 19 hand positions that follow, I include general information on how to position your hands and which organs, conditions, and chakras are helped by each position. Note that only some of the hand positions directly treat the seven major chakras.

Starting at the head

Reiki treatment generally starts at the head. Head positions are good for recipients who have colds, tension headaches, sinus infections, allergies, earaches, migraines, and toothaches and need stress release. The head positions also establish a sense of balance in not only the head area but also through the whole body. Because these positions treat the brain, they also affect the rest of the body.

The positions used on the head are among the most important of all hand positions.

1. **Eyes and face (see Figure 10-1): Place your hands over the recipient's closed eyes with your hands to each side of the nose and fingers resting on the cheekbones. Your thumbs rest on the third eye.**

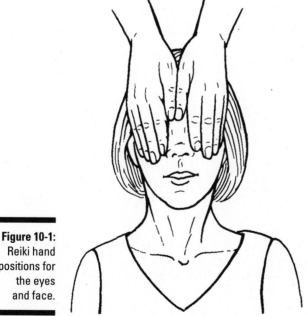

Figure 10-1:
Reiki hand positions for the eyes and face.

Some people use a tissue to protect the eyes. Treating here relaxes the recipient and takes them into the Reiki experience, which is like being between waking and sleeping.

This position opens the third eye (sixth) chakra, which helps improve issues of vision, both through the eyes and intuitively. The sixth chakra is associated with the pituitary gland, lower brain, nervous system, ears, nose, and eyes.

2. **Top of the head (see Figure 10-2): Place your hands over the top of the head with your wrists touching and fingers pointing down toward the ears.**

You may want to move your hands away from the hair and hover over the crown. You may not want to spend too much time here, but stay long enough to ensure that the crown area is open.

This position opens the crown (seventh) chakra, which aids the recipient in feeling spiritually connected and is associated with the upper brain and pineal gland.

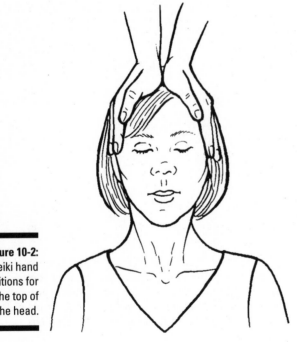

Figure 10-2:
Reiki hand positions for the top of the head.

3. **Temples (see Figure 10-3): Rest your hands on both sides of the forehead, between the eyebrows and the hairline, with the fingers lightly touching the cheekbones.**

This position aids in balancing the brain, relieves headaches, and helps to connect spiritually. You might sense the throbbing of blood vessels in this tender area.

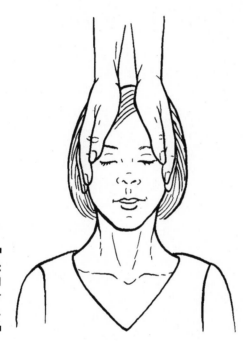

Figure 10-3:
Reiki hand positions for the temples.

4. **Ears (see Figure 10-4): Put your hands over the ears.**

This position promotes equilibrium, treats the inner and outer ears and the jaws, and quiets a busy mind.

5. **Beneath the head (Figure 10-5): Place your hands under the head. Do this by rolling the head to one side, putting one hand underneath, holding the head with that hand while you roll the head to the other side, and put your other hand beneath. Try to hold the bottom of the head, *medulla oblongata,* so your fingers are just touching the top of the neck.**

This relaxing position treats the sixth chakra (third eye) and also treats the back of the head.

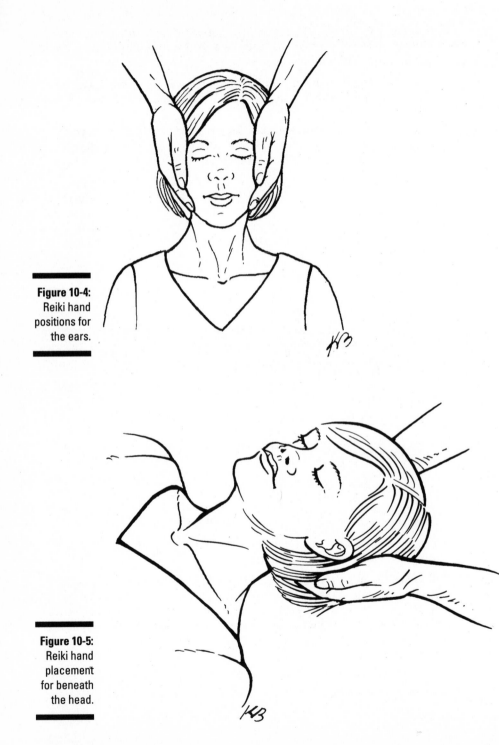

Figure 10-4:
Reiki hand
positions for
the ears.

Figure 10-5:
Reiki hand
placement
for beneath
the head.

Moving down the front of the body

The throat and neck positions serve as the transition to the trunk of the body. You are probably still standing or sitting behind the recipient as you perform the next three hand positions.

6. **Throat (see Figure 10-6): Let your fingers touch each other as you cup the bottom of the throat with your hands. Be gentle and keep your hands around but not touching the throat.**

   This hand position, which helps the thyroid and parathyroid gland, vocal cords, larynx, and lymph nodes, treats the throat (fifth) chakra that controls the throat and neck. This is the seat of expression and communication. Use treatment here to help the recipient speak up, speak his mind, speak for himself, and speak his truth. It's good for writer's block too!

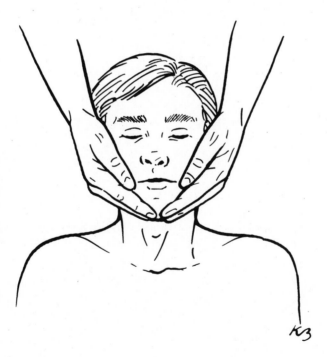

Figure 10-6:
Reiki hand position for the throat. Make sure your touch is light, not tight.

This position is not for everyone because some people are squeamish about having someone else's hands near their throat. You can try keeping your hands about a hand's width away from the throat.

7. **Collarbone (see Figure 10-7): Rest your hands on the sides of the neck with your fingers pointing toward the center of the chest.**

Figure 10-7:
Reiki hand
positions
for the
collarbone.

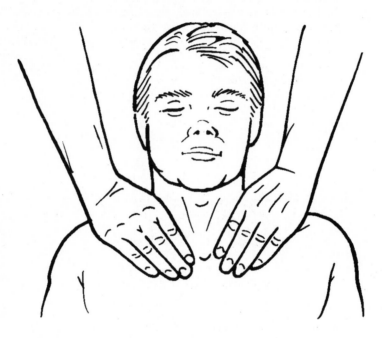

This position gives Reiki to the thymus area, which is between the throat and heart chakras. The thymus gland is important for immune function.

For this next position, place yourself either behind or on the side of the recipient (it all depends on the logistics of your height, their height, and how far you can stretch!).

8. **Back of the neck and front of the heart (see Figure 10-8): Put your left hand beneath the neck area and your right hand over the top of the center heart area.**

This position combines treatment of the back of the neck with the heart. You are treating two areas simultaneously: the throat chakra and the heart chakra, which helps with expression from the heart, or speaking one's truth. This position is good for treating high blood pressure; actually, any position on the neck helps with high blood pressure.

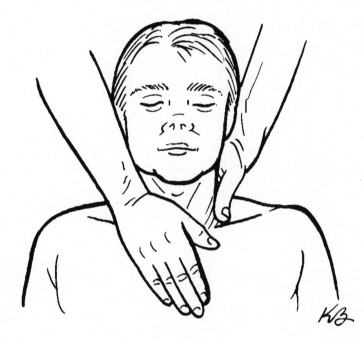

Figure 10-8:
Reiki hand positions for the back of the neck and the front of the heart.

For the next four positions, stand (or sit) on either side of the Reiki recipient.

9. **Heart (see Figure 10-9): Place your hands in a T, one hand placed horizontally above the breasts and one hand between the breasts placed vertically.**

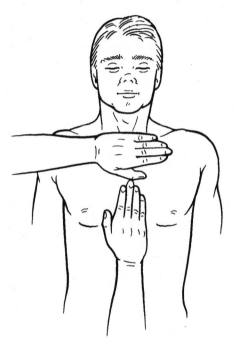

Figure 10-9:
Reiki hand positions for the heart.

Treating the heart (fourth) chakra controls all things having to do with the circulatory system, including the heart, veins, and arteries; the lungs (which are related to both heart and throat chakras); the breasts; and the thymus gland. Opening the heart chakra with Reiki increases the flow of love, air, and nurturing that can be received and given. When the heart chakra is open and flowing, the recipient experiences forgiveness and a sense of love and compassion.

With the next three positions on the abdomen, you can use your hands as in Figure 10-10, with your hands one in front of each other in a line, or as in Figure 10-11, with your hands next to each other, thumb to thumb.

10. **Upper abdomen (see Figure 10-10): Put your hands in a line underneath the chest area.**

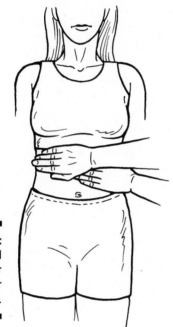

Figure 10-10:
Reiki hand positions for the upper abdomen.

This position treats the digestive organs (stomach, liver, gallbladder, and intestines) as well as the spleen.

The solar plexus, or pit of the stomach (third chakra), is treated by both positions 10 and 11. The third chakra is associated with power and self-esteem and the pancreas gland. Treat the solar plexus to help with diabetes, liver disease, and gastrointestinal disorders.

11. **Middle abdomen (see Figure 10-11): Move your hands down about one hand width below position 10 to treat the middle part of the abdomen. Place one hand on top of the navel and the other hand below the navel.**

    This position treats the pancreas, gallbladder, and large and small intestines.

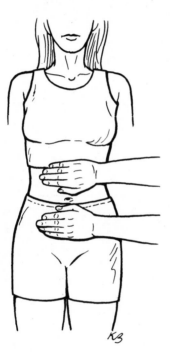

Figure 10-11:
Reiki hand positions for the middle abdomen.

12. **Lower abdomen and sacral area (see Figure 10-12): Place your hands on the lower abdomen, one in front of the other, with your hands and arms away from the genital region. Or instead, you can place your hands in a slight V shape.**

This position treats the sacral (second) chakra, reproductive organs, bladder, and pelvic area. The belly is called the *hara* in Japanese and is considered to be the seat of the body's energy. The second chakra is associated with sexuality and creativity. The reproductive organs, which have energetic centers here, represent creation of all types, from babies to books. Emotions are commonly stored in the second chakra, which can lead to problems in the reproductive system and lower back.

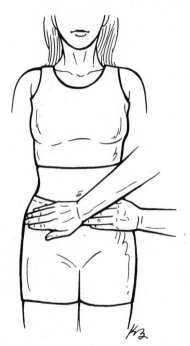

Figure 10-12:
Reiki hand positions for the lower abdomen.

At this point, you may want to include treatment of the root (first)chakra. For some recipients (if you know them well or have discussed beforehand), you can treat a bit lower on the pelvic area, taking care to avoid the genitals. Or you can treat with your hands above the body (see the section "Using Reiki without Touching the Body," later in this chapter).

Treating the root (first) chakra covers the bladder, the tailbone (coccyx), and sciatic nerves; is associated with the adrenal glands; and is related to issues of sexuality, feeling supported, and feeling connected to the earth (grounded). Like a tree, you need good roots (chakra) to provide sustenance and support from prevailing winds. Sexual issues are generally associated with both the first and second chakras.

Switching to the back of the body

To work on the back, you have to ask the recipient to turn over. The person may be deeply resting, so this can take a minute to achieve. The recipient lies on her stomach, with her head resting on a pillow or on a special neck rest that is attached to the massage table. You stand or sit at the side of the table.

When the recipient has complaints about back problems, treating the back can be very helpful. Another benefit of working on the back is to access some of the chakras more easily from behind.

Note that some people have longer backs, so you may need to add an extra hand position or two to cover the entire back!

13. **Upper shoulders (see Figure 10-13): Put your hands on the top of the shoulders, under the neck.**

    Reiki helps relieve some of the tension and neck and shoulder aches, which are common in this region. You are also giving treatment to the back of the throat (sixth) chakra here, when your hands are near the neck.

14. **Shoulder blades (see Figure 10-14): Take your hands down a few inches to rest on the top of the shoulder blades on the back of the heart area.**

    This position treats the back of the heart (fourth) chakra, the heart, and the lungs.

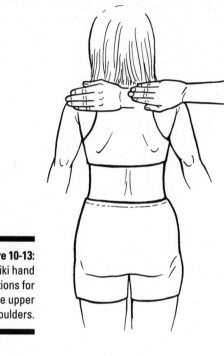

Figure 10-13:
Reiki hand positions for the upper shoulders.

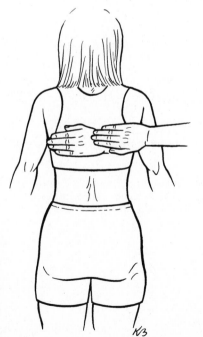

Figure 10-14:
Reiki hand positions for the shoulder blades.

15. **Waist area (see Figure 10-15):** Place your hands on the back of the waist area.

    This position treats the kidneys, the adrenal glands, and the back of the solar plexus (third) chakra.

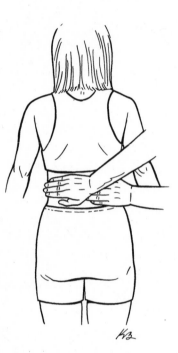

Figure 10-15:
Reiki hand
positions for
the waist.

16. **Lower back (Figure 10-16): Rest your hands on the hollow of the lower back just above the buttocks.**

    This area is another place of tension for many people. This position helps release tension in the lower back and treats the sacral (second) chakra.

    Some practitioners treat the buttocks, which gives Reiki to the root (first) chakra. Use this position with discretion (and permission) or treat with your hands above the body.

Figure 10-16:
Reiki hand
positions
for the
lower back.

Don't forget the legs and feet!

The original standard hand positions didn't formally include the legs and feet. Most people, including myself, like to be treated on the legs, ankles, and feet. You can perform these positions while the recipient is lying on her stomach or on her back. You stand to the sides of the table when treating the knees, but you can stand or sit at the base of the table when holding the feet or ankles. As always, try to make yourself comfortable when working.

   17. **Knees (see Figure 10-17):** Hold the knees on either side: top or bottom.

       A nice treatment for knees is to cup them underneath with one hand and put the other hand on top. Many people have pain in their knees from overexertion or injury.

   18. **Ankles (see Figure 10-18): Put one hand on the back of each ankle.**

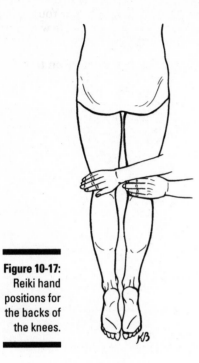

Figure 10-17:
Reiki hand
positions for
the backs of
the knees.

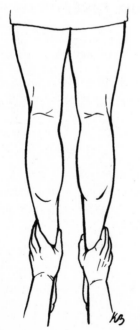

Figure 10-18:
Reiki hand
positions for
the ankles.

Doing so helps to balance the energy of the right and left legs. You can also work on one ankle at a time by holding the top of the ankle with one hand and the bottom of the ankle with the other hand.

19. **Soles of the feet (see Figure 10-19): Place your hands firmly on the back of the feet.**

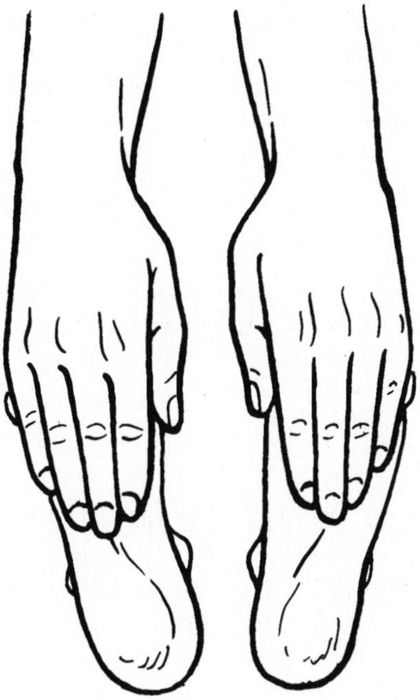

Figure 10-19: Reiki hand positions for the feet.

Some people don't like to have their feet touched, but if you hold firmly on the bottom of the feet, most people can tolerate that. This position brings the Reiki energy down to the feet, which helps ground and balance the energy in the body.

Balance the treatment on both sides of the body. For example, if you treat the right ankle, then treat the left ankle at the same time or afterward.

Considering additional Reiki positions

The positions that I discuss in the preceding sections cover most of the body, but you may feel that additional positions are useful.

- ✔ **Shoulder and hand:** Hold the left shoulder with one hand and the left hand with another. Repeat on the right side.

- ✔ **As your intuition tells you:** You may feel drawn to treat the wrists, elbows, upper arm, thighs, side of the hips, or sides of the abdomen. It all depends on the information you get from the recipient before and during the session and from your intuition.

- ✔ **Over the recipient's hands:** She might have her hands folded over her abdomen. Instead of moving her hands, you can put your hands over hers.

Respect the recipient's boundaries. If you feel that the first chakra (genitals) or breasts need treatment, perform Reiki with your hands well above the body (see the section "Using Reiki without Touching the Body," later in this chapter).

Knowing Where to Go and When to Leave

When you're new at Reiki healing, you may wonder how to know where to put your hands and when it's time to move to the next position.

One way of Reiki knowing is to decipher the Reiki sensations in your hands. As you perform Reiki more frequently, you may start to sense the following:

- ✔ **Tingling, pulling, or heat in your hands as they pass over certain areas of the body:** You feel these sensations in some areas but not others. See the section "Byosen Reikan Ho: Scanning the body," later in this chapter.

- ✔ **A sense of energy passing through your hands to the position you are holding on the body, almost as if a magnet is holding your hands in place:** The recipient is "drawing" the Reiki energy to her.

Your hands hold the key to knowing what to do during a Reiki session.

Deciding on hand placement

The beauty of using the standard hand positions is that you don't have to question where to put your hands; you just follow the numbers of the hand positions! Another way to perform Reiki is to use an intuitive approach to decide hand placement. Most practitioners use a combination of standard positions and intuitive techniques. And you want to remain flexible. For example, if someone has a liver problem, place your hands directly over the liver in addition to or rather than a standard hand position.

Following your intuition, which just means inner knowing, or the sensations in your hands to determine where to put your hands during a Reiki session is the subject of the next two techniques.

Guided by spirit: Reiji Ho

This Japanese method (Ho) prepares you to be guided (ji) by spirit (Rei). Use this method to increase your awareness of Reiki guidance (intuition).

1. **Stand and put your hands in the Gassho position (see the figure in Chapter 9).**

   Set your intention: to connect with Reiki.

2. **When you feel that you've connected with the Reiki energy, bring your hands (still folded) up to your forehead and rest there for a moment (see the figure in Chapter 9).**

   You and your hands are now ready to start a Reiki session! Trust that your hands are guided to go to the right positions.

3. **At the end of the Reiki session, when you no longer feel guided to put your hands on any part of the recipient's body or aura, conclude with a Gassho.**

This simple exercise powerfully sets the stage for intuition to flow. Use it alone during a session or alongside the other techniques described in this chapter.

Byosen Reikan Ho: Scanning the body

Use Byosen Reikan Ho to sense where the recipient's body needs to heal. With your hands held above the recipient's body, move your hands over the surface of the body. (See Figure 10-20.) Note any changes in sensation, which might be temperature changes of hot or cold, a tingling, pain, or itchiness. When you feel this change, keep your hands in this area (either on the recipient's body or just above) and apply Reiki energy.

You can use this technique before a treatment, in which case you scan to get information that you will use during treatment. If you scan during the Reiki session itself, keep your hands above the body while scanning and stop to give Reiki when you sense it is needed.

Byosen means illness, Reikan means intuition or inspiration, and Ho means method.

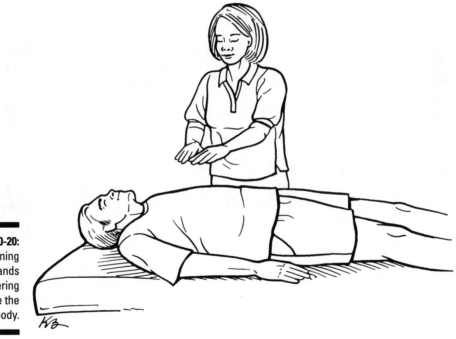

Figure 10-20:
Scanning
with hands
hovering
above the
body.

Moving on

The next part of the art of performing Reiki is to know when to pick your hands up from one position and move them to the next position. You can use a clock to help you, or you can decide on a certain number of breaths; for example, you may choose to spend three minutes or nine breaths in each position. Or you can use your intuition and observation to sense when it's time to move on.

The following signs let you know it's time to move on to the next hand position:

- ✔ The sensation that led you there has ended. This could be a tingling or heat sensation.
- ✔ You get an intuitive message to go somewhere else.
- ✔ The recipient sighs or alters her position.

These signs let you know the energy has been received in that area.

Despite all I've said about hand placement, it helps to know that Reiki energy knows exactly where to go. So you can rest assured that wherever your hands are or wherever they go is perfectly fine! Reiki will flow.

If you find that the recipient flinches or seems uncomfortable with certain positions, ask the person about it or simply move your hands to give Reiki above the body, or move to another position.

Using Reiki without Touching the Body

A very useful aspect of Reiki is that it can be performed without any contact with the recipient's body. Reiki works with your hands on the body or above the body, because the energy associated with your body, your aura (see Chapter 2), extends beyond the physical body. You can send Reiki with your hands hovering over an area of the body.

The hands-off techniques give you more options for treating others. You can use these techniques as part of a regular Reiki session or as the main course of treatment for people who can't or don't want to be touched.

Use the hands-off technique when treating any areas you can't touch, such as burns or the genital area.

Beaming Reiki energy from across the room

Sending energy across the room is similar to distant Reiki (see Chapter 15) except that the person is still in the same room as you. You can stand away from the recipient and hold your hands up at shoulder level. Feel the Reiki energy leave your hands and treat the recipient's entire body and aura at once. You can also use beaming to treat a particular area on the body.

This technique is useful for children or pets who may not let you get near them for hands-on or even hands-just-above-the-body treatment.

Using your breath and your eyes

The following two techniques come in handy when you're working on someone and have your hands on one place but feel the need to also send Reiki to another place. You can send Reiki through your eyes (or breath) to reach the third place (the first and second being where your hands are). In this way, your breath and your eyes are extra "hands of Reiki." You can use the following techniques during a normal Reiki session, when treating objects, and with long-distance healing (see Chapter 15).

Gyosi Ho

The Gyosi Ho method of healing is done by staring. Here's how to use it:

1. **Connect with the object or person to whom you want to send Reiki through the eyes.**

   Do this by gazing softly.

2. **Stare at the spot where you are sending the Reiki and let the energy flow from your eyes.**

   You can visualize Reiki symbols (Chapter 8) in your eyes and follow your gaze.

3. **When you finish focusing on one area, return your eyes to a soft gaze.**

   You can now look at another spot to send Reiki.

Koki Ho

Koki Ho is a method of healing done with the breath. Here's how to use it:

1. **Prepare yourself by concentrating the Reiki energy in your body (see Chapter 9 for techniques).**

   You can follow the procedures for Gassho or contracting the Hui Yin (See Chapter 9).

2. **Breathe in and bring your breath down into your belly.**

   This is also called hara breathing (*hara* is Japanese for belly).

3. **Imagine or draw with your tongue the Cho Ku Rei (or another symbol) on the inside of your mouth.**

4. **As you exhale, blow the symbol or Reiki energy toward the part of the recipient's body you want to treat.**

Balancing Chakras with Reiki

The *chakras* are a set of seven major energy centers that encompass the physical, mental, and spiritual layers of the energy body (see Chapter 2). The standard hand positions listed in the earlier section "Examining Full-Body Hand Positions" cover all the chakras.

Some practitioners give the chakras emphasis, knowing that having a balanced chakra will bring many of the organs into balance as well. When treating the chakras, you can use the any of the techniques outlined in this chapter and the rest of the book. Byosen scanning of the chakras allows you to sense with your hands where there is an imbalance in one of the chakras (see the section "Byosen Reikan Ho: Scanning the body," earlier in this chapter). To treat a chakra, you can do any of the following:

✔ Send Reiki directly to the chakra with your hands above or touching the body.

✔ Send Reiki with your eyes or your breath.

✔ Use your hands in the front and back of the chakra (separately or simultaneously).

✔ Move your hands as you hold them above the chakra: Move them in a clockwise and/or counterclockwise position or tap the air above the chakra.

✔ When working on all the chakras, start with the first and move up to the seventh chakra.

✔ Try connecting chakras by holding two at one time, for example, the heart chakra and the sacral chakra.

The ideas I list here are suggestions. Use your intuition while treating the chakras.

Chapter 11

Applying Reiki to Yourself

. . . .

In This Chapter

▶ Exploring the benefits of self-Reiki

▶ Getting ready for self-Reiki

▶ Finding out the hand positions

. . . .

*B*efore you try to help others through Reiki, using Reiki on yourself is an important and essential step. By doing self-Reiki, you'll see the truth and value of two age-old pieces of advice, "Healer, heal thyself" and "Practice makes perfect." And the benefits to you of regular self-Reiki sessions are great indeed.

The regular self-application of Reiki enables you to heal your body, mind, emotions, and spirit. Healing resolves issues, illness, and blocks so you can experience enlightenment, joy, or even bliss!

Self-Reiki is covered in the first level of Reiki training, after you have received your first attunements (initiations) to the Reiki energy flow (see Chapter 7).

In this chapter, I discuss the importance of making time for yourself and describe the standard hand positions to use as a basis for a Reiki self-treatment.

Putting Yourself First

If you don't put yourself first when it comes to Reiki, no one else will. You probably know how important relaxing and taking care of yourself are for your health, but that doesn't necessarily mean that you actually take the time you need for relaxation and stress release. You'll discover, however, that finding ways to fit Reiki into your schedule makes good sense.

Most 1st degree Reiki classes teach self-Reiki, and many teachers suggest or even require a 21-day (3-week) practice of self-Reiki (see Chapter 7). This 21-day cycle is just about enough time to develop a new habit, so by practicing self-Reiki for the 3 weeks, you give yourself a new life-enhancing practice. Twenty-one was also the number of days that Mikao Usui spent meditating on Mount Kurama, where he had his revelation about Reiki!

Discovering the benefits of self-Reiki

Like any Reiki session, self-Reiki gives you the benefit of the universal energy flowing into your body. Reiki can help you relax, remove tension, and heal your body, mind, and spirit. By doing Reiki daily, you can help maintain a high level of health.

During self-Reiki, you might enter the dreamlike state of meditation and find that you see images or get another form of inspiration. Write down any ideas that come to you during your sessions (see Chapter 19 for more info on keeping a Reiki journal). You can also keep track of any health benefits you find while performing Reiki regularly.

Self-Reiki also prepares you to be a better Reiki practitioner for others. By treating yourself before treating others you do the following:

✔ Open yourself to be a clearer and more open Reiki channel

✔ Put yourself in the mind-set that's more likely to receive intuitive information

✔ Set the intention to honor yourself

To get the full benefit of the relaxation and healing that Reiki brings, try to give yourself Reiki on a regular basis. Like all things, the more attention and time you give to your self-Reiki, the more benefit you get. Because self-Reiki keeps your energy running smoothly, you can look at self-Reiki as a form of preventive medicine.

Creating ways to incorporate self-Reiki

It's up to you to make the time and effort to give yourself Reiki — no one will do it for you (unless you book a Reiki session with another practitioner; see Chapter 5).

Giving yourself a quickie Reiki session

You can give yourself a quick spot of Reiki as needed! Some people call this "spot Reiki" or a Reiki mini-session. You don't perform a full session but use Reiki on an as-needed basis. So if you trip and hurt your foot, you can sit down and give your foot Reiki for a few minutes.

If you're feeling stressed, you can give yourself Reiki while waiting in line at the supermarket — as long as you do so discreetly! You can just touch your chest or your hand, which won't look out of the ordinary. Or use Reiki if you are suffering with sleeplessness in the middle of the night, taking a bath, or talking to a friend on the telephone. Whenever you feel the urge, you can put one hand on a part of your body and intend the Reiki to flow.

Here are some ways to incorporate self-Reiki into your day:

✔ Schedule self-Reiki sessions in your appointment book.

✔ Give yourself Reiki every morning before getting out of bed.

✔ Give yourself Reiki every night before going to sleep.

The time you allot for self-Reiki can vary. You can give yourself a luxurious hour-long session of about three to five minutes per position. Another option is to devise a shorter session for yourself that runs 15 minutes.

Preparing to Give Yourself Reiki

Just as you would prepare to give a Reiki session for someone else (see Chapters 9 and 13), you can set the stage for a special experience for yourself and boost the levels of Reiki you're channeling. You can do several things in advance of self-Reiki in order to enhance the experience:

✔ Use one or more of the meditation and focusing techniques listed in Chapter 9, such as Joshin Kokyu Ho and Seishin Toitsu, before treating yourself.

✔ Use intention (to set the Reiki energy flowing), intuition (to know where to put your hands and when to move them), and integrity (to remember to treat yourself with the utmost of respect).

✔ Make your personal self-Reiki session special by setting the stage with music, candlelight, aromatherapy, or any other relaxing or sensual pleasure. Do for yourself what you would do for others!

Treating Yourself with Reiki

Use the hand positions described in this section when giving yourself a full self-Reiki session. An advantage of giving Reiki to yourself, as opposed to being in a spa or clinic, is that you can choose where and when to perform the Reiki. A full session lasts about an hour, but you can add or subtract minutes to fit your own needs and schedule. If you have less time, skip some of the hand positions. If you have more time, you can linger on each position or add more positions (see the section "Being creative with positions," later in this chapter).

In terms of what to wear, you can be in your pajamas or your work clothes, as long as you're comfortable. Removing any heavy jewelry, glasses, a watch, or belt is always a good idea. You can be seated in a comfortable chair or lying on your bed.

You can use your self-Reiki sessions for relaxation purposes or for healing of a serious illness. In either case, the more time and effort you dedicate to practicing self-Reiki, the more you get out of it.

Listing the self-Reiki hand positions

If you're a beginner to self-Reiki, I suggest you go through the following 15 positions in the given order, for a set amount of time on each position: 30 seconds to 5 minutes each, depending on how much time you have.

After practicing this series of self-Reiki positions once or twice, you can read Chapter 10 to get more detailed information about the benefits of each hand position and tips on knowing when to move to the next position.

One note on carrying out the hand positions: Your fingers can be touching or not touching. Although some Reiki experts give rules on such things, I feel that using the most comfortable position for you is the best approach.

Starting at the head

Start your session by placing your hands on your head and face:

1. **Eyes: Begin your self-Reiki session by covering your eyes with your hands, with your fingers on either side of your nose and fingers pointed upwards. Breathe deeply as you begin to relax into the self-Reiki session. (See Figure 11-1.)**

2. **Top of your head:** Gently cover your crown at the top of your head with fingers pointing toward each other and just touching. (See Figure 11-2.)

3. **Back of your head:** You can use two variations for working at the back of your head. For the first position, put your hands on the back of your head with fingers facing upward and pointer (second) fingers just touching (see Figure 11-3). For the alternate position, place your left hand at the base of your head and your right hand just above, with each hand facing toward the opposite ear while gripping the head.

   Use the position that feels most comfortable for your arms. Both of these positions are very calming.

4. **Side of your face:** Hold your hands on the side of your face with fingers pointing upward. See (Figure 11-4.)

   Your hands are resting on the sides of your cheeks just before your ears. This position relieves facial tension and is good if you have dental pain.

   An optional position here is to hold your hands with fingers facing upward over your ears.

Figure 11-1:
Begin your
self-Reiki
session by
placing your
hands over
your eyes.

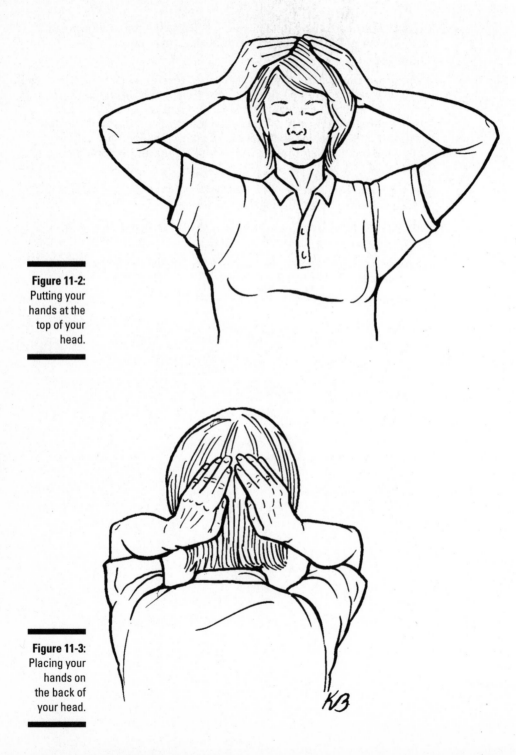

Figure 11-2:
Putting your
hands at the
top of your
head.

Figure 11-3:
Placing your
hands on
the back of
your head.

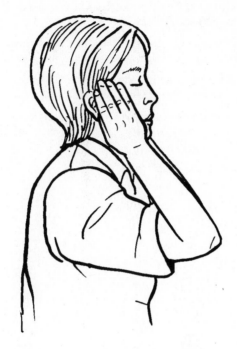

Moving down the front of the body

From your face, you gracefully move your hands down your body to give Reiki to your throat, chest, and abdomen.

5. **Throat (see Figure 11-5): Treat your neck by cupping your hands around your throat.**

   Hold your wrists together and let your fingers form a ring around your neck.

6. **Throat and heart (see Figure 11-6): Place your left hand over your throat and your right hand over your heart.**

   You can also use the opposite hand formation, if that feels better to you!

7. **Upper chest (see Figure 11-7): Place both hands on your chest area above your breasts, with fingers facing each other.**

8. **Upper abdomen: Place your hands just under your breasts, on your upper stomach, with fingers facing each other. (See Figure 11-8.)**

   Positions 7 and 8 are close to your heart chakra, but you can also cover your breasts directly when you work on yourself.

9. **Middle abdomen: Place your hands on your abdomen, with hands on either side of your navel, with fingers facing each other. (See Figure 11-9.)**

Figure 11-5:
Self-Reiki
hand
positions for
the throat.

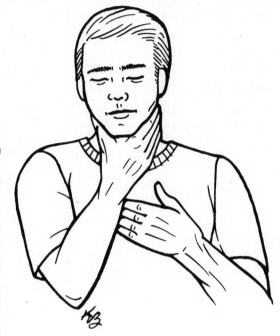

Figure 11-6:
Self-Reiki
hand
positions for
the throat
and heart.
Your hands
should
touch
lightly, not
tightly.

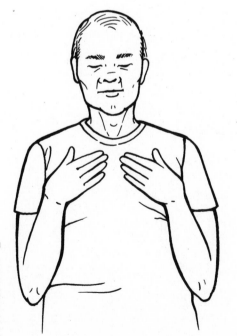

Figure 11-7:
Hand
positions for
your upper
chest.

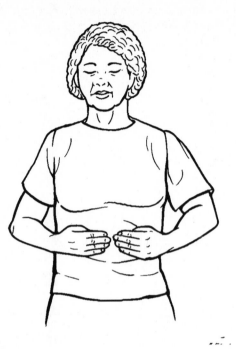

Figure 11-8:
Hand
positions for
your upper
abdomen.

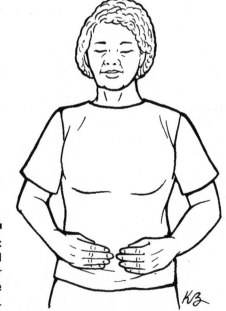

Figure 11-9:
Hand
positions for
your middle
abdomen.

10. **Lower abdomen: Put your hands with fingertips just touching, in a V shape pointing downward over your belly. (See Figure 11-10.)**

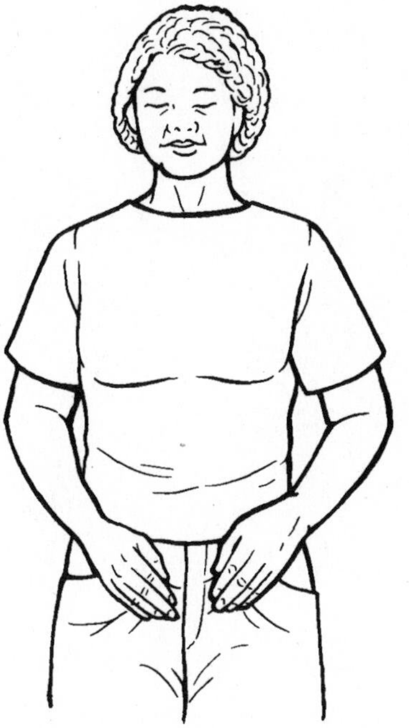

Figure 11-10:
Hand positions for your lower abdomen.

Switching to the back

Which positions you reach on your back, and how you reach them, depends on your flexibility! Do the best you can to reach some areas of your back.

11. **Shoulders: To reach your shoulders, put your hands behind your head and down onto your shoulders. (See Figure 11-11.)**

    An optional position here for the very flexible is to reach behind your heart area, in the middle of your shoulder blades.

12. **Waist: Reach around and put your hands on your middle back around the back of your waist. (See Figure 11-12.)**

13. **Lower back: Move your hands to rest on your lower back, parallel to your hips. (See Figure 11-13.)**

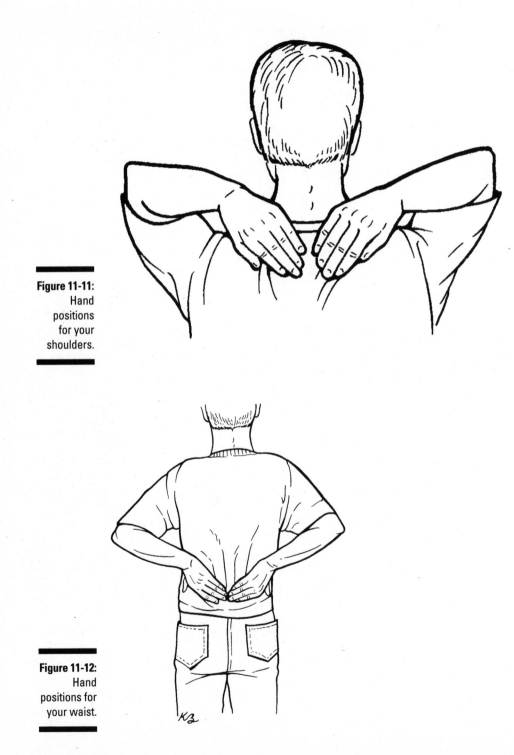

Figure 11-11:
Hand
positions
for your
shoulders.

Figure 11-12:
Hand
positions for
your waist.

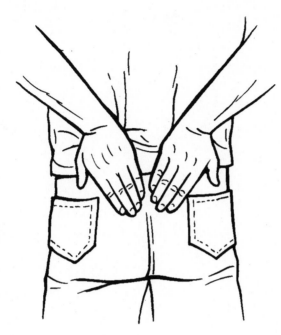

Figure 11-13:
Hand
positions for
your lower
back.

Don't forget the legs and feet

Some people leave out their legs and feet, but you should include them if you have problems with these parts of your body. And it helps to feel that the session really covers your entire body when you include the legs and feet.

Treating your legs and feet is probably easiest if you sit in a chair and bring one leg up at a time to reach your hands. Or if you lie down, you can bend your legs to reach your knees.

The last two positions aren't illustrated, but I know that you know where they are. I leave it to you to find a way to give Reiki to your ankles and feet, because how you hold these positions really depends on your flexibility.

14. **Knees: Cover your knees with your hands (see Figure 11-14).**

15. **Ankles: Place your hand around your ankle.**

16. **Feet: Reach to your feet and hold the bottom of each foot.**

    You can hold each foot one at a time.

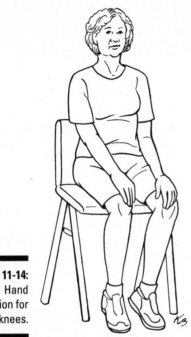

Figure 11-14:
Hand
position for
the knees.

Being creative with positions

Use the standard hand positions as a starting point to discover what works best for you. When you feel comfortable with the positions I describe earlier, you may want to branch out with other positions.

Here are some ideas that work for me, but everyone is different so use what works for you.

✔ Treat yourself from the front and back of your body simultaneously. Here's what I mean:

• Put one hand on the front of your neck by your throat and another hand on the back of your neck. This position allows the throat chakra energy to really expand!

• If you're limber, you can put one hand in front of your heart and one behind your heart on your back.

• Another great position is to put one hand in front of your belly and one on your lower back.

• You can nurture your knee with one hand cupping it from behind and another hand gently soothing it on the top.

✔ You can also add positions covering or hovering over your breast (heart chakra) and/or groin (root chakra). Neither of these is considered a standard position because of sensitivity toward inappropriate touching of sexual organs. But when you're working on yourself, you can give yourself a boost in these areas.

✔ Add other positions as you need or like, such as on your wrists, arms, thighs, or ankles.

Check out Chapter 10, which describes how to give a Reiki session to someone else, for more ideas on using Reiki. It's always good to try new hand positions on yourself first.

Treating yourself for illness

Self-Reiki is especially invaluable for people who have chronic illnesses like cancer, which may have complex causes and effects in the body that need sustained treatment over a period of time. Some hospitals offer Reiki training to their patients as a form of take-home self-care. When you can give yourself Reiki, you'll be able to schedule an appointment with yourself daily.

If you're dealing with a serious or long-term illness, you also will probably want to visit a Reiki practitioner for complementary support of any medical treatment you are undertaking.

You may also want to learn Reiki so that you can give healing energy to yourself between sessions with your practitioner.

Chapter 12

Reiki Rocks! Using Crystals with Reiki

*T*he ancient art of crystal healing relies on the subtle energy emanations of different crystals (see Chapter 2 for info about subtle energy). Crystals are used nowadays in medical machinery and quartz watches, as well as to adorn the body as jewelry. Crystal healing is increasingly recognized as a useful complementary medicine.

The use of crystals for healing is a separate practice from that of Reiki, but many Reiki practitioners like to have crystals on hand and may use them alongside Reiki. Using crystals with Reiki is like having an extra pair of hands!

Crystals are the mineral formations from deep within the earth. They come in different shapes and colors. You've probably seen clusters of crystal quartz or lavender-colored amethysts and been amazed by their intricate beauty. Each crystal has its own special energy.

Crystals are a sparkling expression of the beauty of nature. You can't help but admire their quality of color, form, and sometimes even the scale. Wonder, awe, admiration, and inspiration come from observing or being in the presence of crystals. For a person who is skeptical whether crystals impart any magical qualities, just liking beautiful objects is a reason to have crystals in the Reiki room, or anywhere else for that matter.

Are you crystal crazy?

A basic elementary school lesson teaches students how to classify matter into one of the three kingdoms: animal, plant, or mineral. In this scheme, animals and plants are considered to be alive, while minerals are considered inert and lifeless. However, as with plants and pets, people who love crystals tend to collect strays and new crystals when they travel.

Are you one of those people who feel that crystals are special and have their own unique subtle energies? Here's a fun quiz to see whether you're a closet crystal hugger:

✔ Have you ever found yourself gazing into a crystal, entranced by its beauty?

✔ Do you collect rocks and carry them from place to place when you move?

✔ Do you have a lot of crystal jewelry?

✔ Have you gone digging for crystals?

✔ Is your house being taken over by members of the mineral kingdom? (If you've become a rockhound or crystal collector, this is a real possibility.)

If you've answered yes to any of these questions, you're probably caught by the crystal spell. But remember that you don't need to acquire a lot of crystals to enjoy them!

You don't *need* to use crystals to practice Reiki, but because many Reiki practitioners combine these two forms of energy work, I present information you can use if you want to try your hand with crystals.

Exploring the Healing Power of Crystals

Just look at a crystal and see where it leads. You may find that crystals trigger a feeling, memory, or journey of some sort. Even if you're not sure about the metaphysical properties of mineral crystals, crystals can be useful for a variety of other reasons:

✔ People need certain minerals (the substances from which crystals are made) to survive. Iron, potassium, magnesium, and other minerals are essential for cellular activity.

✔ People wear gems or precious stones as jewelry and adornment. Think of wedding rings, birthstones, and earrings.

✔ Traditional Chinese medicine practitioners use minerals along with botanical and animal product herbs.

You may want to use crystals the next time you meditate. Try holding a crystal or gazing at it during meditation.

Sensing the energy of crystals

Just as you have an aura and transmit your own unique energy (see Chapter 2), crystals also have their own energy. Each type of mineral, such as a diamond or amethyst, has its own signature energy. Within each type, the individual stones may also have slight variations.

When you're choosing jewelry for example, you might look at two similar malachite earrings, but one pair will look better to you. That's the lure of a particular crystal — you're intuitively drawn to the exact crystal that you need for a particular situation.

Each crystal emits an energy. You can sense this energy the same way you sense energy with Reiki.

Knowing the lore of crystals

People have believed in the power of crystals for centuries and many are fascinated by the lore, or stories, associated with crystals. Many ancient cultures have used minerals, crystals, or gems, including the Egyptians, Chinese, Indians, and Native Americans.

Some people believe that certain crystals or gemstones (a precious form of crystal) can do the following:

- Enhance perception (think of a crystal ball)
- Give protection
- Heal disease

Information that is available on different crystals and their healing powers for different ailments is based on the centuries of information gleaned from ancient cultures.

Reiki and crystals can go hand in hand, working together to aid intuition and healing. In terms of healing, they both work at all levels of the body and the aura (see Chapter 2).

Table 12-1 shows how crystals are associated with the chakras (discussed in Chapter 2) and some of the symbolic rulerships they're thought to have.

Take this table as fun reading and a starting point when looking at associations of certain crystals with each chakra. The color association is a good place to start when you use crystals, but each crystal is more complex than just a color. For example, clear quartz contains all the colors and works at every level of healing. The same thing can be said of the more expensive diamonds. Now you know why I include quartz and diamond along with the seventh chakra, which is traditionally associated with violet.

Table 12-1   Various Types of Crystals and Their Associations with the Chakras

Crystal/Gemstone	Chakra	Name	Color	Symbolic Rulerships
Agate, bloodstone, hematite, red garnet, ruby	1st chakra	Root	Red	Good fortune, aggression, high energy
Carnelian, coral, moonstone	2nd chakra	Sacral	Orange	Emotions, comfort, security
Amber, citrine, tiger's-eye, topaz, yellow sapphire	3rd chakra	Solar plexus	Yellow	Vitality, success, joy, strength
Emerald, green jade, kunzite, rose quartz, watermelon tourmaline	4th chakra	Heart	Green and pink	Abundance, richness, bliss, harmony
Aquamarine, blue sapphire, chalcedony, turquoise	5th chakra	Throat	Blue	Understanding, loyalty, wisdom, protection
Azurite, calcite, lapis lazuli, sodalite, quartz	6th chakra	Third eye	Indigo	Communication, logic, creativity, rationality
Alexandrite, amethyst, clear quartz, diamond, selenite	7th chakra	Crown	Violet	Ambition, spiritual awareness, clearing away obstacles

Making rainbows with cut glass crystal

Wedding registries and fine drinking glasses may come to mind when you think of crystal. Or you may think of those beautiful sparkly cut-glass crystals that throw rainbows all over the room in bright sunshine (or moonlight for that matter). Although crystal glasses that have a musical ring and rainbow-producing glass crystal balls are beautiful, they're entirely different from the mineral crystals that are the subject of this chapter. I learned Reiki in a studio that had crystals hanging in windows with plants. These elements created a beautiful ambience for the Reiki clinics that were held twice weekly.

While glass crystal is beautiful, it doesn't have the same energy properties as the crystals that come from minerals of the earth.

Distinguishing between Crystals, Rocks, and Gems

When you decide to use crystals along with Reiki, it helps to know just what type of stone you have or which type of stone to look for. Here's some background on where crystals come from and which ones are gems.

You might sense the earth as solid, but deep within our planet, molten lava or magma bubbles away. Natural disasters such as earthquakes and volcanoes result from the constant activity and eventual release of pressure from the steam of hot magma.

Thankfully, the earth's surface is a solid layer that contains mountains, rocks, sand, and crystals. If you went on a hike through desert mountains, where the earth's crust is more revealed due to the absence of abundant plant life, you might find the following:

- ✔ **Elements:** The chemical components of the earth are called elements. Silver, gold, and iron are examples of elements that on their own make up crystals. The chemical symbols for these elements are Ag for silver, Au for gold, and Fe for iron.

- ✔ **Minerals:** Most minerals are made from combinations of elements. Two or more elements combine to form a mineral. Chalcedony, for example, is a type of mineral formed by the chemical elements silicon (Si) and oxygen (O_2) to form silicon dioxide (SiO_2). Other elements may combine with the silicon dioxide to give other minerals different colors. Red chalcedony is formed from silicon dioxide plus iron.

✔ **Crystals:** The repeated arrangement of minerals into distinct geometric shapes is called a crystal. The geometric pattern or shape is unique to each type of crystal. Crystals are fascinating because of this beautifully ordered construction.

✔ **Rocks:** A rock or stone is a hard substance formed from minerals or petrified life forms. Crystals are frequently found within rocks.

✔ **Gems:** A gem is a crystal stone (or pearl) that is considered precious due to its ability to be cut, polished, and used in jewelry or other products. Diamonds, emeralds, and pearls are examples of gems.

Some gems come from living things rather than minerals. This category includes pearls, coral, amber, and jet. Like their mineral counterparts, these remnants of life also emit a subtle energy, and though they are not really crystals, they are included in the practice of crystal healing.

I focus on crystals for the remainder of this chapter. But remember that crystals are made of minerals, which are made of elements. Crystals are sometimes considered gems (which will make them more expensive to obtain), and crystals are found in rocks.

Many crystals used for healing purposes are reasonably priced, including the powerful clear quartz crystal that is used to amplify healing. Herkimer diamonds, for example (which aren't really diamonds but a type of quartz found mainly in Herkimer County, New York) are clear stones. Colored types of quartz are also available, including smoky quartz and rose quartz.

Finding the Right Crystals for You

Crystals are widely available at specialist stores and on the Web. You may even find some crystals when you go out hiking (although this depends on where you go and whether taking crystals or rocks home with you is legal).

Considering the crystal's shape

Crystals vary as a result of different alignments of elements in the geometric lattice shape that forms the crystal. In addition, each crystal is found in different outer forms, either as a result of natural formation or from cutting the natural stone. Here are the different shapes of crystals:

- **Crystal ball:** The ball-shaped crystal is famous in lore as the medium of the gypsy fortuneteller. The practice of using a crystal ball to see through time is called *scrying*.

- **Wand:** You can use crystals in a wand shape for Reiki healing. Try programming the wand with Reiki energy (see the section "Giving Your Crystal a Reiki Charge," later in this chapter). One idea is to "draw" the symbols by using the crystal wand as a pencil over the part of the body you want to send healing to.

- **Points:** Many crystals end in points. During healing, the point can be turned toward the recipient to bring in energy and turned away from the recipient to draw out energy.

You can find crystal shapes with many other names, including double-terminated, cluster, geode, egg, and pyramid. The same healing energy is found in a crystal no matter whether it is polished or unpolished, cut in one particular shape, or uncut.

Don't be confused by the plethora of crystals that are available. Instead, use your intuition to lead you to the right crystal to use alongside Reiki healing and your intention will lead you to use it in the right way.

Choosing which crystal to use

If you're considering using crystals for your own Reiki healing or the healing of others, try one of these methods to choose which crystal to use:

- **Energy scanning:** Use your hands to sense the energy of the different crystals. This technique is similar to the technique used to scan before giving a Reiki treatment (see Chapter 10).

- **Meditation:** Close your eyes and see which, if any, of your crystals come to mind.

- **Pendulum:** Some people use a crystal pendulum to get a message, such as yes or no for a particular crystal (see Chapter 2).

If you're working with a Reiki recipient, you can ask the person to pick a crystal. The person will intuitively pick the crystal he or she needs at that time.

Know that whichever crystal you do use is the right one. Trust your intuition and the inherent wisdom of the crystal and the healing process as a whole.

Before using crystals in healing, apply the same principles you would use in a regular Reiki session. Use integrity, intuition, and intention. Say a prayer of healing intent before choosing and using your crystals.

Staying Crystal Clear: Cleaning a Crystal's Energy

Crystals have their own special intrinsic energies. Most crystals also take on the energies of people or situations around them. A crystal that has taken on other energies may have less effect of its own, or you may even detect some of the negative energies of others.

The importance of cleansing and charging your crystals is really part of connecting with your crystal and asking for its highest potential for healing.

If you use crystals for healing yourself or others or if the crystals have been sitting around your house for a while, you'll want to clean them. Just like washing your countertop between meals or painting your walls to freshen them up, your crystals need regular cleaning attention. If you want your crystals to help you as much as possible, they deserve the best treatment, so keep them clean.

Knowing how to cleanse your crystal

Crystals need to be cleaned to remove dust and dirt, fingerprints, and even energy imprints from people or situations. Take care when cleaning to avoid harming a delicate crystal. Check with an expert in crystals or a crystal book (see the Appendix) to find out more about how to clean individual crystals. Here are some things to use to clean your crystals:

- **Distilled water:** Sprinkle or run the crystals under pure water.
- **Sunlight:** Set your crystals (except amethyst, which may fade) in bright cleansing sunlight.
- **Moonlight:** Let your crystal absorb the power of the moon.
- **Salt:** Cover your crystals with salt. Discard this salt when you're finished.

- ✔ **Incense:** Pass the crystal through the smoke of a cleansing incense such as sage; this technique is called *smudging*.

- ✔ **Soil:** Some folks bury crystals in the soil to remove particularly negative energy. You can wrap the crystals in cotton or another natural material before putting them into the ground.

- ✔ **Reiki:** You can use Reiki to cleanse your crystal. Put the crystal in your hands and use the Cho Ku Rei, or power, symbol (see Chapter 8 for info about Reiki symbols). Or try the Japanese technique of Jakikiri Joka Ho.

Jakikiri Joka Ho: Another way to clean crystals

This Japanese Reiki method, Jakikiri Joka Ho, breaks away negative energy for cleaning inanimate objects. The meaning behind the name of this method can be broken down like so:

- ✔ *Jaki* means "bad energy."
- ✔ *Kiri* means "to cut."
- ✔ *Joka* means "purification."
- ✔ *Ho* means "method."

Use this method on crystals (or any other nonliving object) by doing the following:

1. **Hold the crystal in your left or nondominant hand.**

2. **Set your intention to cleanse the crystal of all negative energy.**

3. **Hold your dominant hand over the crystal and perform three quick chops (like a karate chop) in the air just over the crystal.**

   The crystal is now ready to be programmed or charged with energy.

If you want, you can perform Gassho with your hands in a prayer position (see Chapter 9) before and after this technique.

Giving Your Crystal a Reiki Charge

Crystals have their own intrinsic energy, but they also respond to the Reiki symbols (see Chapter 8). In crystal therapy-speak, adding an energy to a crystal is called *charging* it. Another word you may hear is *programming* your crystal, which could mean adding a Reiki symbol or adding an intention, such as healing or manifesting abundance.

By charging your crystal with Reiki, you embed the crystal with Reiki, which can then be transmitted (and amplified) through the crystal.

Before giving Reiki, make sure the crystal is cleansed (see "Staying Crystal Clear: Cleaning a Crystal's Energy," earlier in the chapter).

You can give any Reiki energy or symbol to a crystal by holding the crystal in your hands and sending Reiki out through your hands while visualizing the symbol and saying the symbol's name three times out loud or to your self:

- ✔ Give the Power symbol (Cho Ku Rei) for basic empowerment. Even if you've used Cho Ku Rei for cleansing, I would give the symbol's energy again.

- ✔ Give the Distance symbol (Hon Sha Ze Sho Nen) if you will use the crystal for distance healing.

- ✔ If you're a Reiki Master Teacher, you can even give your crystal an attunement so that it is a Master Teacher too!

After the Reiki crystal is charged, it will send the Reiki symbol continuously. When placed in a room, a crystal charged with the Power symbol Cho Ku Rei will continuously send that cleansing energy into the room.

If you haven't been initiated into the symbols yet (see Chapter 8), you can send Reiki through your hands to the crystal without using the symbols. And if the crystal is too big to place in your hands, just put your hand or hands over the crystal and send Reiki that way.

An advanced Western Reiki technique is to construct a healing grid with crystals. The grid is simply a set of crystals lined up in a determined formation (such as a circle or octagon). Reiki practitioners charge a set of quartz crystals with Reiki symbols and use these crystals to construct a healing grid that continuously sends Reiki as distant healing to loved ones who have their photos placed on the grid. You could place pieces of paper with someone's name or other objects within the circle of quartz crystals. By using the Reiki-charged stones as well as an intention of healing, you set a powerful healing in motion.

Bringing Crystals to the Reiki Table

After you have some crystals at hand and you've cleansed and charged them with Reiki energy, you can use them to aid in the Reiki session.

You might think of Reiki energy as coming from heaven and crystal energy as coming from earth. In that way, Reiki and crystals complement each other during a Reiki treatment.

Knowing which crystals to use

As you use crystals more often, you'll gain the confidence and experience to choose which crystals to use for treating different ailments. If you haven't used crystals before, you may run into a lot of advice from different people telling you which crystals are right for you. However, if you check in with your intuition regularly, you'll know which crystal is right. If you should be using a different stone, you'll know that too. If you read enough books and speak to enough people, you'll hear differing information about which crystals to use. For that reason, developing your own intuition and the confidence to follow it is key.

Each of the chakras (see Chapter 2) is associated with different colors. You can choose crystals with these colors to help treat energy imbalances in a particular chakra (refer to Table 12-1).

You might start your journey with crystals with a set of chakra-balancing stones that contains a set of seven polished crystals associated with each of the chakras. Try holding each of these crystals and meditating with it to see how the energies differ.

When you determine that a certain chakra is unbalanced, you can use a crystal associated with that chakra during your treatment. For example, you can use rose quartz to treat the heart chakra.

Placing the crystals during a Reiki session

The crystals are helpers in the process of Reiki healing. You can choose from many ways to bring them into your session:

- ✔ Wear crystal jewelry so that the energy is coming through you and is around you while you treat with Reiki.

- ✔ Keep crystals in the room. In this way the energy is always flowing to keep Reiki energy strong.

- ✔ Put crystals under the table. While you work on the top of the table, the crystal can send energy through the bottom of the table. I place crystals under strategic locations, such as the heart chakra.

- ✔ Give the recipient a crystal or two to hold. This lends a sense of comfort.

- ✔ Place crystals on the recipient's body or just around the body. For example, you can place a rose quartz in the middle of the chest on the heart chakra and clear quartz above the head. Use Table 12-1 to get some ideas of crystals to use at different chakras.

Continuing with the theme of the healing grid, described earlier in this chapter, another advanced technique is to place cleansed and charged crystals around a Reiki recipient in a grid. What this means is that a set of stones is placed at designated positions on or around the recipient's body. This technique combines Reiki with crystal healing techniques. If you want to work with crystals in this way, I suggest you seek out a teacher who includes crystals in the Reiki course or find a specific course in using crystals with Reiki. Use Chapter 7 for suggestions on how to find a teacher and course: You'll have to inquire specially to see who offers classes that include crystals.

Part IV
Sharing Reiki with Others

The 5th Wave   By Rich Tennant

"I appreciate your sharing your dreams and wishes for starting your own Reiki practice, but maybe I should explain more fully what we at Make-A-Wish Foundation are all about."

In this part . . .

You're ready to take the techniques you found out about in Part III and begin to channel the Reiki energy to help others. I tell you how to design a Reiki session of your own from start to finish, and I describe community events like Reiki shares and circles, where you can give and receive Reiki with other Reiki practitioners and also bring Reiki to your community. This is a great way to meet other people interested in Reiki and practice your new skills. If your Reiki recipient is far away, use the long-distance techniques that I explain to send Reiki across both time and space — pretty amazing stuff.

I also describe how to combine Reiki with other forms of healing, including medicine, massage and other body work, and therapeutic work. Increasingly, Reiki is used in medical situations, including emergency medicine and before and after surgery to augment the medical treatments.

When you're ready to start your own Reiki practice, check out the final chapter in this part for tips and advice on things to consider to make your practice a success.

Chapter 13

Putting Together a Reiki Healing Session

A Reiki session is like a live performance. Each one is different, and each requires that you, as the Reiki practitioner, be something of a "live wire," because you are the actor through which the Reiki energy flows. The Reiki recipient is your receiver, or audience. For a successful "show," you must set the stage for healing and prepare yourself to let the energy flow through you.

Just as you would read a script before reading the lines of a play, read Chapter 9 to discover how to prepare yourself to channel the energy and Chapter 10 to review the positions and techniques to use.

This chapter is about what it's like to work one on one with someone in an individual session. Your role is to be open and ready for the Reiki to come through you. You set the stage by getting the room ready for Reiki. You guide the recipient through your attitude and kindness. By maintaining a sense of nonjudgment and love, you give the recipient a sense of ease and relaxation.

A Reiki practitioner doesn't control the outcome of healing. The intention of Reiki is to provide the highest level of healing. Spirit determines the form that the healing takes.

Finding Your Reiki Style

Before starting a Reiki session, get a feel for your own personal style of working with Reiki. Each Reiki practitioner has his or her own style of working. You may learn from your Reiki teacher, but eventually you make the techniques your own. Here are some tips on developing your own style:

✔ Become knowledgeable about different Reiki techniques (listed throughout the book).

✔ Go to different Reiki circles and participate (see Chapter 14). You'll discover what you like best as you experience different techniques.

✔ Try out different techniques. You can use the techniques in this chapter or vary the symbols you use (see Chapter 8). Practice the meditation and focusing techniques in Chapter 9.

✔ Combine your knowledge of Reiki techniques with your developing intuition. In this way, you give each recipient a uniquely tailored Reiki session.

Preparing Yourself to Give Reiki

The more time you spend preparing yourself before giving Reiki, the calmer you'll be, and the more pleasant the experience will be for you and the receiver. Here are some ways to become ready to give Reiki:

✔ **Consider your clothing.** Be sure that you're comfortable and that your jewelry or clothing won't get in the way of the treatment.

✔ **Wash your hands and brush your teeth.** You are working near someone's body and their nostrils. Personal hygiene is important so the recipient isn't distracted by what you had for lunch. Washing your hands is a good step to take before any Reiki session and in between sessions.

✔ **Become present and connected to Reiki energy.** Detach from what you were doing before the session and get in the spirit of the Reiki session to come. Just taking a few deep breaths and connecting for a few minutes will help you feel centered, grounded, and connected. I discuss techniques to increase your Reiki flow more thoroughly in Chapter 9.

Come to the Reiki session with a clean body and spirit. This advice may seem obvious, but don't perform Reiki if you are under the influence of alcohol or illegal drugs. Some people avoid caffeine and nicotine before a session. These substances overload the body and may reduce your ability to channel energy.

Getting Your Surroundings Ready

The Reiki room needs to be clean, neat, and quiet so that you can create a comfortable space where healing can occur. The following advice can help you create such a room:

- **Locate an appropriate space.** The best option is to have a dedicated room for Reiki that you can set up and leave it as you like. If you use a room that does double duty for other tasks, try to keep clutter and other distractions to a minimum.

- **Play soft gentle music.** Music is soothing and can help you and the recipient relax and take in the Reiki energy. Have a selection of different types of music: instrumental, New Age, chanting, or anything else you find that helps you get in the Reiki mood.

- **Have the following supplies on hand:**

  - Tissues

  - Drinking water and cups

  - Pillows and blankets

- **Use candles and incense with discretion.** Candles are good at setting a mood, but the smoke from incense or candles can irritate some people. Some recipients may be sensitive to certain fragrances, so ask before burning such objects.

- **Create a spot where recipients can hang their jackets and store their personal belongings.**

- **Keep the room clean and vacuumed.** Keep clutter to a minimum (see more info about this topic in Chapter 18).

- **Keep the room energetically cleaned.** Use plants, crystals (see Chapter 12), sunshine, and air purifiers.

Before a session, you may want to open a window, burn some incense (but watch for lingering smoke), say a prayer, or otherwise clear the room of stagnant energy. (See the section "Cleansing the Reiki room," later in this chapter, for more information on clearing energy.)

Merging Different Healing Practices

If you have professional training in other healing modalities, by all means combine them in your practice. Tell the person beforehand which healing practices you will use. If the recipient wants only Reiki, respect that wish. Chapter 16 describes how to combine different healing techniques with Reiki.

If you don't have professional training or proper licenses to practice other healing techniques, then don't use them. You can practice massage on your husband in the privacy of your home. But if you incorporate massage into your Reiki session and you aren't licensed to do so, you risk legal action.

Familiarize yourself with the legal aspects of Reiki, which I discuss briefly in Chapter 17, but you really need to consult experts who are knowledgeable about the laws where you live.

Considering Ethics and Boundaries

The relationship between Reiki giver and Reiki receiver is based on trust. The recipient must be able to feel comfortable and trust that you will do her no harm.

To treat a recipient with due respect goes beyond not purposefully harming her. You must also follow these guidelines:

- ✔ Never touch a recipient's private parts. Don't touch the genitals, the breast area, or the buttocks.

- ✔ Be clear about your intentions. State your intentions to yourself, to spirit, and to the recipient. See Chapter 9 to read about intention and prayer in Reiki.

- ✔ Avoid making promises. Don't say that Reiki will cure a disease. Are you really sure of that? Don't keep someone from pursuing other types of healthcare. See Chapter 16 to read about other types of healthcare.

The higher your level of integrity, the better the Reiki session will be. The recipient will pick up on your high level of ethical integrity and is more likely to trust you and the Reiki healing.

The International Association of Reiki Professionals has produced an excellent Code of Ethics (see the Appendix) that you can use as checklist to make sure that your own ethics are in order.

Recognizing that each person or situation is unique

From your training and experience you develop a personal style for giving a Reiki treatment, but you should alter this for each recipient. For example, a person who has problems with movement won't be able to comfortably turn over in the middle of the session. If someone comes to you with a specific issue, you may modify or at least incorporate information about this issue into your session. For example, you may need to repeat the intention to heal or change the order or course of your treatment.

To help you determine appropriate Reiki usages, Table 13-1 shows when to use different Reiki techniques. Some of these techniques are discussed later in this chapter.

Table 13-1	Knowing When to Use Different Reiki Techniques		
Technique	*Before Session*	*During Session*	*After Session*
Dry washing (Kenyoku Ho technique)			Yes
Beaming Reiki (see Chapter 10)	Yes		Yes
Reiki with hands above body (see Chapter 10)		Yes	
Reiki with hands on body (see Chapter 10)		Yes	
Aura cleansing	Yes		Yes
Cleansing Reiki room	Yes		Yes
Protecting yourself	Yes		

Like all things in life, balance is essential. Be flexible enough to alter your style to fit the Reiki recipient. But also maintain the style and structure of a session that you need to keep Reiki flowing for you. Life would be boring if each of us were exactly the same.

Sharing information with others

The Reiki recipient may reveal information to you about herself or others. This information is confidential, so you shouldn't repeat it to anyone else.

During meditation or Reiki sessions, you enter a quiet and sacred space. At these times, messages may come for you or the Reiki recipient. An important ethical issue is how much information to share with the recipient and when to share it.

Use your intuition to guide you on what is appropriate. This matter is personal, and some people are open to receiving intuitive information and others are not.

When you treat another person, you're doing sacred work, so it's best to err on the side of not hurting anyone else. Sometimes the practitioner wants to show off his psychic or intuitive abilities, or is excited to share information received during a session. Before sharing any information with the recipient, ask yourself, "Will sharing this information help?"

Respecting boundaries

The responsibility for healing lies squarely with the person who is receiving Reiki. When the recipient asks you for Reiki, she is asking for help with her own healing process. Your job is to be a conduit for this energy. Knowing your role in the healing process, and staying within those boundaries, is important for you and the recipient.

Boundaries get muddled when the practitioner takes on the responsibility for healing someone else or when the practitioner doesn't take care of her own healing needs.

Sometimes healers get confused about how to help people. In the desire to be of service, you may get tangled up in other people's affairs or go beyond your comfort zone. If that happens, pull back and look at yourself. See where you need more healing or self-love. Decide how much time you can give before or after a session for telephone calls or consultation. Be clear with recipients who need more time and energy than you can give and refer them to other professionals as needed.

The greatest gift that you, as a teacher or healer, can give to others is to be healthy yourself. When you have worked through your own issues and removed your own energy blocks, the light and love you can then channel is obvious to others.

Having confidence in your abilities as a Reiki practitioner lessens the need to have to prove to anyone how good you are or the need to fix others. You can gain confidence by working on your own healing and practicing the techniques offered in this book.

Reiki is a limitless energy that flows through the practitioner. If you feel depleted after a Reiki session, then you're trying too hard. After a Reiki session, you should feel enlivened by the Reiki energy that has been flowing through you.

Going through the Session

The Reiki session has a beginning, middle, and end, just like three acts of a play. The beginning sets the stage, the middle holds the energy, and the end closes things off nicely. How you run things depends on how much time you have. The average session lasts about one hour, but you may schedule shorter or longer periods.

Starting the session

The way that you start the session sets the tone for the Reiki healing. After you calm yourself and clear the room of clutter and stuck energy (see the section "Cleaning and Protecting," later in this chapter), you're ready to begin.

This is the time to connect with your recipient and prepare the person for the Reiki session. The following tips can help you prepare the recipient for Reiki:

✔ Make sure the person is comfortable on the table. Add bolsters, pillows, or blankets as needed.

✔ If the recipient is new to Reiki, explain what you will do during the session and what she can expect (recipients can expect to feel very relaxed).

✔ Ask whether the recipient has a particular intention or need for this Reiki session.

✔ Say a prayer or intention for the session, such as "We come together for the highest level of Reiki healing today."

✔ Use the aura cleansing technique (see the section "Exploring the technique of aura cleansing," later in the chapter) to prepare the recipient for Reiki.

Start with Byosen scanning (see Chapter 10), Reiji Ho (see Chapter 10), or go right to the first hand position of the standard Reiki session (see Chapter 10).

Taking notes mid-session

Watch the clock and about midway through the session ask the person to turn over if you will also be working on the other side of the body. Most practitioners start by working on the front of the body while the recipient lies on her back. But choose the positions that work best in each situation. If the recipient is having back troubles, you may want to focus entirely on the back, with the recipient lying on her stomach.

At this midway point, you can note whether you're running fast or slow and change the amount of time on any hand position. By using your intuition (see the section "Receiving Guidance through Intuition," later in this chapter), you can determine whether you need to change the course of the treatment. For example, you may be running slow and sense that the person needs more time on the heart area, so you decide to reduce the amount of time spent on the knees and ankles. Or you make a note to yourself to come back to the heart when you finish working on the abdomen.

Ending the session

The session ends when you feel that the recipient has taken as much energy as possible or you must stop because of the time on the clock. Be sure to do the following at the close of the session:

✔ **Seal in the Reiki and protect the recipient.** When you end the session, perform an aura cleansing (see the section "Exploring the technique of aura cleansing," later in this chapter) to seal in the Reiki you have just given. You can also say a prayer of closing, such as this one:

"Thank you spirit for providing Reiki healing to [insert name of recipient] today. May she take away only that which is for her highest good. May she be cleared of any stagnant or lower energy, which is now transformed to light. May [insert name of recipient] be bathed in light and protected as she integrates the healing performed today."

✔ **Cleanse and protect yourself.** You do this by using Kenyoku Ho, or dry bathing (see the section "Using the Kenyoku Ho technique," later in this chapter).

✔ **Make sure the client is grounded.** Reiki can make the recipient feel spacey. It's kind of like the feeling when you just wake up from a good dream, and you don't necessarily want to wake up and get out of bed! You can help the client by holding on to the client's feet at the end of the session. Make sure the recipient sits for a while or walks around before exiting.

✔ **Share feedback with one another as appropriate.** The recipient may have questions about the session or want to share some thoughts or reactions. You might share information such as "You seem much more relaxed now." Remember to take care in presenting information or giving advice to someone else (I discuss this in the section, "Sharing information with others," earlier in this chapter). If you're not a therapist or doctor, don't give psychological or medical advice.

✔ **Plan for another session.** You can give the recipient a business card or make an appointment for a future date.

✔ **Receive payment.** If you didn't get paid at the beginning of the session, you can do so now.

Receiving Guidance through Intuition

You are being guided during a Reiki session. You receive that guidance through your intuition. You may experience intuition as a gut feeling, instinct, or insight. You may not even realize what's happening, but you get a thought to "move to the next position" or "put your hands over the heart." This is the type of intuition I am talking about in this situation.

As you develop confidence in using intuition, it becomes your most important tool in knowing exactly how to format the Reiki session for each person to cater to their individual needs. Two Reiki techniques rely on intuition: Reiji Ho and Byosen Reikan Ho (see Chapter 10). For Reiji Ho, you are guided where to put your hands next. For Byosen Reikan Ho, your hands are guided to parts of the body that have disease or need Reiki. Both of these techniques require that you follow your inner knowing or intuition to know where to place your hands during a Reiki session.

A great way to develop your intuition is to practice giving an intuitive Reiki session with an open-minded Reiki partner (perhaps one of your classmates from Reiki training). Don't move your hands until you get a "message" telling you where to go next. An intuitive message might come in one of the following ways:

- **Inner vision:** Close your eyes and see whether an image comes to mind. For example, you might see a picture of a right shoulder.

- **Sensations:** See whether you feel in your own body a tingling sensation. If you feel a new sensation (meaning that it's not your own long-term knee problem but something that seems to have just arisen), then put your hands on the recipient's body in that place.

- **Thoughts:** You may get a thought such as "put your hands on the jawbone."

- **Sound:** You may hear or sense the word "breathing," in which case you can focus Reiki on the nose and lungs.

If nothing comes to you, just pick the next position out of a hat. Imagine that you are reaching into a hat with pieces of paper with different body parts listed. Pick out a piece of paper. What does it say? Go there.

Ask the recipient for feedback: You might say, "I don't know why, but I got the signal to put my hands on your left elbow. And the person might tell you, "I banged my elbow on the car door this morning!"

The more you're open to intuition and follow it, the better you'll become at using and interpreting your intuition.

When you're able to trust yourself and follow your intuition, Reiki sessions may not be what you were expecting, but they'll help the recipients. They may even ask you how you knew to put your hands in just the right place. See Chapter 9 for more information.

Cleaning and Protecting

As a Reiki practitioner, you don't have to worry about blood or body fluids as doctors or dentists do. But you are getting close to another person, and during the releasing that goes along with Reiki, some of the stagnant energy may be released.

You don't need to be frightened of stagnant energy, which is also called "negative energy" or "lower-vibration energy." Stagnant energy shows up in lots of places for lots of reasons, such as in a sickroom that hasn't seen sunlight or fresh air for a while or a crowded supermarket where you can barely move through the aisles.

The solution for a Reiki practitioner is to be conscious of protecting yourself, the Reiki recipient, and the room from "picking up" or keeping any negative energy. And you want to clear away any stray negative energy that has landed on you or in the room. Use these techniques to keep everything fresh as a daisy:

✔ Aura cleansing to protect the recipient before and after a Reiki session

✔ Kenyoku Ho to protect you after a Reiki session

✔ Power symbol protection (see the section "Protecting yourself," later in this chapter) and cleansing (see the section "Cleansing the Reiki room," later in this chapter) before a Reiki session

Exploring the technique of aura cleansing

Have you ever noticed the freshness of the air after a heavy rain — when the sun comes out and a rainbow forms in the sky? After a Reiki session, you feel that sort of freshness. Any energy that is inside of you that is stuck or dense will wash away. By performing an aura cleansing, you protect against any low energy coming back. The *aura* is the energy field surrounding the body. Read more about the aura in Chapter 2.

Follow these steps to cleanse the aura:

1. **With the Reiki recipient lying down in a comfortable position, keep your hands above the body and sweep your hands from the top of the head slowly down the body to below the toes.**

2. **Repeat Step 1 two more times.**

By working on the aura before starting treatment, you remove some of the resistance to the Reiki. Consider it similar to the prewash cycle at a carwash or on a washing machine.

After the Reiki session, cleansing the aura helps seal in the balancing that has just been given and protects the aura from picking up more "debris." You can compare this step to applying a wax or other product to a car to protect it after you wash it.

Using the Kenyoku Ho technique

The Kenyoku Ho, or dry bathing, technique, taught by Mikao Usui, refers to the process of cleaning yourself without water. Ho means method, and Kenyoku means dry bathing.

With the intention of cleansing, you take your right hand and clear your left side and then with your left side you clear the right hand. Follow these steps:

1. **Starting with your right hand over your left upper chest near the shoulder, run your hand across your chest toward your right hip and fling energy off your hip.**

2. **Repeat the process with your left hand over your right upper chest near the shoulder. Run your hand across your chest toward your left hip and fling energy off your hip.**

3. **Repeat this process two more times.**

Or you may choose this method:

1. **Put your right hand over your left upper chest and run your hand up over your shoulder and down your left arm, flinging the energy off your fingers.**

2. **Put your left hand over your right upper chest and run your hand up over your shoulder and down your right arm, flinging the energy off your fingers.**

3. **Repeat Steps 1 and 2 two more times.**

Here's one last method:

1. **Put your right hand on your left inner wrist and fling the energy over your palm and off your fingertips.**

2. **Put your left hand on your right inner wrist and fling the energy over your palm and off your fingertips.**

3. **Repeat Steps 1 and 2 two more times.**

Use any or all these methods to remove energy from yourself after a Reiki session.

Protecting yourself

The Power symbol Cho Ku Rei (Chapter 8) is cleansing and protective. Use it before a Reiki session to keep any stray energy from being attracted to you. Here are two techniques involving the Power symbol that you can use to protect yourself before performing Reiki.

✔ Draw the Cho Ku Rei with your fingers or entire hand on each of your chakras, starting with the first chakra and work your way up to the top of your head (the seventh chakra). (I discuss chakras in Chapter 2.) As you draw the Cho Ku Rei, say the name to yourself or out loud three times.

✔ Draw a large Cho Ku Rei with your fingers or entire hand over your chest area, incorporating your throat (fifth chakra) down to your solar plexus (third chakra). Say the name Cho Ku Rei three times as you draw the symbol.

You can also set an intention, such as "I am protected as I perform this Reiki session." You can use this intention in addition to the Power symbol protection or on its own if you find yourself in a rush.

Cleansing the Reiki room

Before performing a Reiki session, cleanse the room of any lingering energy by drawing the Reiki symbol Cho Ku Rei (Power symbol) with your fingers or entire hand and saying its name three times. Here are two different ways to use Cho Ku Rei in a room:

- ✔ Put Cho Ku Rei in every corner of the room. If you can't see or reach every corner, you can intend that the Cho Ku Rei energy reach each corner by staring at the corner, tapping your hand towards that corner, or blowing the energy toward that corner. Remember to get both the top and bottom corners. This technique takes longer but is good for rooms with lots of stagnant energy.

- ✔ Send Cho Ku Rei to the ceiling, floor, and all four walls. This quicker method is good to use before a Reiki session in a room that is otherwise kept energetically clean.

You can also set the intention: "This room is cleansed, purified, and ready for Reiki healing today." You can do this in addition to using the power symbol or by itself if you're really in a rush.

Chapter 14

Experiencing Reiki in a Group

. . . .

In This Chapter

▶ Discovering group Reiki events

▶ Feeling the power of group Reiki

▶ Considering a Reiki retreat

▶ Introducing Reiki to the public

. . . .

*Y*ou can experience Reiki in ways other than a one-on-one session or in a class setting. Reiki practitioners and teachers organize different group events to spread the word about Reiki to the public, share Reiki with others, and provide a continuing education and support system for Reiki practitioners.

A Reiki event such as a Reiki circle or share is a great way to meet up with other people interested in Reiki. You can discover more about Reiki firsthand, find a Reiki teacher, exchange Reiki sessions with others, and share Reiki with your local community.

In this chapter, I explain the different types of Reiki events and list the reasons they might interest you. I also describe how being with a group enhances the effects of Reiki. This chapter also addresses how both someone who has never experienced Reiki and someone who has recently trained in Reiki may benefit from attending a Reiki event.

Participating in Reiki Events

Reiki events are generally targeted to one of the following:

✔ **The general public:** This group includes *anyone* who is interested in Reiki.

✔ **Reiki professionals:** This group consists of those who have had some level of Reiki training.

If you're not sure whom the event is for, ask the organizer. Note also that many events are open to both the general public and Reiki professionals.

To define what type of Reiki events to look for, I provide a variety of terms for different Reiki events:

- **Reiki circle** means a group of people coming together to experience the healing power of Reiki. The word "circle" implies that at some point, the group sits or stands in a circle. In general, Reiki circles are open to the general public. Reiki circles are sometimes called *healing circles* or *Reiki healing circles*.

- **Reiki share** or **Reiki exchange** refers to the sharing of Reiki healing among practitioners. The terms Reiki circle and Reiki share are sometimes used interchangeably, so check with the organizers to be sure. A Reiki exchange implies that both people in the exchange are practitioners.

- **Reiki talks** or **workshops** are generally for Reiki practitioners of all or some level (see Chapter 7) and provide continuing education on subjects such as crystals or additional techniques.

- **Reiki retreats** are group events in which a group of Reiki practitioners get together to have a retreat. Reiki talks and group Reiki are usually part of the program.

- **Reiki clinic** is usually in the setting of a healthcare or healing facility and focuses on bringing Reiki to the general public, usually in the form of one-on-one healing.

Finding Reiki events

To find out about local Reiki events, check your local newspapers or community bulletin boards (such as those at libraries and healthcare centers) or ask alternative health practitioners. Two general types of groups sponsor Reiki events:

- **Local Reiki groups or organizations:** A sponsor may be one lone Reiki practitioner in your town or a city- or state-wide organization of Reiki practitioners from different branches. Many Reiki events are somewhere in between and are organized by a handful of practitioners who live in a given town.

- **Reiki branches:** A particular Reiki branch may sponsor an event. Usually, people from all Reiki branches are welcomed at such events.

The cost of Reiki events varies. Some local Reiki events are free of charge or accept donations. Generally, Reiki talks, shares, and circles are priced reasonably so that many people can attend.

Larger-scale events that attract people farther afield are usually advertised in Reiki-specific resources like magazines, Web sites, newsletters, or e-mail lists (see the Appendix for more information on resources).

After you begin training in Reiki, join a local or regional Reiki organization. One of the many benefits is notification about Reiki events. Check out the Appendix and ask your Reiki teacher to find out about organizations near you.

What to expect

Each Reiki event is unique, but it usually includes one of more of the following activities:

- ✔ **Talks or presentations:** The topic might be Reiki in general for the general public or a specific topic of interest to Reiki professionals.

- ✔ **Meditation, passing energy, and distance healing:** See the sections "Meditating in a Reiki group," "Passing energy around in a circle," and "Sending distant Reiki as a group," later in this chapter. Reiki circles, shares, exchanges, and retreats usually include these Reiki spiritual practices.

- ✔ **Reiki healing sessions:** Reiki tables are usually provided, and you receive treatment from one or more Reiki practitioners. See the sidebar "Experiencing group Reiki" and the later section "Harnessing the Power of Group Reiki." All Reiki events except Reiki talks include some form of Reiki healing sessions.

Reaping the benefits

In addition to giving or receiving Reiki, Reiki events offer other benefits. For example, you get the opportunity to do the following:

- ✔ Meet other people in the Reiki community
- ✔ Learn new things about Reiki

✔ Make new friends

✔ Find a Reiki practitioner or teacher

✔ Obtain Reiki clients for your business (if you're a practitioner)

Anyone who has trained from 1st-degree Reiki onward (see Chapter 7 for a discussion of Reiki training) can participate in an exchange of information and healing with other Reiki professionals or help bring Reiki to the community.

In terms of offering Reiki to the public, some circles allow anyone to participate in group Reiki, and others require that you have finished 2nd-degree Reiki training. Each group has its own guidelines for who can perform Reiki. In some cases, photocopies of your training certificate (see Chapter 7) are required if the group doesn't know you.

Allow yourself to receive Reiki. Even if you feel you want to give Reiki to others, remember that you deserve to receive Reiki too.

Harnessing the Power of Group Reiki

When Reiki practitioners and interested members of the public experience Reiki together, the intentions for healing and spiritual connection cause the energy levels to soar, providing a boost to everyone present.

Giving group Reiki sessions

Imagine the energy you feel when one person performs Reiki. Now multiply that by many people performing Reiki. You get the idea. When more than one practitioner lays hands on a recipient, that is *group Reiki*. The Japanese term for group Reiki is Shu Chu Reiki.

When groups of Reiki practitioners get together, energy levels are high, and the experience can be joyful and fun. Performing Reiki with other practitioners is a great way for new Reiki practitioners to gain confidence and experience. You can also learn new tricks by watching how other practitioners carry out a session.

The usual Reiki session involves one practitioner treating one recipient. When you have multiple practitioners and multiple recipients, there are many possible configurations for giving Reiki:

✔ Multiple Reiki tables with one person giving the Reiki to each recipient

✔ Two or more Reiki tables, but with two or more people giving the Reiki to each recipient

✔ One Reiki table with all practitioners giving Reiki to one recipient at a time

Group Reiki is the same as any other Reiki session. Before performing Reiki, make sure to prepare the room for Reiki and set your intention for the session (see Chapters 9 and 13).

The layout of hands for group Reiki depends on the number of practitioners performing Reiki. See Figure 14-1 for an example of the layout of hands during group Reiki.

Here are some ideas for group Reiki:

✔ One person may act as the leader and work on the head areas. This person is usually the one to indicate when the Reiki session has ended (unless you are using a set amount of time, such as 15 minutes).

✔ One person can work on the left side of the recipient, and another person works on the right side, mirroring the same positions. For example, each person can hold the shoulder and hand of the opposite side of the body.

✔ When many people are performing Reiki on one person, finding a place to put your hands can be difficult! If that is the case, you can beam Reiki to the recipient and move yourself a little farther away from the crowded table. Another option is to give Reiki to some of the practitioners who are performing Reiki on the recipient.

Experiencing group Reiki

People often come away from group Reiki very pleased with the experience.

For example, Joe of Southern California reports that he felt incredibly relaxed and soothed at his first Reiki session. He found a Reiki circle and experienced a few people placing their hands on his body. He immediately drifted off in a dreamlike state. He had a vision of his grandfather's home, with a green lawn and flowering plants. This image brought him a sense of comfort and peace. Having come to the Reiki circle

an open-minded skeptic, he left more convinced of the value of Reiki.

Karl was planning on having heart surgery in a few days. He attended a Reiki circle and invited all of his Reiki friends. It was standing room only as every person attending put his or her hands on Karl's body. What an energetic send-off before surgery! Karl felt relaxed and peaceful and knew that he had done all he could to prepare for the operation. His surgery was successful.

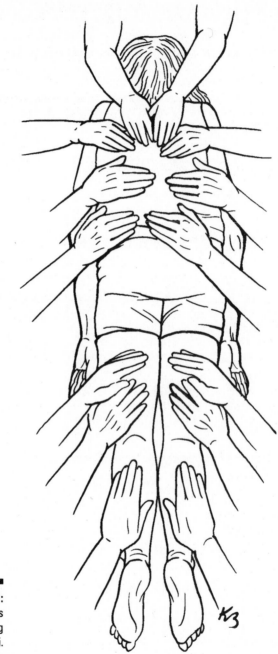

Figure 14-1:
Many hands
performing
Reiki.

Meditating in a Reiki group

Most group Reiki circles start with a brief (or not so brief) meditation, which is always a powerful experience. In most cases, it is a guided meditation, which means that one of the group members leads by talking everyone through the meditation. You close your eyes, get comfortable in your chair or seat on the floor, and take a few deep breaths. The meditation helps get folks centered and spiritually connected before beginning the Reiki.

Passing energy around in a circle

Here's the circle part of Reiki circle. You don't need to be a Reiki practitioner to pass or run energy. All you have to do is visualize energy or white light passing through you. The group leader guides you through this technique. Here's a summary of the technique for passing energy in a Reiki circle (in which everyone is either standing or sitting):

1. **Hold hands with the person on your left and right.**

   Your left hand is on the bottom facing upward and your right hand is on the top facing downward.

2. **Sense the energy coming from the person on your left into your left hand and through you out of your right hand to the person on your right.**

3. **Imagine the energy passing around the circle in a counterclockwise position.**

   You might sense a pulse of energy going around the circle.

Sometimes the leader will tell you to switch hand positions and send the energy in the opposite direction.

Variations of this technique are used in both Western and Japanese Reiki. Reiki Mawashi is the name of the technique in Japanese, which means "to pass on spiritual energy."

Sending distant Reiki as a group

Another part of a Reiki circle or Reiki share is praying or sending Reiki to others who are not present. (I describe this form of Reiki, known as distant Reiki, in Chapter 15.) Each group has its own preferences, but generally, all the people at the meeting can say the names of people to whom they want to send Reiki. Another method is to write down the name of a person to send Reiki to and put it in a box or in another designated area. Then the group as a whole sends distant Reiki to all the people mentioned.

Reiki circles can send distant Reiki to the earth, political leaders, or troubled areas or situations.

Receiving a group Reiki session

A highlight of Reiki circles and shares is the giving of Reiki to people who want it. Generally, the Reiki session is shorter at a Reiki circle than at a private session (which I describe in Chapter 13). Because the energy is more intense when you have more than one practitioner working on a person, the session can be completed more quickly.

Group Reiki is an incredibly powerful experience, and I recommend that you give it a try! The energy sensations can feel much stronger than during a normal Reiki session. You probably won't know which practitioner has what hands where because people change position. But you'll feel so wonderful that you won't care anyway!

Group Reiki can be a great way to get a surge of Reiki energy to remove stuck energy or start the healing process for long-standing illnesses.

By attending the same group regularly, you get to know the practitioners and get a level of trust that will allow you to feel secure enough to release deep-seated emotional blocks.

Going on a Reiki Retreat

A retreat is a time away from your normal activities when you can get quiet and work on your spiritual connection. Reiki fits in perfectly with a retreat situation. Retreats can be as short as a day or a weekend.

Different Reiki branches or regional Reiki societies organize retreats yearly or more often. You can get all the benefits of a Reiki circle: meeting new people, learning new techniques, and finding time for your spiritual growth. The retreat is like a longer version of a Reiki circle, with quiet time added in. Check with the individual organizers to see if you need to have Reiki training to attend the organized retreat and, if so, which level of training is required.

Another possibility is to attend a retreat organized by your spiritual or religious group and use Reiki in addition to the meditation and quiet times that are included in the retreat.

To find out about retreat schedules, I suggest that you ask your network of Reiki pals (Reiki teachers, practitioners, and friends) and check Reiki magazines and organizations (listed in the Appendix). For retreats that are not specific to Reiki, you have a wide choice. Start by considering a particular spiritual practice, such as Buddhist or Christian retreats, which are most commonly found. Or consider a retreat at a particular location. You'll find books and magazines devoted to these topics at your bookstore and library. You might even find a retreat center in your locale by looking in the phone book.

If you can't make it to an organized Reiki retreat, make your own by scheduling a quiet time to focus on Reiki. You can schedule quiet time at home or away and spend time meditating, giving yourself Reiki (see Chapter 11), reading spiritual books, and being in nature.

The origins of Reiki retreat go back to Mikao Usui, who took a 21-day retreat of meditation and fasting that led to his enlightenment; this spiritual retreat was documented on his memorial stone (see Chapter 3).

Taking Reiki to the Community

A group of Reiki practitioners can organize events at places within the community, which is a great way to introduce people to Reiki. After you have commitments from enough practitioners and found enough portable Reiki tables and a place to hold the circle, you're ready to go! You may find that even people who have never even heard of Reiki before you advertised your circle will be interested enough to attend.

Here are some different categories of organizations and events that may offer Reiki healing circles or that may let you present a Reiki talk or healing event:

✔ **Health-related:** Hospitals, hospices, nursing homes, health fairs, and health food stores

✔ **Religious or spiritual:** Places of worship or spiritual meetings

✔ **Metaphysical:** Metaphysical bookstores and New Age fairs

✔ **Animal-related:** Animal shows and meets, farming events, holistic pet stores, veterinary offices

✔ **Community:** Libraries, schools, and universities

If you want to bring Reiki to lots of different types of people, I suggest you join an existing Reiki circle (See "Finding Reiki events") or start your own.

Chapter 15

Sending Reiki Where Needed

• •

In This Chapter

▶ Looking at ways to send Reiki over distance and time

▶ Considering the permissions issues of distant Reiki

▶ Preparing to send distant Reiki

▶ Giving distant Reiki

▶ Healing yourself

▶ Giving Reiki to groups of people at once

• •

*R*eiki just flows when you place your hands on yourself or on someone else. But what if the person you want to heal is on the other side of the earth? A valuable Reiki technique called distant Reiki allows you to channel the Reiki energy and send it to anyone, anywhere.

Call it distant Reiki, long-distance Reiki, healing in absentia, or nonlocal or remote healing, this powerful technique lets you send Reiki anywhere in the world. Distant Reiki techniques are taught in 2nd-degree Reiki training and use the Reiki symbols. In fact, the third Reiki symbol is called the Distance symbol or the Connection symbol because it allows Reiki energy to cross any boundaries of space and time.

In this chapter, I describe different methods you can use to send distant Reiki. After you use distant Reiki to heal at a distance, you may want to try other creative uses of Reiki healing, including the following:

✔ Going forward and backward in time

✔ Healing specific situations

✔ Healing specific places

As you can see, Reiki can heal many situations. I particularly enjoy using most of the techniques described in this chapter because of the breadth they add to my Reiki practice. It's like Reiki is at my fingertips always, available to help wherever and whenever it's needed.

Like a Prayer: Understanding How Reiki Can Be Sent

Most people understand the concept of sending a prayer long distance. You can pray for someone in the same room or far away. Like prayer, Reiki can be sent in any situation. Also like prayer, Reiki can transcend space and time.

After you study 2nd-degree Reiki, you learn how to perform distant Reiki (see Chapter 7 for more about Reiki training). Follow all the guidelines for distant Reiki as you would for regular Reiki sessions, including the following:

- ✔ Use your *integrity* to make sure the Reiki is being sent in good faith (preferable to have permission).

- ✔ Use your *intention* for the Reiki energy to be transmitted to a particular person, place, time, or situation. Intend for the highest level of good for the recipient and for protection for you and the recipient.

- ✔ Use your *intuition* to know how to structure the long-distance Reiki session.

For a powerful group experience sending distant Reiki, check out a Reiki circle or share, which sends distant Reiki to individuals and situations by placing them figuratively in the middle of the circle. See Chapter 14 for information about Reiki circles and Reiki in the community.

Sending Reiki to people who are far away

The basic and most common use of the distant Reiki technique (see the section "Performing the Distant Reiki Session," later in this chapter) is to send Reiki long distance. The recipient may be in the hospital or in another country. The distance doesn't matter because Reiki can transcend any distance.

When you send distant Reiki, you can also set the time it is received. For example, you can send Reiki to an overseas relative at 8 p.m. your time and intend for the Reiki to be received at 9 a.m. her time. In this way, you combine the features of crossing both time and space during the distant Reiki session.

Sending Reiki to the future

Going into the future lets you send Reiki ahead to important events such as exams, competitions, job interviews, or dental appointments. Because you may not be available at a particular time to send Reiki to someone (or even yourself), this technique comes in handy as a way to preset the Reiki to flow. When you send the Reiki, you can state the time and place and person who is to receive the Reiki and the situation if you know that information.

For example, if you want to send Reiki to someone who is about to have surgery and you know the time and place of surgery, state something like this: "This Reiki healing is intended for Melinda Jones that she may receive the highest level of healing and care during her heart operation at 10 a.m. Monday at Francis Hospital. May she respond well to the surgery and heal quickly and fully."

Some people like to send the Reiki to the patient before and after the surgery and to the surgeon for the time of surgery. I suggest you follow the suggestions that your teacher gives you and use your intuition to find the best procedure for any situation.

Sending Reiki to the past

The ability to send healing backward in time allows you to help heal previous experiences. No, unfortunately this doesn't mean you can alter history, but you can heal what results from it.

Because people tend to hold onto past experiences, both good and bad, much of the healing done in the present time or now is actually healing the leftovers from the past. For example, suppose that you have been suffering for years from neck pain from a past car accident. You can return to the scene of the accident — in your imagination — and send Reiki to yourself and anyone else involved. Doing so requires good use of imagination and visualization.

Set your clear intention for the specific past experience or time period you want to focus on for the Reiki session.

Sending Reiki to different places and situations

Out of necessity or a desire to heal, practitioners have found creative ways to use Reiki. For example, Reiki is an excellent way for people to send immediate healing energy to any situation, near or far.

Note that you should apply all techniques of intention, integrity, and protection as described in this chapter when sending Reiki to a place or situation.

Helping to heal the earth with distant Reiki

Just like the crystals discussed in Chapter 12, the earth itself is receptive to healing with Reiki. Natural disasters that harm the earth include fires, volcanoes, and tidal waves. The earth is also affected by the actions of humans, including pollution and destruction of rain forests. The earth includes the rocks and minerals, soil and sand, plants and trees, and animals of all types. For all to coexist peacefully, a balance exists which mirrors our own individual energy systems.

The earth provides every need we have for sustenance. If you feel the call, send Reiki energy to the earth. You can send Reiki to the earth in a general way, and the energy can be taken where needed. Or you can send Reiki to specific places on earth, such as a continent, ocean, forest, or wherever you are drawn to send the energy.

Helping to heal conflicts on earth

You can use Reiki to heal anything, including inanimate objects (see more about this in Chapter 18) or even situations, such as the following:

- ✔ **Traffic accidents:** When you hear of an accident or pass an accident on the road, you can send Reiki to all the people involved.

- ✔ **Wars:** With an intention of resolution and peace, you can send Reiki to the victims of war, who are many.

- ✔ **Political situations:** During contentious elections, you can send Reiki so that the differences among political parties of different ideologies are healed soon after the election.

- ✔ **Natural disasters:** When a tsunami, earthquake, or tornado strikes communities or countries, you can send Reiki to those situations immediately upon hearing the news.

The techniques to send Reiki to any of these situations are the same as any distant Reiki session. You may wonder what the ethics are when sending Reiki to a situation. Because getting permission from all parties in a war or natural disaster is impossible, you can intend that Reiki go to all who want it. You're not sending Reiki to any particular individual but making this healing energy available to those who need it.

I've heard it said that the news, which can be pretty horrible at times, provides a template of people and situations that need prayer or healing. If you want to practice sending distant Reiki and don't know where to start, just open the newspaper.

Reiki on a larger scale

The Reiki community comes together and uses Reiki during times of personal, national, and international need. In most of this chapter, I describe individual situations. But Reiki is also valuable when a larger-scale need for healing exists.

Reiki and September 11, 2001

On the morning of September 11, 2001, when I heard about the unfolding events, including the destruction of the Twin Towers (which I had seen go up during my childhood) in New York, I felt drawn to send Reiki. Months later when I visited the actual site of destruction in lower Manhattan, I sent Reiki to the site. When I flew over the area and could see where the towers used to stand, I sent Reiki from the airplane. I was able to "sense" the towers perhaps as an amputee still feels a lost limb.

I know that many Reiki practitioners and Reiki circles around the globe sent energy around this terrorist attack.

Reiki and the December 2004 tsunami

I sent Reiki as soon as I heard of the tsunami in Southeast Asia, and looking at the images on television, I sent Reiki energy to those locations. I took a globe (I had a children's beach ball of the earth) and held my hand over the parts of the world affected. I also printed out a map of the region and beamed Reiki that way.

William Rand of the International Center for Reiki Training (see the appendix for more information) sent out an e-mail to his e-mail newsletter subscribers requesting that they send Reiki to the region.

At every Reiki circle I attended, energy was sent to the victims of the devastating tsunami.

Reiki and 2005

London terrorist attacks and Hurricane Katrina, 2005

As this book goes to print, Reiki practitioners around the world are sending Reiki healing to all those affected by these devastating events.

Getting Permission to Send Distant Reiki

When you work on someone in person, you have implied permission to do Reiki or else the person wouldn't be there! Distant Reiki presents a challenge of making sure the recipient wants to receive the Reiki you want to offer.

This Reiki technique touches on important ethical issues of healing and boundaries between the healer and person being healed, which I discuss further in Chapter 13. The keyword is integrity, which should be maintained in distant Reiki just as it is with face-to-face Reiki.

The decision of whether to heal and how to receive such healing lies entirely with the individual. Don't force your intention to channel healing on someone else. If your offer of Reiki is refused by one person, you can always find someone who does want to receive the Reiki healing energy.

Receiving consent from the recipient

Generally, you should give Reiki long distance only after you receive a clear request from the person who will receive the Reiki. This request can be in the form of a written or verbal request, such as "You can send Reiki to me anytime" or "Please send me Reiki so my knee heals from this surgery."

The request for Reiki is like a green light, giving you the okay to send Reiki to this person, following the manner of the person's instructions. If the call for Reiki is for a specific situation, you must inquire before sending Reiki for another situation. A general call for Reiki at anytime is a permanent green light — unless you later hear otherwise from the person.

Sometimes you'll receive a request for Reiki on another's behalf. If you aren't sure of the person's consent, you can take one of the following courses of action:

- **Choose not to send Reiki.** This is the easiest and clearest course of action to take. You have a firm resolve that you send Reiki only when directly requested.

- **Connect with the person and get an intuitive consent.** Meditate and get a picture in your mind of the person whom you want to connect with. You are connecting with the purpose of finding out by way of your intuition if the person is open to receiving Reiki from you. You might get an image of the person or sense an energy. Ask the question in your mind: "Do you want to receive long-distance Reiki from me?" If you get a clear yes or no, then proceed accordingly.

  I generally don't send Reiki to individuals who don't request it. But if I get a request on another person's behalf ("please help my father, son, or sister"), I use the intuitive approach to see if I can proceed. In one case, I connected with a friend's sister and heard: "I can do it on my own; I can take of myself. I don't need your help, thank you very much." When I told my friend this, she told me it sounded very much like her sister. I did not send Reiki in this instance.

  You might get a response such as "Okay, whatever" from a teenage boy or "Please, anything to help" from an elderly person in pain. In these cases, send Reiki to the person.

- **Send Reiki with a specific intent that it flows only where it is desired.** You can send Reiki without explicit approval, but first make clear in your mind that, if the person in question doesn't want Reiki, the energy will go to the earth or to some other person who wants it. You might say, "I am sending this energy to John, but if he doesn't want or need it, let it go to someone who does need it."

You may have strong feelings one way or another about getting permission to send Reiki. Follow what feels right for you.

All over the world, people pray for one another without necessarily asking if the recipient wants that prayer. Some practitioners use this logic to send Reiki without getting permission. But most agree that the path of most integrity requires getting permission.

Sharing what you learn with the recipient

Using long-distance healing requires you to connect with another person (or situation) and helps build your intuitive skills because intuition is your only sense of what is happening. I discuss intuition and Reiki in Chapter 9.

While performing distant Reiki, you're using your intuitive senses and may therefore receive intuitive information about the recipient. If you feel that the recipient would value and want this information, by all means tell the person. As discussed in Chapter 13, use discretion, respect, and confidentiality with all information received during a Reiki session.

Getting Prepared for Distant Reiki

After you get the hang of sending distant Reiki, you'll be able to send the energy in a variety of environments. But to get started, find a quiet place and time where you won't be interrupted. You need to focus on the following:

- **Grounding yourself and connecting with spirit:** Just like an in-person Reiki session, you need to make that spiritual connection so that you are in the best position to channel Reiki. Read Chapter 9 for tips on preparing to channel Reiki.

- **Channeling the Reiki energy:** You are not sending your own energy, but channeling Reiki energy. Make sure you feel the flow of Reiki before connecting with the recipient.

- **Connecting with the recipient:** After your channels are open and you're transmitting the Reiki energy, picture the recipient (See the section "Using visuals for the distant session," later in this chapter) and send the Reiki energy.

- **Keeping energy clean between yourself and the recipient:** Make sure to use any techniques you would normally use in a face-to-face Reiki session. In particular, remember to disconnect from the session and wash your hands or use the other techniques described in Chapter 13. Setting intention is also important for protection of energy. The point is to keep your energy to yourself and other people's energy to themselves.

Performing the Distant Reiki Session

When you study 2nd-degree Reiki (see Chapter 7), your teacher will provide you with techniques to use. The first few times you perform distant Reiki, it's best to follow the same procedure as an in-person Reiki session and your teacher's instructions or the technique outlined in the section "The distant Reiki technique," later in this chapter. But as you grow in confidence, you can use intuition to guide you more and more.

Using visuals for the distant session

Because you don't have the recipient in front of you, you need to find a way to "see" what is going on during the session. You can choose from different things to help you visualize or represent the distant Reiki recipient in your mind.

You can use a substitute prop to represent the recipient:

- **A teddy bear:** Use the teddy bear as a replacement for the individual and hold the teddy bear and give it Reiki.

- **Your knee:** The top of your knee can represent the person's head, and you can move your hands around your leg to give Reiki to different parts of their body.

You can picture the recipient by using one of the following:

- **A photograph:** You can stare at the photo, or you can hold the image between your hands and send it Reiki.

  On the back of the photograph, write the person's name, date of birth, profession, or any other information that you can get to help you focus on the person during the healing.

- **Your imagination:** Visualize the person in your mind. You may see the person as a vague mass of energy (like the aura described in Chapter 2) or have a clear picture of the person's body lying on a Reiki table.

I have used all these techniques. I find a teddy bear to be too small for my hands and generally use the imagination technique. But I am known to have a very vivid imagination! Try these techniques out for yourself and see what works for you.

In distant Reiki, your intuition or imagination is particularly valuable because you won't be receiving information directly at that time. You can't see with your eyes whether the person is sighing, crying, smiling, or coughing.

The distant Reiki technique

Here is the basic method I was taught to perform distant Reiki.

1. **First obtain permission (see the section "Getting Permission to Send Distant Reiki," earlier in this chapter)**

2. **Visualize and say the names of the following symbols aloud three times each:**

    • Hon Sha Ze Sho Nen (Distance symbol)

    • Sei Hei Ki (Emotional symbol)

    • Cho Ku Rei (Power symbol)

3. **Say the name of the receiving person three times.**

4. **Picture the recipient in your mind.**

5. **Repeat Step 2.**

6. **Begin the Reiki session exactly as you would in person.**

    See "Using visuals for the distant session" to determine which method you will use during this distant Reiki session. In your mind's eye, visualize what you're doing.

7. **Cleanse the aura (see Chapter 13).**

8. **Use the standard Reiki hand positions (see Chapter 10).**

    For a full session, start at position 1 and end at position 19.

9. **End the session with an aura clearing (Chapter 13).**

10. **Cleanse yourself with dry bathing (Kenyoku Ho) as described in Chapter 13.**

Because different teachers provide different variations on Reiki techniques, you may encounter advice for this method that's different from what's shown here.

Mikao Usui used distant healing methods, which he called Enkaku Chiryo Ho. (Enkaku translates to "remote or sending," Chiryo to "treatment," and Ho to "method.") This method uses the visualizing technique of photographs, if available, to send Reiki to people at a distance, even if the distance is just another room in the same building.

Creating the session structure

Just as you develop your own style of performing Reiki for a regular Reiki session (see Chapter 13), you can also develop your own style of performing distant Reiki. You can use any of the techniques outlined in Chapter 10 or 13 during a distant Reiki session. In place of the full session I describe in the section "The distant Reiki technique," earlier in this chapter, you can do the following:

✔ Use a brief spot treatment of places that need attention.

✔ Work with the aura or other sense of energy you have of the person. You may feel that one part of the person's aura or a particular chakra (see Chapter 2) is out of whack or needs smoothing and you can send Reiki to that area.

As for an in-person session, continue to send Reiki until you sense that what is needed at this time has been achieved. So if you sense that the recipient's energy is askew near the hip area (the second chakra), continue sending Reiki in your mind until you feel that the skew has been healed. You may sense that the area of the body is pulsing with energy as if it's now plumped up with Reiki energy, or you may sigh yourself, which signals that a shift has occurred.

For your first few distant Reiki sessions, use your friends and family and elicit their feedback. Their response to your distance treatment can help you with future distant Reiki sessions.

Using Distant Reiki to Heal Yourself

You can use distant Reiki for yourself in the following ways:

✔ **Sending to yourself in the present time:** While sitting in meditation, you can imagine yourself and send Reiki to yourself.

✔ **Going to the past:** As you recall or feel stuck by prior events in your life, make the decision to send Reiki to these situations. When you heal your past wounds, you get the benefit now.

✔ **Going to the future:** Try sending Reiki to your future self. Go one month or even years into the future. You can think of a certain event of the future such as a vacation, retirement, wedding or just send to the future with no event or time frame in mind.

You may receive a message when you send Reiki to yourself. When I send Reiki to a future self, I usually receive a positive message. It's as if my future self is more evolved and more loving than I am now and "she" wants to help me!

You can use any technique on yourself. In fact, it's best to put yourself first in order to learn and practice any technique but also so that you gain the benefit of Reiki healing.

Sending Reiki to Many at Once

Many Reiki practitioners use distant Reiki regularly and have multiple requests for healing. Different techniques allow you to send healing regularly to more than one person:

- ✔ **Reiki box:** Write down the names of the people or situations you are sending healing to and put the paper with the names into a box. Reiki the box regularly and you send Reiki to all requests inside the box! Note that you can use a beautiful ceramic bowl or any other object as long as it's intended for Reiki.

- ✔ **Crystal grid:** You charge the crystals with Reiki energy and place them in a set pattern and with a specific intention. Crystals are used to enhance the energy sent at a distance. (You can read more about crystals in Chapter 12.)

- ✔ **Boards with photos and names of people to be healed:** Use a bulletin board or any other type of surface where you can attach the names or photos of people requesting Reiki. You can beam the energy to the requests on the board. Read about Reiki beaming in Chapter 13.

Using Reiki to connect from a distance

I had a friend from the southwest United States who regularly sent e-mails to a group of people. I occasionally sent e-mail to him too. One day, my e-mail was bounced, so I tried it again, but it still didn't go through.

I became concerned, because I knew that "George" had a heart condition. I did an Internet search for his name and found an article of someone with the same name receiving an artificial heart. Was this my friend George? I found a picture of a man in bed with all sorts of apparatus, downloaded this picture onto my computer, and sent distant Reiki. Whether or not it was my friend, this person could use Reiki, I sensed. Over many months, I never deleted that picture from my computer, and I occasionally tried out the e-mail address, but it was always returned.

One day as I was writing this book, I got an e-mail from George! Yes, the man in the picture was him, and yes, he did have an artificial heart and then a heart transplant but is recovering now. I was delighted to hear of this miracle! I feel that Reiki helped me feel connected to him, even when I was distant and wasn't exactly sure what was going on. Did Reiki help him? It surely made a contribution, no matter how small, that, along with the medical help he received and prayers from others, gave him more time on Earth. We truly are all connected. We just forget it much of the time. Distant Reiki is a way to sense the connection among all people.

Chapter 16

Combining Reiki with Other Health Practices

- -

In This Chapter

▶ Considering the healing properties of Reiki

▶ Incorporating Reiki into medical care

▶ Helping treat pain with Reiki

▶ Using Reiki with bodywork and counseling

▶ Seeing how Reiki can help with addiction problems

- -

Reiki is a gentle spiritual energy that heals. It provides relaxation, stress release, and a soothing touch. Reiki energy brings about the highest good and can be used to enhance the effects of any other treatment. In this chapter, I describe how to use Reiki as a powerful tool in your healthcare toolbox to complement any other healing practices.

Discovering How Reiki Heals

Reiki supports your innate healing abilities. Your body has a marvelous ability to heal and protect itself from harm. Sometimes, though, this inner healing ability just doesn't work and what results is pain or illness, or to put it another way, dis-ease.

Seeing Reiki as energy medicine

From the perspective of energy medicine, any dis-ease is caused by an imbalance in your body's energy. The energy imbalance, which could be caused by an energy block or stagnation of energy, ultimately manifests physically or emotionally as pain or disease.

Conventional medicine treats symptoms and sometimes the biological cause of the problem. Energy medicine treats the underlying pattern of energy that makes you susceptible to disease. Reiki restores your body to harmony so it can self-heal and restore itself to health.

Reiki is a high-level intelligent energy that has the ability to balance the subtle energies of your body at every level: physical, mental, emotional, and spiritual (see Chapter 2). No matter where your disease has occurred in terms of an energy imbalance or where the disease has manifested, Reiki gets to the root of the problem, which ultimately solves the problem.

The practitioner's role is to help the Reiki energy. The recipient is always in charge (even at a subconscious level) because Reiki only flows to the place where it is needed. The intrinsic wisdom of the body "knows" to pull in Reiki energy. The observant Reiki practitioner will feel the pull of the recipient's energy by sensing "I have to put my hands over there."

Supporting the healing process with Reiki

REMEMBER

So what does the harmony that Reiki provides do for the person who is experiencing disease? Reports from individual Reiki recipients indicate that they experience the following after one or a series of Reiki sessions:

- ✔ Relief of muscle tension, pain, anxiety, and stress
- ✔ Quicker healing from tissue damage from surgery or radiation
- ✔ Fewer side effects from medications such as chemotherapy
- ✔ Positive attitude and feeling more energetic
- ✔ Better ability to focus and concentrate

Deciding on how many Reiki sessions to have depends on your individual needs (see Chapter 5). While you get some benefit after just one Reiki treatment, longer-term illnesses probably require longer-term treatment.

I now describe two ways that Reiki helps, which could provide support for all types of illnesses; reducing stress and removing energy blocks.

Using Reiki to reduce stress

The application of Reiki reduces the effects of stress, which is a major factor in many illnesses. Reiki can lessen tensions, relieve sleep problems, improve breathing, and make it easier to smile. When relaxed, the body has a better chance to perform its own healing miracles.

A friend from London with chronic health issues said, "I use Reiki on myself — it's been one of the only things that has helped me over the last few years — to relax and to reestablish sleep patterns."

Releasing energy blocks

Reiki heals at a deep level by removing energy blocks. As old stuck energy is released, channels within the body open up. This release of stuck energy may bring about crying, coughing, sighing, or other physical manifestations. After releasing stuck energy, Reiki recipients report the following effects:

✔ A weight has been lifted.

✔ Dreams are more vivid or yield interesting information.

✔ Insights to difficult issues or problems may occur.

Each person receives the amount of Reiki healing that is best for the person at the time.

In the days of Mikao Usui and Chujiro Hayashi (see Chapter 3), people attended daily Reiki clinics for months at a time to receive treatments. Today, most people receive Reiki less often and use Reiki as an adjunct to other types of healthcare.

The conventional medical system aims to provide life-saving interventions in the forms of medicines, surgeries, and other treatments. When you have a heart condition, cancer, manic depression, or other serious condition, it would be foolhardy or even life threatening to shun or postpone these treatments in the face of a serious illness.

Reiki is not a substitute for medical or psychological attention. If you have a serious condition, you must pursue life-saving medical or psychological intervention first, and then consider adding Reiki treatments. If you postpone necessary medical treatment, you risk your disease getting worse.

Now that I've told you all that Reiki can do for you, I must also tell you what you should not rely on Reiki to do:

✔ **Diagnose:** Although a Reiki practitioner may get some insights into a recipient's problems, this doesn't qualify the practitioner to make a diagnosis. To find out about an illness, visit a medical practitioner who can run a battery of tests to provide clinical information.

✔ **Cure:** Reiki doesn't promise to cure a disease, but it will certainly help you achieve a feeling of peace and serenity. In conjunction with other medical treatment (see the section "Adding Reiki to the healing toolbox," later in this chapter), healing can be achieved, which in some cases means a cure.

Healing doesn't necessarily mean a cure. In some situations, healing means simply to be at peace, whether that is during the recuperative process or even the dying process. The Reiki practitioner can only assure the availability of healing energy; he can't control the outcome of healing.

Steps for the healing journey

You might use Reiki as a one-time stress release or engage the use of a Reiki practitioner (see Chapter 5) as a long-term partner in healing a health issue. To get the most from Reiki in your efforts to heal, try the following:

✔ **Determine your health goals.** What are you trying to achieve with this treatment? To get over back pain? To recover from surgery? To be able to run again? When you have specific goals, you know what you're working toward.

✔ **Pay attention.** When you try Reiki or any other treatment, see how it makes you feel and note whether it is helping. If not, consider trying something else.

✔ **Be willing to change.** Reiki as an empowerment tool may bring to your attention changes that you need to make. For example, you may need to get more sleep or exercise. Or you may need to eat less at night. If you don't make changes, then nothing else changes. Or put another way, if nothing changes, then nothing changes.

✔ **Be persistent.** You may need to go through this list over and over again. Healing is a huge endeavor and may require more than pills or surgery can give you. You may need to redefine your health goals, try something again, note the effects, and make more changes, over and over again.

Don't give up on the road to healing — which is also the road of self-discovery and enlightenment. Every challenge that comes before you can teach you great things.

Integrating Reiki into Medical Care

The fact that Reiki is becoming more accepted in hospitals and other healthcare settings is exciting. Reiki has so much to offer as part of a healthcare package. In this section I describe how Reiki fits in with conventional medical care as well as alternative medical care. Actually, all medical care of every type is now being called *integrative medicine,* which puts it all together in a healthy package.

Adding Reiki to the healing toolbox

Maintaining good health is a full-time job. Many tools, including Reiki, contribute to well-being. Health requires self-care and a balancing act of the following:

✔ Rest and sleep

✔ Food and drink

✔ Movement and play

- Work and chores
- Community and spirituality
- Intimacy and connection with others

Creating a good balance of these parts of your life is related to your physical, mental, emotional, and spiritual well-being. If you find that your life lacks the balance that promotes good health and your health is suffering, you may need to seek professional help for the following:

- Diagnosis and treatment of medical conditions
- Medicines or supplements
- Surgical procedures
- Reiki or other energy work such as acupuncture, Qigong, and homeopathy
- Bodywork such as massage, chiropractic, or physical therapy
- Talk therapy and emotional release work
- Addiction recovery treatment

Reiki works with all the self-care and professional-care tools that I mention in this section.

Reiki and healthcare professionals

Nurses and doctors are learning Reiki and using it in their clinical practice. Other healthcare practitioners such as emergency medical technicians, massage therapists, and other types of "bodyworkers," social workers, and other types of mental health practitioners are also learning Reiki to add to their toolbox to heal others.

When a doctor or nurse who has learned Reiki places their hand on a patient, Reiki flows. I think this is the way medicine was always meant to be practiced. It is the healthcare professionals who are leading the way to bringing Reiki into the hospitals, clinics, and into the healthcare system in general so that patients can have a choice of different tools for their health.

Healthcare professionals who are also Reiki practitioners are also working on designing and carrying out studies to find out which diseases can most benefit from Reiki treatment.

Reiki and different healthcare conditions

When you consider that Reiki reduces stress and that stress is a factor in so many illnesses, it makes sense that Reiki can help so many illnesses. I list below some of the different conditions where individuals have reported benefiting from Reiki.

- Addictions
- AIDS/HIV
- Arthritis
- Attention deficit disorder
- Autism
- Back pain
- Burns
- Cancer: breast, colon, endometrial, lung, throat; leukemia
- Crohn's disease
- Depression
- Diabetes
- Endometriosis
- Fibromyalgia
- Heart condition
- Hepatitis C
- High blood pressure
- Hypothyroidism
- Insomnia
- Irritable bowel syndrome
- Kidney stone
- Lupus
- Migraines
- Multiple sclerosis
- Neck pain
- Stroke
- TMJ (TemporoMandibular Joint Disorders)
- Toothache
- Uterine fibroids

This list gives you an idea that Reiki is applicable to many different disorders. Reiki can provide supportive healing for these and many other medical conditions.

Reiki in hospitals

The benefits of Reiki have not gone unnoticed by the medical profession. Increasing numbers of hospitals are offering Reiki to their patients. In some cases, the regular medical and nursing staffs provide Reiki, and in other cases, separate units or volunteers provide Reiki.

Ask your doctor and other medical staff to see whether the following treatments are available in your hospital:

- ✔ Inpatient Reiki treatment before or after medical procedures
- ✔ Outpatient Reiki treatment
- ✔ Reiki training so you can give Reiki to yourself when you get home

When looking to see if your hospital offers Reiki, you can check to see if they have a department or section that deals with integrative medicine or mind-body medicine.

Reiki and medicines

Reiki helps the body use any medications, including pharmaceuticals, over-the-counter medications, herbs, or supplements. You can perform Reiki on the pills or vials of medication or give a Reiki treatment to the person who is on medication. Reiki helps by

- ✔ Reducing the negative side effects of medication
- ✔ Promoting the positive effects of medication

You may wonder how Reiki can do these seemingly miraculous things. Reiki is an "intelligent" energy that aims to provide the highest good. The highest good is to benefit from the medicine as quickly as possible. Reiki can help that happen.

Don't discontinue any medication until directed to do so by a healthcare professional. If a change of medication seems warranted, check with the professional who prescribed it.

Reiki in the waiting room

Joy, a friend of mind who is a Reiki Master told me, "I gave Reiki to my husband as he was waiting to have an angiogram, which helped him to relax and not to tighten up before his procedure. I noticed there was another woman giving Reiki to her husband. Then I was sent to a second waiting room where I introduced myself to Lisa (who turned out to also be a Reiki practitioner).

After two hours went by, Lisa received a page to pick up the phone. She was advised that her husband had to receive a quadruple bypass. Lisa became hysterical, and I immediately offered her Reiki, which helped her to become calmer. So Reiki is not only for the patient but also to support their families."

The synchronicity and connection that Reiki can bring continued between these two families. Joy soon discovered that her husband also needed quadruple bypass surgery. When Joy and her husband attended the pre-op appointment, they met Lisa again, and she told them that her husband had come through his surgery successfully. Joy's husband had surgery the next day, after receiving lots of Reiki energy, and he too is recuperating well. Reiki can help the healing process for the entire family.

Examining Reiki medical studies

Most of the information on the usefulness of Reiki in medical situations is from anecdotal evidence. An anecdote is a story from one person such as:

My sister didn't have to have her knee replacement surgery after she tried Reiki!

This anecdotal evidence, or story, is interesting but there is no evidence that other people who try Reiki will have the same result.

Previously, most people studying Reiki didn't have the resources or experience to perform controlled scientific studies on groups of people who try Reiki.

Reiki is a subtle energy, and its effects may also be subtle compared with other types of treatments. As someone who went to graduate school in epidemiology, which is the study of diseases, I would like to also point out that it takes special methodology in terms of both study design and analysis to "prove" a treatment or cause for any disease and it is common to find that studies differ in their results. Given all of that, I believe that soon the medical studies will prove what Reiki practitioners see all the time: the miracles of healing that Reiki can provide.

Four different Reiki clinical trials are currently registered on the Web site of the National Center for Complementary and Alternative Medicine (NCCAM) at http://nccam.nih.gov/ (see the appendix for more information):

✔ Efficacy of Reiki in the treatment of fibromyalgia

✔ Effects of Reiki on painful neuropathy and cardiovascular risk factors

✔ Reiki/energy healing in prostate cancer

✔ The use of Reiki for patients with advanced AIDS

The results from these and other studies should help you understand which illnesses or conditions can best benefit from Reiki from a clinically relevant standpoint.

Because Reiki is an energy medicine, some practitioners also look at studies on other forms of energy medicine such as therapeutic touch, Qigong, and polarity therapy. Any illness or condition that responds to another form of energy medicine may also respond well to Reiki.

I supply resources to investigate studies on Reiki and medicine in the appendix.

Using Different Reiki Techniques for Illness or Pain

When you use Reiki to treat a specific illness or pain, you can take a variety of approaches in the way you conduct the Reiki session:

✔ Perform the standard hand positions on front and back of the body (see Chapter 10). By doing so, you know that all parts of the body are covered.

✔ Use your knowledge of anatomy to focus energy on the body part in question (see Chapter 2 for an illustration of the body). The study of human anatomy aids you in your Reiki practice.

✔ Decide which chakra energy center is associated with the problem and focus on that chakra (see Chapter 2 for a description of the seven-chakra system).

✔ Use your intuition to know exactly where to place your hands. Read about the Reiji Ho approach (see Chapter 10), in which you use your intuitive skill, and the scanning technique (see Chapter 10) in which you let your hands sense the areas of the body needing attention.

✔ Follow *The Original Reiki Handbook of Dr. Mikao Usui,* written by Mikao Usui and Frank Arjava Petter, which gives some advice on how to treat certain illnesses (for more information, see the appendix).

You may use any combination of the techniques above to treat a physical illness in conjunction with the pursuit of necessary medical care.

Reiki energy flows to the parts of the body where it is needed. Even when you don't know exactly where to put your hands, intend for Reiki to heal for the highest good, and that is exactly what will happen!

Observe the situation. If someone is ill, try using Reiki, but if it doesn't seem to be helping, then add another technique to the healing toolbox.

Using Reiki in Special Situations

What is wonderful about Reiki is its ease of use. You don't need special equipment — just a pair of hands from someone who has studied Reiki (see Chapter 7). Because you can give Reiki with just the touch of a hand or even send it from across the room (see Chapter 10), Reiki can be used in many different situations.

Reiki in first-aid situations

In a situation requiring first aid, after you perform necessary measures and call for professional medical care, you can use Reiki to help calm down anyone who is injured and promote quicker healing. For example, if someone sprains their ankle, you can give them ice and also apply Reiki.

If you are sitting in the emergency waiting room, you can apply Reiki while waiting (see the sidebar: "Reiki in the waiting room"). In the case of serious accidents, apply Reiki after you have called emergency services and while you are waiting for the ambulance. While the ambulance crew is working on the person, stand back and beam Reiki from across the room (see Chapter 10) or send distant Reiki (see Chapter 15).

Reiki and surgery

Reiki can be helpful both before and after surgery. Before surgery, Reiki helps your body prepare for the operation to come. The better the condition before surgery, the quicker you will heal and recover. After surgery, Reiki helps the body recuperate.

Surgery acts on a physical level to repair or remove damaged tissue. Reiki helps on an energy level to help the surgical patient relax, reduce anxiety, and prepare the patient for the changes that surgery brings.

Some people like to send distant Reiki to the surgeon and surgical team or for the best outcome for the person undergoing the surgery (see Chapter 15 for more about distant Reiki).

Reiki during labor and birth

Reiki provides a gentle touch during the emotional and special time of child-birth. A husband, mother, or best friend may want to learn Reiki and be pre-pared to help the mother-to-be through labor. Or a staff member who assists in the birth may also be a Reiki practitioner. See Chapter 6 for a story about how Reiki helped during a difficult birth to give the mother peace of mind despite the pain of contractions and fear of bleeding.

Reiki brings a spiritual energy to the sacred process of birth.

Reiki and chemotherapy or radiation

The methods used to kill cancer cells can also wreak havoc on the healthy cells. Chemotherapy and radiation are effective in killing different types of cancer, but they can also cause difficult-to-manage side effects like insomnia, nausea, and fatigue.

Reiki works to keep your body balanced during chemotherapy or radiation therapy. By using Reiki before the start of anticancer treatment and during the treatment process, the body's inner harmony is better maintained. This can help lessen side effects and reduce the time it takes to recover fully.

Reiki around the time of death

As a gentle and noninvasive treatment for people at the end of their life, Reiki is often used in hospitals, nursing homes, and hospice situations. Reiki helps the person accept their situation and lessens pain and anxiety. The use of Reiki also brings about a sense of calmness and peace, which brings relief to both patients and their family at this time of transition.

More and more hospice nurses and other people who work with people at the end-of-life are receiving Reiki training. I was encouraged to find out that our assigned hospice nurse (who met my dad only the day before he died) had studied first-level Reiki. The Long Island Reiki Association had a presen-tation on "Reiki at the End of Life," which I attended a few months before my dad died. I heard the stories of various people who had used Reiki, including nurses who helped their patients die with dignity and peace. See Chapter 6 for my experience with using Reiki around the time of death for both of my parents.

Matching Reiki with Bodywork

Any type of treatment that uses a hands-on approach is a natural partner for Reiki. When the hands are placed on the body for massage, physical therapy, chiropractic work or other types of bodywork, they can also transmit Reiki.

Reiki works at the level of the body's energy, and the massage or physical therapy work on the muscles and joints themselves. Together, these treatments can help the recipient work through deeply held patterns of strain or pain.

 Some classifications of bodywork include Reiki as a type of bodywork, presumably because Reiki involves hands on the body. But Reiki doesn't involve movement of muscle or manipulation and is better classified as "energy work."

One problem with different classifications is that all healing deals with the same underlying problems, but each form of bodywork approaches healing from a different angle.

Bodywork and energy work together make a winning combination. As a massage therapist, chiropractor, or other type of bodyworker you can use Reiki in any of the ways discussed in Chapters 11 and 13.

I start you off on your journey combining Reiki with your bodywork practice with these suggestions:

- ✔ If the person is sitting: Put your hands on the person's shoulders and stand quietly for a few minutes while giving Reiki energy. Or you can hold your hands gently on the crown chakra.

- ✔ If the person is lying: You can use any of the hand positions listed in Chapter 10. On the front of the body, try holding your hands over the heart chakra and the sacral chakra. On the back of the body, hold the neck (back of the throat chakra) and the lower back (sacral chakra) simultaneously.

- ✔ Before and after the session: Use the aura cleansing technique to "sweep" away energy before and after your session.

I'm sure you will enjoy using Reiki to enhance your work.

When the client is relaxed with Reiki, the bodywork part of the treatment is easier and more effective. Reiki also helps seal in the change in body structure and movement to better effect longer-term improvements.

Combining Reiki and massage

I admit it: I love to receive a good massage. And I particularly love it when a practitioner combines massage and Reiki. I've reached the point where a massage without some type of energy work feels like something is missing.

On the other hand, I once had a Reiki session during which the practitioner told me, "You need a massage for your shoulders." That Reiki practitioner wasn't licensed to practice massage, but she sensed that I needed more than what Reiki could give me — at least in terms of my shoulder tension.

Using Reiki with Counseling

A therapist friend who is also a Reiki practitioner says, "your issues are in your tissues," where tissues refers to the components of the body. This is the basis of mind-body medicine: What is in your mind is in your body and what is in your body is in your mind. She realizes the limitations of talk therapy on its own and recommends Reiki to some of her clients. She is not alone. More mental health practitioners realize the value of bodywork and energy work in the resolution and transformation of emotional issues. Therapists who know Reiki may give Reiki to clients, or they may recommend a Reiki practitioner to their clients.

Reiki works to release energy blocks and can help release and bring to light long-standing blocks (see the section "Releasing energy blocks," earlier in this chapter).

If you're seeing a mental health counselor, schedule an appointment the day after a Reiki session. Issues are likely to come up during a Reiki session that you'll want to discuss as soon as possible with your therapist. Although Reiki helps to bring up issues, a trained mental health practitioner will be able to then help you work through the insights and feelings that are raised.

Reiki brings in a gentle, loving touch that also helps to heal broken hearts and mend unimaginable hurts.

Using Reiki to Change Habits and Heal Addictions

Whereas a habit can be simply annoying or bothersome, an addiction is downright dangerous. You can be addicted to anything from food to pills to cigarettes to sex. Alcoholism, drug addictions, eating disorders, and gambling addictions are notoriously difficult — but not impossible — to overcome.

Reiki has a role in helping to overcome habits and addiction by reducing the effects of stress and promoting overall well-being.

Overcoming addictions

Reiki has great potential to help people with addictions heal while they're also trying other therapies, regardless of which of the following they're doing:

✔ Going to an inpatient treatment center

✔ Seeking psychiatric or psychological help

✔ Attending a 12-step recovery program

Reiki can help people with addictions do the following:

✔ Stay calm during the withdrawal period

✔ Provide them with new ways of coping with the ups and downs of life

✔ Connect to spirit and a feeling of bliss (without suffering a hangover the next day)

Trying a technique for addictions and habits

If a Reiki recipient has a habit or addiction he wants to heal or you are working on your own habit or addiction, you can try this healing technique, which is also called *deprogramming method* and *mental technique.*

1. **Choose a time to perform the technique to remove addictions and change habits.**

   You can use this technique during a Reiki session (see Chapter 13) or a self-Reiki session (see Chapter 11).

   If you use this technique outside of a Reiki session, make sure the recipient has already relaxed and is open to receiving Reiki by performing an aura cleansing (see Chapter 13) or meditating (see Chapter 9) before using this technique.

2. **Make an affirmation stating the intention to heal. Here are some examples:**

   - I am free of nicotine addiction.

   - I treat myself with loving kindness.

   - I enjoy nutritious life-enhancing foods.

3. **Put one hand on the upper forehead and one hand low on the back of the head over the bump, or occipital ridge, just above the neck.**

4. **Imagine the first three Reiki symbols (Chapter 8) and say each name out loud or to yourself: Hon Sha Ze Sho Nen, Sei Hei Ki, and Cho Ku Rei.**

5. **Say the affirmation in your mind or out loud three times. Keep your hands in position until you feel the affirmation has "taken."**

For this technique, experiment with your hands to see which hand position feels the strongest (for me, it's the right hand on my forehead and left on the back of the head).

If you use this technique without symbols, that method is similar to the Japanese technique called Nentatsu Ho, or method for sending thought. The Japanese technique Seiheki Chiryo Ho (healing habits technique) is almost identical to this technique, except that the Distance symbol isn't used.

The single most important tool you have is your intention to heal yourself. Repeated use of this technique or any of its variants is necessary for success. Getting substances out of your body takes time. You need at least a month to change your behavior to a new habit, and you need more than that to learn new ways of coping without a substance or habit.

Chapter 17

Becoming a Professional Reiki Healer

*Y*ou may decide to take Reiki beyond using it for just yourself and your family and enter the world of professional healing. Some people give Reiki on a volunteer basis, and others use Reiki healing to create part or all of their income. In any case, practitioners must follow the highest level of integrity in their work.

In this chapter, I discuss what it means to be a Reiki healer and things to consider as you build a successful practice. Even volunteer work is a business of sorts — it just doesn't charge for services. The same standards of practice that I discuss in this chapter apply for Reiki volunteer work; you just don't have to concern yourself with receiving money from individuals.

Making a Business out of Reiki

I know that reading the words "Reiki" and "business" in the same sentence will upset some people. Some folks aren't happy that anyone charges for a healing therapy such as Reiki. In this world, however, healers of all types charge for their services, whether they're massage therapists, doctors, or chiropractors. It makes sense that someone who practices Reiki also needs to make a living.

To make a business out of Reiki, you have the following options:

- ✔ You can add Reiki to your existing therapeutic practice (see Chapter 16). This works if you're already a professional such as a social worker, nurse, or physical therapist and want to include Reiki as part of the services you offer.

- ✔ You can work as an employee providing Reiki at a healthcare or healing center.

- ✔ You can start a small business providing Reiki on either a part-time or full-time basis.

Because most people are in the third category — wanting to provide Reiki as a self-employed practitioner — that will be the focus of this chapter.

When you are self-employed, it's up to you to pay taxes and report any earnings to the tax office in your state or country. Employ an accountant to help you with financial issues such as taxes. Consulting your local tax office can provide very useful information on setting up a small business, bookkeeping, deductions, self-employment, and other tax issues.

Maintaining High Standards

It's essential to keep your intentions clear: to be a pure channel for Reiki energy and maintain the highest level of integrity and healthy boundaries (see Chapter 13). When Reiki practitioners hold to high standards of practice, more people are likely to consider Reiki as a potential treatment.

Some Reiki practitioners have an overwhelming desire to heal others. Other people like to use Reiki but don't feel comfortable calling themselves a healer. Between these extremes is a healthy balance of knowing your limitations but also knowing your skills as a healer.

The role models of healers in our society range from religious figures to your family doctor. Mikao Usui is a role model for Reiki practitioners, and he modeled humility, flexibility, and personal growth.

The road to becoming a healer is longer than a three-day Master Reiki class.

From my own experience as both a Reiki practitioner and Reiki recipient and thereby observing many Reiki practitioners in action, I suggest the following:

✔ **Get training and more training.** You'll feel more confident as a practitioner when you know you have the knowledge and skills you need. But don't use this to feed your insecurity, as in always feeling you are never enough. You are enough, and you deserve to allow yourself the skills to be the best you can be.

✔ **Use a mentor or other professional feedback.** Seek support from your Reiki teacher or other professional healers. Most healing professions have supervision for new healers to address issues that inevitably arise.

✔ **Join professional organizations.** These groups offer a way to stay in touch with other Reiki healers and find out about new issues that can affect you.

✔ **Follow the laws in your state.** You should not only keep informed but also stay on the right side of the law. In some cases, this means changing the way you practice so that you follow the law of the land. See the section "Knowing the legal issues of practicing Reiki," later in this chapter.

✔ **Practice from the highest level of integrity.** Know your place as a healer. See Chapter 13 for the details about ethics and boundaries.

✔ **Ask for feedback.** When you teach or give a Reiki session, you can ask the students or recipients for feedback, either verbally or in the form of a questionnaire.

✔ **Continue your own healing.** First and foremost, you must heal yourself. This task is ongoing and gives you the experience and compassion to help others. See Chapter 19 to read about personal growth and Reiki.

✔ **Plan your classes or sessions.** Think through the syllabus for your class or content of your Reiki session. Incorporate any changes that arise from feedback from your mentor or students.

✔ **Respect money.** Professionals charge their clients for their time and services. You have spent time and energy to gain the abilities to use Reiki. Charge enough for your services so that you're compensated enough not only to survive but also to live fruitfully.

Most of you have other roles in addition to your role as a Reiki practitioners. For example, I am a Reiki practitioner and also a writer. You might be a nurse, doctor, massage therapist, artist, insurance salesman, mother, or teacher. Your own life experience comes in handy because the people you see for Reiki sessions or classes are also incorporating Reiki into their lives. You can show them how to use Reiki in their lives by your example.

Remembering that you are a facilitator of healing

People come to Reiki because they are ready to raise their energy, solve their own problems, and remove blocks — they're ready to heal. They come to you as a facilitator to help them make the connection to the Reiki energy. In this sense, you are like the tubing through which Reiki energy flows.

Keep the Reiki Principles (see Chapter 4) foremost in your mind when practicing Reiki, and consider this principle: Just for today, I will be humble.

Knowing your place as a Reiki professional

In addition to the boundaries I discuss in Chapter 13, remember the following:

- ✔ Distinguish your professional and personal relationships. If you make friends with your clients and your friends become your clients, the relationships can get muddled very quickly. Are you going to be able to continue to get paid and maintain a professional atmosphere around someone who has become your friend? When you have clients who are also friends, you must work even harder to maintain professional boundaries (See Chapter 13). Otherwise, if things get messy, you could lose your client or, even worse, your friend.

- ✔ Don't practice medicine or massage unless you are licensed to do so. Don't give advice about what people should eat or what herbs to take. You can advise them to consult a nutritionist or doctor or acupuncturist. Beyond that, you are there only to practice Reiki.

Planning Your Reiki Business

As a professional Reiki practitioner, you need to establish a place to do Reiki and set prices for your work, among other things. These things are all part of your business plan. The more effort you put into a business plan, the more you'll get out of it. Here are some suggestions to consider in your business plan:

- ✔ **Set your goals for your Reiki business.** What do you want to achieve? Do you have a financial goal? Do you want to serve a certain number of recipients? Teach a certain number of courses? Be as specific as possible. You can also set up one-year, three-year, and five-year plans.

- ✔ **Make a list of supplies needed.** Supplies include everything from a massage table to tissues and paper towels to a water cooler.

- ✔ **Plan a marketing strategy.** How are you planning to attract clients or students?

  - Think of the people you're trying to attract. Where do they live? How old are they?

  - Consider planning a word-of-mouth campaign through telephone or e-mails.

  - Promote yourself by introducing yourself at local businesses, such as health food stores, massage salons, spas, and chiropractors' offices.

  - Develop a Web site.

  - Write a print or e-mail newsletter.

  - Speak at local establishments.

  - Sponsor an open house or other promotional event to attract clients or students.

- ✔ **Plan for advertising.** Decide whether you'll advertise in newspapers, magazines, or newsletters or on the radio or the Internet.

- ✔ **Create promotional material.** Either do it yourself or hire a professional artist or printing company to produce flyers, brochures, and business cards.

- ✔ **Decide how you'll process and manage money**. You need to set up a business checking account, bookkeeping strategies, and credit card accounts (to receive payment).

This list may seem long, but planning a business is a big job. Take it step by step and note how other complementary and alternative therapists are succeeding (or not) in your area. Learn from other people's mistakes.

Getting business assistance

When starting your new business, plan ahead as much as possible. Consult a professional accountant or small business analyst for advice.

Also, you must know what money you have to invest in your business and what type of income you need to make. By setting your financial goals, you will have an idea of your target.

If you're one of those people who hates to talk or think about money, it's time to get over that attitude if you want to make a go of your business of helping people heal through Reiki.

Knowing the legal issues of practicing Reiki

Reiki is a relatively new treatment, and the legal and political worlds have not yet decided how to deal with it. Here are the two most important issues to consider:

- ✓ **Liability insurance:** It makes good business sense to have some sort of insurance. Your local Reiki organization should be able to inform you of options in your area.
- ✓ **What you are legally able to do:** In some locations, it's illegal to practice any type of bodywork (including Reiki) unless you have a massage license. Consult your local Reiki association, state health department, or a lawyer for advice.

Pricing your services fairly

As you set up shop, you need to come up with the prices for your services. You may decide on a sliding scale fee or other special rates that you want to offer.

Check out the usual rates for Reiki sessions and classes in your area and also find out the cost for a local massage. Generally, the price of a Reiki sessions and a massage are similar, though Reiki is sometimes priced a little lower.

You need to be able to cover all your costs and also provide yourself with adequate compensation for your time and efforts.

Finding the perfect healing space

You don't need much for Reiki, but you do need to provide a space for healing to occur. Location is critical because you want to be easily accessible to the people who will come for Reiki. Sometimes the location that will reach the most people is in the middle of a city! Read more about space for Reiki sessions in Chapter 13.

Depending on how often you teach Reiki, you can rent a space to use occasionally or use your home or a public space, such as a room you can rent at your local library or community center. Also consider spaces where yoga classes are taught. The size of the room depends on how many students you have in your class.

Using your home as your Reiki space has pros and cons. Here are the pros:

✔ Convenience

✔ Less expensive than other options

✔ Use as a tax deduction (speak to an accountant about this)

✔ Control over noise and other disturbances

Considering the Reiki table

Most Reiki tables are simply massage tables adapted to use for Reiki. First consider the following features of a Reiki table.

✔ **Weight of the table:** Will you be leaving your table in one spot or carrying it around from place to place? Consider a lighter weight table if you'll be frequently moving it around. Each extra pound of table can make a difference to your arms and shoulders!

✔ **Faceplate:** When the Reiki recipient is lying on her stomach, you may want to use a faceplate, which is an appendage to the table that holds the face. Although massage therapists need to have the face properly supported during the pressure of massage, a faceplate is optional during Reiki, and not all Reiki practitioners use the faceplate.

✔ **Table legs:** Because the Reiki practitioner may sit while performing Reiki at the head and foot of the Reiki recipient, it's useful to have a table with legroom. Some massage tables come with legroom, or the company

may offer a special end plate to adapt the table for Reiki use.

Here are some tips for finding a Reiki table of your own:

✔ If you see a table you like at a Reiki share (see Chapter 14), ask the practitioner for the name of the brand.

✔ Check out your local massage supply shop.

✔ Ask your Reiki Master or other Reiki friends.

✔ Check out the classified ads in newspapers.

✔ You can find tables through many of the Reiki resources listed in the Appendix and by doing a search for "Reiki table" on the Web.

✔ Popular brands of tables include Earthlite, Stronglight, and Astra Lite.

Then you have the fun part of picking out the color or getting a nice cover for your table! Consider what will enhance your client's experience.

Considering your Reiki classes from start to finish

If you want to teach Reiki as part of your practice, think about how you will present your classes. Also consider the following:

✔ Which classes will you teach?

✔ What are the prerequisites?

✔ Where will you teach?

✔ How long is each class?

✔ What is the cost?

See Chapter 7 for ideas on how to plan your Reiki classes. Here are other things you should consider doing:

✔ **Creating Reiki class outlines:** Create a course syllabus that includes how each day of class will proceed, including topics to be covered, attunements, and lunch breaks.

✔ **Producing Reiki course materials:** You can use this book or another source as your class materials, or you can produce your own materials. Remember that you can't just photocopy information from different books and pass it to your students. Doing so can be considered copyright infringement! You're better off choosing certain books for your students to purchase and supplementing as necessary with material that you prepare yourself.

✔ **Designing certificates:** Follow your Reiki Master Teacher's suggestions for producing certificates. You may have a seal and may need to purchase certificates and use a fine pen or your computer to individualize each certificate.

Your Reiki teacher should teach you how to prepare a Reiki class. But like developing your own style when giving Reiki (see Chapter 13), you'll also develop your own style when teaching Reiki.

Using your home as your Reiki space also has its downside:

✔ Possible disruption to your family

✔ Loss of privacy

✔ Concerns about security

✔ Loss of space in your home for personal use

Sometimes Reiki space within a home also may appear less professional when family knickknacks are on display or the telephone is ringing for your children.

Getting the right equipment

You don't need much equipment for Reiki, but you do need the following items:

- **Reiki table:** This item is the same as a massage table except that a Reiki table has room to put your legs under the front and back of the table when sitting at a chair.

- **Chairs:** You need a chair to sit on when giving Reiki, and if you have room, you may want to provide a chair for the recipient to rest in after the session.

- **Bolsters and pillows:** You put these items under the recipient's head and/or knees during a session.

- **Music system:** Your sound system can be simple or more elaborate but all you need is a low volume during a session or class.

If you want, you can add extras like plants, rugs, and wall hangings to personalize the space.

Being Part of the Reiki Community

The advantages of joining your local Reiki circle are many (see Chapter 14 for a discussion of Reiki circles, shares, and retreats). As a professional Reiki practitioner, you can

- Network with other Reiki practitioners.
- Find new clients or mentors.
- Share your information with others.
- Work with others in your community to raise awareness of Reiki healing.

Dealing with the competition

If you're feeling competitive about or fearful of other Reiki practitioners, that is a sign that you need to get a better business plan or do some Reiki on yourself to deal with fears of abundance.

Here are some affirmations to work with:

"There is enough for everyone. There is enough to go around."

"I am guided to develop my Reiki practice by spirit and the power of Reiki."

What you put out into the world is what will come back to you!

Staying up-to-date in the world of Reiki

Even though Mikao Usui developed Reiki in the 1920s, the world of Reiki is still changing. For example, the history of Reiki taught to most Reiki masters before 2000 or so probably taught more myth than fact. If you haven't read a more recent book on Reiki (like this one) or kept in touch with Reiki associations, you might have missed the fact that research in Japan has come up with more accurate information on Reiki history (see Chapter 3 for details about Reiki history and Chapter 20 for info about Reiki myths). Here are some reasons to stay current:

✔ If you don't keep up with the world of Reiki, you may teach your students incorrect information.

✔ If you don't keep up with legal issues about Reiki in your state, you may miss important information that could directly affect you.

✔ If you don't keep up with health issues related to Reiki, you may not find out when Reiki is covered by health insurance (keep your fingers crossed) or when your local hospital is looking for Reiki practitioners.

Keep current about Reiki by reading Reiki books, magazines, and newsletters and being part of a Reiki organization. See the Appendix for information on these resources.

Part V
The Part of Tens

The 5th Wave   By Rich Tennant

" Oh relax! Some of your cat's energy channels
are blocked, but I'm using this to clear the
toilet behind you. "

In this part . . .

Using Reiki in your life can be fun, genuinely helpful, and mind-expanding. The Part of Tens gives you some extra information you can use to take Reiki to the next level — whatever that means for you.

In this part, you can find out how to use Reiki in your everyday life, from energizing your food to protecting your car, and how to use Reiki to expand your personal growth. You also get a chapter on facts that shatter some of the myths surrounding Reiki. Finally, I include some extra non-traditional Reiki symbols for you to check out.

Chapter 18

Ten Uses for Reiki in Everyday Situations

After you study Reiki I or Reiki II (see Chapter 7), you can begin to use Reiki in all sorts of situations. Here's where the word *imagination* comes into play. Apply the Reiki energy to energize or protect anything from your bicycle to your flowers to the food you eat. Or you may want to remove stagnant energy and use Reiki to clear the air. This chapter describes ten different ways to use Reiki in and around your home.

Reiki can do no harm, so you might as well give it a try! In any situation where you can use prayer, you can use Reiki. In any situation you can think of, you can use Reiki.

Helping Plants Reach Their Potential

Plants come in all forms — from ground huggers like moss and grass to colorful flower and vegetable plants to great big trees! Just like people and animals, plants are live beings that can benefit from the Reiki energy.

Reiki can help plants grow, flower, and fruit. Now you may be someone who talks or sings to plants, or you may not. But you'll find that Reiki will help your plants, indoor or outdoor, grow and grow and grow. Here are some tips for using Reiki:

- ✔ Use Reiki on seeds before planting.
- ✔ Send Reiki to plants before pruning or cutting flowers. (I use this method to "connect" with the plant and find out the best spot to cut it.)
- ✔ Use Reiki on any plant that is ailing.
- ✔ Use Reiki on the water before watering plants.

I've heard a rumor that if you give Reiki to plants that have insects, the Reiki will help not only the plant but also the bugs. Supposedly the insects grow in numbers! This myth illustrates the importance of intention when sending Reiki. Set your intention to help the plants, and that's what will happen. As the plant becomes healthier, it's more likely to resist insect attack.

Boosting Your Food's Fortitude

Food nourishes the physical body. Many Reiki practitioners make it a habit to send Reiki to their food just before they eat. Put your hands around the plate of food and send it the Power symbol (see Chapter 8). Leave your hands there while you feel the energy entering and boosting the energy of your food. You'll know when to start eating! Here is what Reiki can do:

- ✔ Bring out the most of the vitamins, minerals, and other nutrients in the food.
- ✔ Reduce any harmful qualities of the food, such as pesticides.

As I mention throughout the book, always remember the three i's of Reiki: intention, intuition, and integrity. *Intend* for your food's energy to be increased, use your *intuition* to know how and when to use Reiki and what to eat and when to stop eating, and have *integrity* with how you use Reiki and food. When using Reiki with food, *integrity* means that you use the best food you can afford, find, and prepare and then send Reiki to it. You can use Reiki on a plate of junk food, but it won't be as healthy as more nutritious fare.

Use Reiki while you prepare food for others. Preparing food with the love of Reiki is a beautiful gift for yourself and others. You can Reiki your family's meals or even your pet's food bowls!

Shoring Up Your Water

Just as you use Reiki to energize and purify the food you eat, you can use Reiki on the water you drink. Charge the water with Reiki when you do the following:

✔ Take a bath

✔ Water your plants

✔ Drink your eight cups of water a day

✔ Boil water for tea

✔ Give water to your pets

The earth's water is constantly recycled. We drink water and get water from our foods, and then we excrete water in perspiration, urine, and feces. Our wastewater enters the water cycle and can become part of water that is evaporated into clouds, becoming rain or snow that feed streams and lakes and oceans. Sending Reiki to water is to connect to this stream of life's necessary elixir.

If you want to send Reiki to the earth, sending it to the earth's oceans, rivers, and lakes, you can help both the physical planet and the people who come into contact with the water.

Making the Most of Your Medicine

If you take any sort of daily pill, whether it's a prescribed medication or pain reliever, consider charging it with Reiki beforehand. I had the experience of taking a necessary prescription medication and then going for a session with a Reiki Master. She knew intuitively that I was taking a medication and suggested that I Reiki the pill before swallowing it.

The advantage of using Reiki on prescription or over-the-counter medications is that you intend to do the following:

✔ Reduce or eliminate dangerous side effects

✔ Maximize the healing benefits of the drug

You can also use Reiki on any vitamins, minerals, or herbal supplements you take. Reiki will boost the healing properties of these nutrients and potions in the same way it boosts the energy in food itself (see the section "Boosting Your Food's Fortitude," earlier in this chapter).

Calming Computer Problems

Reiki works on electronic appliances, including computers. Because I work on a computer (as I type these words, in fact), I have more experience with this type of appliance than most others! Do you ever find that your computer freezes up and just stops working? Or have you experienced lost documents or other computer problems? Try sending Reiki to your computer when it acts up. Better yet, send Reiki to it regularly to prevent a problem from occurring.

If you have Reiki I training, just put your hands on an object, intend for the Reiki energy to flow, and let it happen! If you have Reiki II training, you can consciously use the Reiki symbols (see Chapter 8) or send Reiki at a distance (see Chapter 15).

Although Reiki can help your computer and work life run smoothly, remember that Reiki isn't a substitute for good computer practices. You need to save your documents frequently and use a good antivirus software to protect your computer from viruses, spyware, and other malicious programs. Just as Reiki works with medicine to bring about a cure or healing, Reiki will help you on the job to promote the best possible outcome.

Use Reiki on other objects at your workplace. You can use Reiki on your desk, your mail, your van, your e-mail, your tools, the telephone, your tests, pencils, your stethoscope, your inventory, and even your cash register.

To cleanse inanimate objects, try Jakikiri Joka Ho (see Chapter 12), though personally, I wouldn't use this on a computer unless I had assured backups. But it works for crystals, clothing, and other objects from which you want to remove any negative energy.

Managing Money with Reiki

Here's something that everyone seems to want more of. I'm talking about money in your wallet, bank account, or piggy bank.

You may have the misconception that money is evil. Some people in spiritual circles think that money is bad. Money itself isn't good or bad; what humans do with it or think about it is what brings about problems. Start thinking more positively about money: how you earned it, what you're doing with it, and how other people are connected with it. That bill in your wallet may have touched the hands of hundreds if not thousands of people!

Use the three i's when it comes to money: *Intend* to increase your prosperity, use your *intuition* to learn ways to create more abundance in your life or savings, and use *integrity* in the way you earn your living.

One of the Reiki Principles (see Chapter 4) states, be honest in your work. To have integrity means you're earning your living honestly, and there is no shame in leading a spiritual life that is rich with abundance. (See Chapter 20 for some info about Reiki and money.)

Send Reiki to your money. Your returns will be worthwhile.

Bolstering Up Your Automobile

Cars and drivers need protection. Whether you're driving alone at night, going on vacation with your family, or sending your child to drive alone for the first time, you can use Reiki to add protection. Here are some tips for using Reiki for cars and road trips:

✔ Whether you are a driver or passenger, you can put a Power symbol (see Chapter 8) in the car before starting the trip. Set an intention for a safe journey.

✔ Send Reiki while you're on the road. Send Reiki to any traffic you encounter and definitely send Reiki to any roadside accident. You can also send Reiki to the homes and people you pass by.

You can use these tips not only when traveling by car but also when you travel by boat, train, bus, or airplane.

If you want to protect your loved ones when they're traveling without you, use long-distance Reiki techniques (see Chapter 15).

Cleaning and Clearing Out Clutter

You may sense negative energy as "bad vibes," which you may feel in a room where someone has been sick with the flu or a bedroom from a broken marriage. Perhaps you have moved into an apartment and feel some negative energy from the previous occupants. Whatever the case, use these steps to cleanse your living area or workspace:

1. **Clear out clutter and throw away garbage.**

   I don't need to tell you that waste has negative energy that needs to be removed. Clutter gives a clogging effect, so do what you can to eliminate or manage it.

2. **Remove the grime.**

   Reiki can't take the place of elbow grease! If your home needs to be cleaned, then start scrubbing.

3. **Open the windows and let in the sunlight.**

   Fresh air and bright light have a way of energizing and refreshing a space or item that needs cleansing.

4. **Send Reiki into the middle of the room, the four walls, the ceiling, and the floor.**

   Use the Power symbol (see Chapter 8) and any others you feel drawn to. You can use the same techniques you would use to prepare a room for a Reiki session (see Chapter 13).

Some people send Reiki into every corner of the room. Use your ability to sense energy or imagine energy and send Reiki repeatedly until the room feels cleaner.

You can use Reiki along with other energy-clearing techniques such as sound (drums or clapping, for example) or smoke from sacred herbs (such as sage). You may have a special crystal to use to bring in positive energy as well (see Chapter 12). Keep in mind the three i's of Reiki: Set your *intention* to clear the energy; use your *intuition* to sense when the energy has been cleared; come from a place of *integrity* in your use of the room.

Another way to change the energy in a room is to use Feng Shui (check out *Feng Shui For Dummies,* by David Daniel Kennedy, published by Wiley).

Protecting Loved Ones

You can send Reiki to people in special situations. For example, use the distant Reiki technique (see Chapter 15) to send Reiki to your child on his first day of school or college or to a parent undergoing a medical test or operation. If your friend is moving, you can send Reiki to help her.

If you have children, you may want to trace or imagine a Power symbol (see Chapter 8) surrounding them as they leave for school. You can also do this to a spouse who leaves for work or pets who go outside.

Sending Reiki or giving Reiki to a loved one is a beautiful way to say "I ask the universe to give you the best in this situation." The outcome is then out of your hands, and it's time to practice the Reiki Principle "do not worry" (see Chapter 4 for info about the Reiki Principles).

Shielding Your Home

When you leave your home for work or vacation, you can send it the energy from the Power symbol (see Chapter 8) or any other Reiki symbol you feel drawn to use. However, keep in mind that using Reiki doesn't remove from you the responsibility of locking all your doors and windows, blowing out all your candles, turning off all appliances, and taking any other sensible precautions.

When I send Reiki as I leave home, it's as if I'm telling the house and any beings inside it that I love them and will be back soon! I feel that I can rest assured that Reiki will protect the home from danger.

Of course, you can use Reiki for protection when you're home also. If you find yourself in a dangerous situation when you're in the house, by all means send Reiki immediately while also taking the steps to remedy the situation (such as getting a fire extinguisher or calling 911).

Chapter 19

Ten Uses for Reiki as a Tool for Personal Growth

In This Chapter

▶ Using meditation and journaling

▶ Relying on the Reiki Principles, affirmations, and intuition

▶ Making your intentions known

▶ Approaching life with integrity

M ikao Usui first designed Reiki to be used for spiritual growth, by using the tools of meditation, becoming attuned to energy, and practicing the Reiki Principles. Western Reiki has added to the Reiki toolbox with an emphasis on self-Reiki, journaling, and setting intentions and affirmations.

In this chapter, I list ten different ways to use Reiki for your personal growth.

Personal growth is a lifelong process. I personally experience spiritual growth as an endless cycle of

✔ **Receiving inspiration:** I get new thoughts and ideas when out in nature, meditating, performing self-Reiki, journaling, or talking with someone else. Or I may get the idea from a book or lecture.

✔ **Knowing my truth with intuition:** By this, I mean becoming aware and conscious of what is the right action to take. While reading a book, I may get a moment of clarity about some issue in my life.

✔ **Acting upon inspiration and intuition:** I make it my intention to change. I take action to change something in my lifestyle.

✔ **Coming up against blocks within myself or others:** These blocks can appear as the proverbial brick wall, a stubborn habit, or perhaps as an illness. Sometimes it is another person who is blocking me; in that case, I can use this person's actions as a mirror to see what is inside of me.

✔ **Working though blocks:** I use Reiki and meditation to work through unresolved issues and blocks and continue receiving inspiration to keep on the spiritual journey.

You're never alone in this process of growth as spiritual guidance comes in the guise of teachers, therapists, and other helpers. Don't forget that many other spiritual seekers also journey on this path!

Receiving Healing with Reiki

Making the time and effort to receive Reiki is half the battle! Whether you are new to Reiki or have been practicing Reiki for decades, let yourself experience the beautiful healing power of a Reiki session. To decide where to go to receive Reiki, check out Chapter 5. Or make the time for a self-Reiki session, if you've already studied Reiki. Relaxation comes as deep sighs of relief or shifting of the body as the Reiki energy dissolves blocks within our bodies and beyond (see Chapter 2 for a description of the levels of energy in the body).

I personally experience Reiki as kind of an enhanced meditation, where for the duration of the session, I won't be bothered by telephones ringing or other requests for my attention. During this special time, I can relax into the table and let go completely. I have experienced healing on the table in the form of memories coming up and spontaneously resolving. For example, I have remembered that someone "did me wrong" and then was spontaneously able to forgive the person. Don't worry if tears flow or you have a coughing fit. These reactions are part of the release of internal energy blocks.

As a practitioner, I notice that people come off the Reiki table with a fresh look in their eyes, and sometimes they look many years younger!

At the very least, a Reiki session will lift some of your stress, and you'll often receive inspirational messages that tell you just what you need to hear!

Going Inward with Meditation

Meditation and Reiki go hand in hand. You use meditation in Reiki classes and before Reiki sessions. You may meditate on your own or with a group of people at a Reiki share (see Chapter 14). Meditation aids in personal growth by allowing you to do the following:

- **Quiet your mind:** Meditation gives relief from the endless cycle of thought after thought after thought.
- **Relax:** Relief from endless thinking brings a peaceful feeling. You can drift into a more blissful state of serenity.

✔ **Become conscious:** When the mind is quiet, it's easier to focus on the present moment — the now.

✔ **Feel your energy flow:** During meditation, you're more likely to sense the energy within and around your body.

✔ **Connect with spirit:** Getting quiet allows you to sense the spiritual energy within and around you.

Meditation provides a sacred space to become your true self. Read more about Reiki meditation in Chapter 9.

Honoring the Reiki Principles

Mikao Usui originally intended that the Reiki Principles (which I discuss in Chapter 4) be recited daily as part of a program of spiritual growth. You might see the principles as a gentle reminder toward right living. The beginning phrase, "just for today," points out the importance of focusing on the present moment:

> Just for today,
> Don't get angry
> Don't worry
> Be grateful
> Be honest in your work
> Be kind to yourself and others.

You can't go wrong studying these profound principles that have as much meaning today as when they were first written in the early 1900s in Japan.

Getting Attuned to Reiki

Attunement in Reiki terms means initiation, and a Reiki teacher is the one who carries out an attunement (see Chapter 7). An essential feature of any Reiki class is receiving the attunement, which distinguishes Reiki from other forms of energy work. The Reiki Master prepares the way for attunements by creating a sacred space and taking you through a meditation. The attunement itself takes just minutes.

One difference between the different Reiki levels is that you receive different symbols during the attunement process. With each advancement in Reiki level (1st degree, 2nd degree, and masters), you are attuned to a higher level of energy.

The Reiki symbols are representations of the Reiki energy that is transmitted to you during the attunement process. In other words, you receive the energy of the different symbols (see Chapter 8 for information about Reiki symbols).

Receiving a Reiki attunement opens the path so your personal energy can vibrate at a higher level. The differences in how you feel before and after an attunement may be either subtle or obvious, but you can bet they'll be life changing.

Keeping a Journal

Writing is a wonderful way to gather your thoughts. You may already have a journal or other place to keep a record of your spiritual journey. Many folks record their dreams, inspirations, and personal goals.

Some Reiki teachers ask all of their students to keep a journal during and after the attunement process. Here are some of the things you can keep in a Reiki journal:

- ✔ Class notes while studying Reiki
- ✔ Inspirational messages received during meditation or attunements
- ✔ Feelings, sensations, or ideas that come up while receiving a Reiki session
- ✔ Experiences of your own and your client while giving a Reiki session
- ✔ Free writing or journaling (while writing whatever comes to your head, you may find answers to long-standing problems)

Don't edit. Don't judge yourself. A journal is a learning tool to be cherished, not a place for criticism.

Empowering Your Affirmations with Reiki

Thoughts create reality. It's that simple. If you don't believe me, just carefully observe your thoughts and see how they affect what happens in your life.

An *affirmation* is a type of positive thought that is a confirmation or declaration.

A positive thought leads you to follow your dreams. A negative thought leads to low self-esteem, anxiety, depression, or anger. It's pretty much a no-brainer to decide which type of thought leads to a life of serenity and happiness!

One of the best ways to counteract negative thinking is to give a boost to positive thoughts, or empower your affirmations. This follows the idea that when there is darkness, don't try to fight it; just turn on the light!

To find your own personal affirmations, use your journals, meditation, or friends to come up with ideas.

Affirmations can be the opposite of the negative thoughts that run through and create havoc in your life. Here are some examples:

> I am worthy.
>
> I am worthy of health.
>
> I am worthy of love.

Affirmations can also be expressions of your dreams and desires:

> The world is full of peace and love.
>
> I cherish my new home.
>
> I am connected to God.

Using affirmations is fun and effective. Take these steps to empower your affirmations:

1. **Choose an affirmation.**

   You might want to write down a few and choose the one that's most significant right now.

2. **Write down the affirmation.**

   Perhaps use a special card, piece of paper, or colored ink.

3. **Say the affirmation daily out loud.**

   Repeating the affirmation gives it more power.

4. **For a week or longer, give Reiki to the piece of paper on which you've written the affirmation.**

   If you haven't yet studied Reiki, just imagine white light going to the affirmation.

To add more energy to your affirmation, try the following:

✔ Use the Reiki symbols to add extra energy to your affirmation.

✔ Visualize the affirmation in your mind. Envision yourself feeling or being the affirmation.

✔ Share your affirmation or goal with another Reiki practitioner. You can send Reiki to each other's affirmation!

✔ Take the paper on which you've written your affirmation and embellish it with pictures, stickers or glitter.

You can manifest your dreams, goals, and intentions by using the same methods as outlined for affirmations. Write down the goal, such as "I am a successful Reiki practitioner," and send it Reiki. Empowering your affirmations is related to two other Reiki practices: manifesting with Reiki (see Chapter 1) and Reiki mental technique (see Chapter 16).

Check out the section "Setting Your Intentions," later in the chapter, to read more about the power of being conscious of your goals and motives.

Giving Reiki to Others

Charity and goodwill are the cornerstones of most religious and spiritual practices. The act of helping others is essential to maintain good spirits. The ways to help others with Reiki are many:

✔ Give a Reiki session to your relative or friend.

✔ Join a Reiki share (see Chapter 14) and give Reiki to people in the community.

✔ Send distant Reiki to friends and family who request Reiki (see Chapter 15).

✔ Send distant Reiki to situations like countries at war or to people in hospitals or politicians.

Don't forget that you can also share Reiki with your pets and send distant Reiki to animals in zoos or oceans.

Because the Reiki energy is going through you as you send it out, you also get a benefit when you give Reiki!

Setting Your Intentions

Your *intention,* which is a goal or a plan, is considered to be crucial in Reiki. Set your goal before receiving or giving a Reiki session. The Reiki energy respects your intention (see Chapter 9 for a discussion of prayer and intention in Reiki). You'll really see results when you start setting intentions in other areas of your life. Here are some examples:

- ✔ When you wake up, you can intend to have a great day!
- ✔ Before phoning someone, you can intend for the conversation to go smoothly.
- ✔ Before stepping to the podium, intend to give a great speech.

Setting an intention is saying the following things to the universe:

- ✔ You're available for a great day.
- ✔ You're ready for a great conversation with your mother.
- ✔ You're prepared to speak words of wisdom.

The universe can then step up to the plate to make your goals come true.

Set your intentions for a day filled with abundance, love, prosperity, and health. See the section "Empowering Your Affirmations with Reiki," earlier in this chapter, to really give a boost to your positive thoughts.

Letting Your Intuition Blossom

Call it a gut feeling or a sixth sense, but most people experience *intuition* as knowing something at a deep subconscious level. Intuition means that you just know something, even if you don't have the evidence for it. Most people have had the experience of calling someone who says, "How funny that you called. I was just thinking of you!" Or perhaps you've experienced knowing who was calling before you even picked up the phone!

Intuitive information seems to come out of the blue! Many famous discoveries have been made while someone was in the shower or taking a walk! While the brain is resting from its usual thinking process, inspiration or intuition has a better chance to come through.

Just having inspirational or intuitive ideas isn't enough. For these ideas to have any value in your life, you must put them into effect. Sometimes following inspiration or intuition is more difficult than it seems. A message that says "quit your job" or "leave this relationship" isn't so easy to carry out! The best thing to do is to follow up on your message by meditating regularly and perhaps seeking spiritual guidance.

You may find that your intuition increases after you start using Reiki. Intuition in a Reiki session tells you where to place your hands and when a session is complete. Intuition in life can guide you in so many ways — if only you're ready to listen.

Living with Integrity

Integrity means honesty and uprightness. Feeling good in your own skin is much easier if you're not carrying guilt about your behavior.

- ✔ When you live with integrity, you feel clean and wholesome.
- ✔ When you act with integrity, you have nothing to hide.

Integrity helps to keep your Reiki practice clean. You'll feel good to know you're doing your best job, practicing honestly, using the highest level of ethics, and respecting yourselves and others.

Applying the concept of integrity to your life as a whole is a tall order, but it's also beautifully cleansing! For some ideas on how to use integrity with Reiki, see Chapter 13 and also the appendix, which lists the Code of Ethics of the International Association of Reiki Professionals.

Chapter 20

Ten Common Myths about Reiki

In This Chapter

▶ Revealing the truth about Mikao Usui

▶ Setting the facts straight about Reiki results and payment

▶ Clarifying the role of Reiki in healing and curing disease

Different people have taken Reiki, a universal energy available to anyone, and described it in their own unique way.

Some Reiki myths are stories about Reiki's history that have been found to be untrue. Hawayo Takata, who courageously brought Reiki to the West, told convincing stories about the origins of Reiki that are now known to be false. Most likely, she invented these tall tales based on a good intention: to help Reiki spread in a Christian world that had anti-Japanese sentiment (during the World War II era). As more Reiki researchers uncover the truth of Mikao Usui and the origins of Reiki in Japan, the true history of Reiki is unfolding.

But if you studied Reiki more than a couple of years ago, you may have heard some moving but ultimately false stories about Mikao Usui. Make sure to update yourself on the more accurate history of Reiki that is now available (see Chapter 3).

Other Reiki falsehoods that are still confusing within the Reiki community include concern over who can benefit from Reiki, which Reiki branch is the best, the relationship of Reiki and money, and the relationship of Reiki and medicine. In this chapter, I expose common Reiki myths and set out to debunk them one by one.

Mikao Usui Was a Christian Minister

Truth: Mikao Usui was a Buddhist, not a Christian.

This tall tale from Hawayo Takata included the information that Usui was a Christian minister who had studied in a Western university. Versions of this myth tell how often Usui preached or even said that Usui was trying to discover the healing powers of Jesus.

Mikao Usui was a lay Buddhist priest (lay priests could remain at home with their families), but Usui is well known to have read Christian texts alongside his Buddhist texts.

The religions of Buddhism and Shintoism coexist in Japan, and Usui probably incorporated both of these in his personal spiritual beliefs and Reiki teachings. This doesn't make Reiki a religion (see the section "Reiki Is a Religion," later in the chapter).

Dr. Mikao Usui Studied at the University of Chicago

Truth: Mikao Usui was a learned man, but he didn't study formally at any university.

Part of the Takata myth was that Usui had studied at the University of Chicago in the United States and Doshisha University in Kyoto, Japan. We now know this to be untrue, though Mikao Usui was a learned man through his personal studies.

Though Hawayo Takata called him Dr. Usui, Mikao Usui was not a physician. Takata may have used the "Dr." as a Western interpretation for "Sensai," as he was called in Japan. Sensai is a title of respect given by a student to a teacher.

You Must Believe in Reiki to Benefit from It

Truth: Reiki can help whether you believe in it or not.

Even if you don't understand how Reiki works or have some skepticism, you may be surprised to find that Reiki works wonders to bring about relaxation and calm.

The only time that someone will not benefit from Reiki is when the person doesn't want it, whether at a conscious or subconscious level. This situation does occasionally occur. If someone doesn't want Reiki, you can't force the person to take it at that time. The person may decide he wants Reiki at a later time.

Note the difference between these two situations:

- **Not believing in Reiki:** You may be skeptical about Reiki and don't believe it really works, but you're open to giving it a try.
- **Not wanting Reiki:** You actually resist the energy of Reiki and are not interested in experiencing it.

This myth was addressed in the first-ever Reiki manual written by Mikao Usui. Nevertheless, many Reiki practitioners say that you must believe in Reiki for it to work. You're probably more open to the miracles of Reiki when you believe in it. You're also more likely to come back for a second session or attribute any improvement in your condition to the Reiki healing.

Many people say "I don't believe," because they can't see Reiki with their own eyes. But most *want* to believe and will give Reiki a chance — just in case it does work!

You Must Pay for Reiki for It to Benefit You

Truth: Reiki can benefit you whether you pay for it or not.

Western Reiki has had some controversy over this matter. One of the stories told by Hawayo Takata (see Chapter 3) was that Mikao Usui came down from the mountain and came upon a beggar. Usui gave Reiki to the beggar, but because the beggar didn't pay for Reiki, he didn't benefit.

Because we now know that the beggar story is untrue, the purpose of the paying-for-Reiki story has become confused. This tall tale from Takata may have served the purpose of telling people to always have an "energy exchange" for their work. The concept is that unless you pay for something, it doesn't have value.

Hawayo Takata charged 10,000 American dollars for a Reiki mastership, presumably as a way to give great value to the Reiki teachings. This practice of charging $10,000 to study for a Reiki Master continued with Takata's students. Most Reiki teachers today do not charge such a high fee. As more Reiki Masters have lowered their fees, more people are studying Reiki, and it continues to spread and help more people.

A balance must be reached in the subject of money and Reiki. Seeing money as an exchange of value, the recipients of Reiki or Reiki student must pay what they feel is a fair amount for what you have received. And likewise, the Reiki practitioner must also feel that he is receiving a fair amount for the services rendered.

Do what is comfortable for you. If you can't afford to pay for Reiki at certain locations, find a practitioner, Reiki circle, or teacher that you can work with.

You Should Not Charge for Reiki

Truth: You must earn a living somehow.

This statement is the opposite of the myth that says "You must pay for Reiki for it to benefit you." Clearly there is some confusion about money in the Reiki community!

Any statement that has a should carries a red flag. Who is "shoulding" you? A group of people within the larger Reiki community has a strong belief that spiritual healing and teachings be freely given. In my opinion, this belief stems from a deeper belief that money is evil.

Each Reiki practitioner or teacher must do what is right for him or her. Because the study and practice of Reiki (see Chapter 7) cost money, you may very well want to get reimbursed for your efforts. Don't forget that your time is also an expense.

The decision about whether to charge and how much you charge for your time performing or teaching Reiki is up to you. See Chapter 17 for more on the business of Reiki.

Each practitioner finds his own truth about money. Some healers treat a certain number of clients at their normal fees and then set a portion of that income or their time each week to treat or teach at a reduced cost or no cost for people with fewer financial resources.

There Is Only One Right Form or School of Reiki

Truth: Different forms or schools of Reiki can all provide healing and a link to Mikao Usui's original teachings.

Read about different Reiki branches or schools of Reiki and you could get a massive headache. So many branches and so many claims can lead to confusion when they all state that they are the original Reiki or most powerful Reiki. Any claim to be the only, the best, or the original form of Reiki is false. I think that even if Mikao Usui were alive today he would have many forms of teaching, all of which are valid!

Reiki has diverged since its discovery by Mikao Usui. All teachers who have passed on Reiki have in some way (some more and some less) put their stamp on the teachings. Teachers add a little here and remove a little there. Before you know it, Reiki is practiced differently by various groups. I cover the different branches of Reiki in Chapter 3.

Most Reiki organizations strive to include all branches of Reiki for a sense of cohesiveness for the future of Reiki.

Ultimately, the choice of which of the many schools of Reiki you work with as a client, student, or practitioner rests upon which types of Reiki are practiced in your geographic area. If you have a choice of different types of Reiki, I suggest speaking to and trying out different forms of Reiki and seeing which one fits. Like Cinderella's prince carrying the glass slipper, you can find the right match!

Reiki Is a Religion

Truth: Reiki is a spiritual energy system, not a religion.

Religion and spirituality are two different things. Organized *religions,* such as Christianity, Islam, Judaism, Hinduism, and Buddhism, each have a set of agreed-upon texts, prayers, and practices that individuals follow. Within any religion, *spirituality* flourishes by the group prayer, meditation, and connection with a higher source.

Spirituality can also exist without an organized or formal religion. For example, you may feel most spiritual in a forest or on a beach, which is not bound to any particular religion.

Although Reiki is influenced by its origins in Japan and the religions of Japan, Buddhism and Shintoism, Reiki itself is not a religion.

Reiki can be practiced and received by people of any religion.

You Know How Reiki Will Heal You

Truth: Healing takes many forms.

When going for healing, people have both reasonable and unreasonable expectations. In the West, most people want a quick fix; they want to go to a Reiki practitioner and walk out cured after one session. But it is unreasonable to expect all your problems to disappear forever after one Reiki session! A more reasonable approach is to be open to the experience and let go of your expectations. It is also reasonable to expect to feel better from Reiki, to feel relaxed, and to want to experience that relaxing feeling again. If you adopt that attitude, you're more likely to be impressed with the results.

Do clients heal in one session? Most likely not. Every situation is unique, and some individuals may experience a miraculous change right away. Most folks experience healing like the peeling of an onion. When one layer is peeled, the next layer is revealed. Reiki allows you to uncover the layers to be healed.

If you're uncomfortable after a Reiki session or with a particular healer, you may want to speak with the Reiki practitioner or try someone else next time. You deserve to find a practitioner with whom you are comfortable (see Chapter 5).

Reiki Can Cure Anything

Truth: Reiki can help almost anything, but it doesn't necessarily lead to a cure.

What is meant by the word *cure*? Generally, *cure* means to restore health or remove a disease. A cure can be temporary, as in the transient removal of pain, or it can be permanent, as in the disappearance of a tumor. Can I guarantee that Reiki will remove your tumor? Absolutely not! (See the next section, "Reiki Can Be Used Instead of Medicine.")

Reiki, however, may offer healing properties that contribute to a cure. Reiki helps you to heal by relaxing you, allowing your own internal healing system to function. Stories abound about the wonders of Reiki helping people overcome every type of ailment. Yet there is no guarantee that a treatment that "cures" one person will also "cure" another.

Healers know that healing doesn't necessarily mean restoring health or feeling better. In some cases, people get sicker before they get well. In other cases, healing means the death of the patient who is in the late or end stages of illness.

All humans are going to die. In Reiki circles, death is considered to be a transition to the "other side."

If Reiki were a cure-all, then people who practice Reiki would never die! Consider that Mikao Usui, the founder of Reiki, died at age 62 of a stroke. In fact, Reiki can be used to help people who are in end-of-life situations (see Chapter 16) by providing soothing relaxation.

Reiki Can Be Used Instead of Medicine

Truth: Reiki should be used alongside medicine.

Reiki is considered to be a complementary treatment. If you have a serious illness, Reiki plus medical treatment provides the best of both worlds — which you deserve. If you rely on Reiki alone, you might lose valuable time when you could be saving your life with conventional treatment. With medical treatment alone, you might lose the added benefit of Reiki to boost the power of your medicines and your internal healing system.

I personally believe in respecting the integrity of the person who is ill. If someone doesn't want to use conventional medicine, I wouldn't force the person to do so. However, as a Reiki practitioner, I must be honest about what Reiki can and can't do.

If you postpone life-saving conventional medical treatment while pursuing the possibility of a cure through Reiki, you might contribute to a person's death. Always advise a Reiki client to seek and follow medical diagnosis and treatment.

In Chapter 16 I describe different ways of using Reiki along with medical care. Here are ways to use Reiki alongside medicine:

- ✔ Have Reiki sessions before and after surgery or medical procedures.
- ✔ Use Reiki on your medicine before you take it (see Chapter 18).
- ✔ Send distant Reiki to a relative or friend or even yourself for the time of surgery (see Chapter 15).
- ✔ Send Reiki to your healthcare practitioners so they're in the best frame of mind to help you.

Be open to healing in whatever way you can!

Chapter 21

Ten Non-traditional Reiki Symbols

In This Chapter

▶ Tibetan Reiki symbols

▶ Karuna Reiki symbols

▶ A new Reiki symbol

*L*ike most people, you are probably curious about what the different Reiki symbols look like. In this chapter, I present the images of ten additional symbols that do not directly derive from Mikao Usui's teachings. Feast your eyes on these representations, some of which may be familiar to you from other sources. If you want to delve further into their use, find a Reiki teacher who can initiate (give attunements) to these symbols.

Anyone can imagine or channel a symbol. A symbol may appear to you during meditation, while getting an attunement (see Chapter 7), or while giving or getting a Reiki session.

Check out Chapter 8 for information about the traditional Reiki symbols. Mikao Usui designated four traditional different symbols: Cho Ku Rei (Power symbol), Sei Hei Ki (Emotional symbol), Hon Sha Ze Sho Nen (Distance symbol), and Dai Ko Myo (Master symbol). Some of these symbols listed in this chapter are taught alongside traditional Usui Reiki training in some Reiki branches. Other symbols are taught in one of the non-Usui Reiki branches (see the appendix).

Double Cho Ku Rei

The symbols with spirals, like the Cho Ku Rei, can be drawn in two directions. The Cho Ku Rei is sometimes used in the original counter-clockwise position alongside the Cho Ku Rei in the reverse position or clockwise (Figure 21-1). You may want to experiment with reversed non-traditional Dai Ko Myo as well.

The double Cho Ku Rei is called Kriya in Karuna Reiki (a non-Usui branch of Reiki; see the appendix). This symbol brings "thought into form" and is frequently used for manifesting. You can draw or imagine the double Cho Ku Rei on top of the goals you want to manifest. This is a strong energy that, like the single Cho Ku Rei, is connected to the earth.

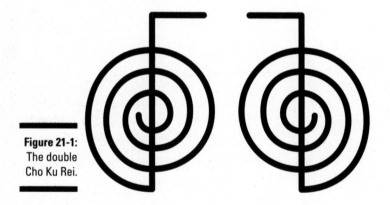

Figure 21-1:
The double
Cho Ku Rei.

Tibetan Dai Ko Myo

Here are two different versions of Dai Ko Myo (see Figure 21-2) that are called Tibetan or non-traditional Dai Ko Myo. Another name for these symbols is Dumo. I was initiated into each of these versions by different teachers, so I provide them here. The Usui Dai Ko Myo (see Chapter 8) is the original and traditional symbol. I find I like these symbols more than the traditional Dai Ko Myo.

Use these symbols in exactly the same way you would use the Usui Dai Ko Myo: during a Reiki treatment or during meditation. In some schools of Reiki, these symbols are used alongside or rather than the Usui Dai Ko Myo, which you find out about in Chapter 8.

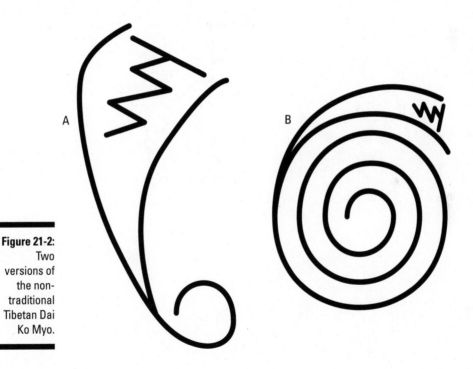

Figure 21-2:
Two versions of the non-traditional Tibetan Dai Ko Myo.

Tibetan Fire Serpent

Some Reiki branches use the Tibetan Fire Serpent (see Figure 21-3) before the attunement process and before a healing session. The snakelike coils represent the Kundalini energy, which is visualized as coiled energy at the base of the spine that surges upward through the body as the coils unwind. The surging energy of the Fire Serpent cleanses and joins the chakras. (See Chapter 2 for more about chakras.)

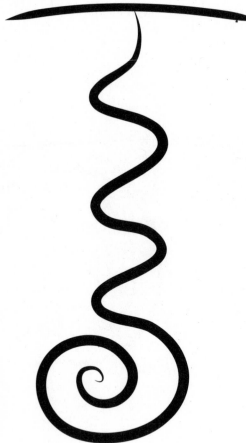

Figure 21-3:
The Tibetan
Fire
Serpent.

Raku

Certain Reiki branches use Raku, a Tibetan symbol (see Figure 21-4), to close the connection between teacher and student after attunements. Some people use it at the end of a session to close the energy between practitioner and healer. Similar to the lightning stroke used in Jakikiri Joka Ho (see Chapter 12), it focuses and grounds (brings into the earth) energy. This symbol is also incorporated into the Tibetan Dai Ko Myo (Tibetan Master symbol) and in an elongated form in the Tibetan Fire Serpent.

Figure 21-4:
Raku.

Zonar

The Zonar symbol (see Figure 21-5) is the letter Z along with an infinity symbol that is drawn three times. This symbol is thought to work across time and space, similarly to the Hon Sha Ze Sho Nen (see Chapter 8). Zonar means infinity or eternity and can be used to heal issues and traumas from the past.

Zonar, Halu, and Harth are the first three symbols used in non-Usui Reiki branches: Karuna Reiki, Karuna-Ki Reiki, and Tera Mai Reiki. See the appendix for references on these branches.

Figure 21-5:
Zonar.

Harth

This symbol combines a pyramid and a cross (see Figure 21-6). Harth is the symbol for the heart and represents infinite love and compassion and means love, truth, beauty, harmony, and balance. This symbol can be used to heal relationships and addictions.

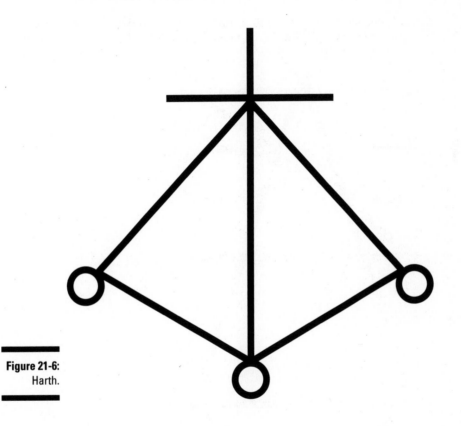

Figure 21-6:
Harth.

Halu

The Halu *(hay-loo)* symbol (see Figure 21-7), an amplification of Zonar, has a Z and infinity sign embedded within it and also has a pyramid added to the top. Similar to the Usui symbol Sei Hei Ki, Halu is used for balance and love. Halu brings about deep healing and dissolves negativity.

Figure 21-7:
Halu.

Antakharana

Various branches of Reiki use the Antakharana symbol (see Figure 21-8) as a tool for meditation and healing. The symbol has a three-dimensional aspect and was used in Chinese and Tibetan meditation practices.

There are several variations of the Antakharana symbol. If you stare at the symbol, you can see that three 7s are attached. I do not personally use this symbol, but it is supposed to work with the aura and to connect to the higher self. You can paste a copy of the symbol under a massage table or on your wall to enhance the effects of Reiki.

Figure 21-8:
Antakharana.

Om

Om is a Sanskrit symbol (see Figure 21-9) used in different Eastern spiritual practices, including yoga. Om represents the sound of the universe and is frequently chanted. It sounds like *"ah-oh-mm"* or *"aum."* Some Reiki branches, including Karuna Reiki, use this symbol. Listening to or chanting the sound "om" helps to connect spiritually. One of my Reiki masters played om chanting music during the attunement process, and I've listened to an om chanting tape during some of the writing of this book.

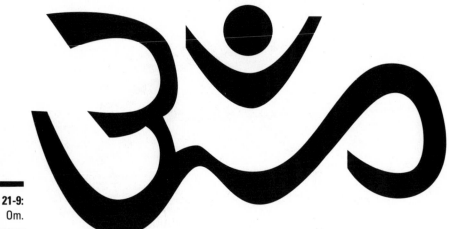

Figure 21-9:
Om.

Shoshana

To inspire you to be open to your intuition, I present here a symbol (see Figure 21-10) that I received intuitively one day while walking at the beach. I drew it in the sand with my fingers. Although this symbol came to me without an initial name, I sense that the name "Shoshana" fits it because it has "Sh" sounding curves at its beginning and end. I sense movement in this symbol: a spinning of the middle bar to anchor it or a twirling of the "S" shapes round and round. I have used Shoshana, which removes energy blocks in the body, for myself and others. The word "Shoshana" means lily or flower in Hebrew.

Figure 21-10:
Shoshana.

Appendix

Great Reiki Resources

M aybe you need to find a Reiki practitioner. Or perhaps you're eager to get initiated so you can start using Reiki yourself. Use this chapter to help you in your search for a Reiki practitioner or a Reiki teacher and to find more information about all things Reiki. Please note that while this list isn't absolutely comprehensive, it will absolutely get you what you need or point you in the right direction. If I did provide every Reiki resource, then this book would overflow!

No one school or type of Reiki is the official or sole Reiki resource.

One of the difficulties in listing Web addresses is that they tend to change frequently, so if you have a problem with any Web site provided here, try going to the home page for any Web site and search for the pages you want from there. Or perform a search on your Web browser (for example, Yahoo! or Google) to find the most recent Web site.

International Association of Reiki Professionals (IARP) Codes of Ethics

When preparing to teach others or practice Reiki on others, before you do anything else, you need to consider their views and take them to heart. That's why codes of ethics are listed first in this appendix. Several codes exist, but the IARP ethics codes for both practitioners and teachers are particularly useful and complete. To join the IARP or find out more about them, go to www.iarp.org or check out the contact information elsewhere in this appendix.

IARP Code of Ethics for Reiki Practitioners:

1. Abide by a vow of confidentiality. Any information that is discussed within the context of a Reiki session is confidential between the client and the Practitioner.

2. Provide a safe and comfortable area for client sessions and work to provide an empowering and supportive environment for clients.

3. Always treat clients with the utmost respect and honor.

4. Provide a brief oral or written description of what happens during a session and what to expect before a client's initial session.

5. Be respectful of all other's Reiki views and paths.

6. Educate clients on the value of Reiki and explain that sessions do not guarantee a cure, nor are they a substitute for qualified medical or professional care. Reiki is one part of an integrated healing or wellness program.

7. Suggest a consultation or referral to qualified licensed professionals (medical doctor, social worker, licensed therapist, and so on) when appropriate.

8. Never diagnose or prescribe. Never suggest that the client change prescribed treatment or interfere with treatment of a licensed healthcare provider.

9. Never ask clients to disrobe (unless in the context of a licensed massage therapy session). Be sensitive to the boundary needs of individual clients. Do not touch the genital area or breasts. Practice hands-off healing of these areas if treatment is needed.

10. Be actively working on your own healing so as to embody and fully express the essence of Reiki in everything that you do.

IARP Code of Ethics for Reiki Teachers:

1. Provide a comfortable area for classes and work to provide an empowering and supportive environment for students.

2. Always treat your students with the utmost respect and honor. It is an honor and a privilege to share Reiki with them.

3. Provide a clear written description of subjects to be taught during each level of Reiki prior to class and list what the student will be able to do after taking the class.

4. Be willing to discuss the proportion of time spent on each subject in class and the amount of practice time available.

5. Be respectful of all other's Reiki views and paths.

6. Be working to create harmony and friendly cooperation between Reiki Practitioners and Masters in the community.

7. Act as a beacon within Reiki and in your community by doing the best job possible.

8. Work to empower your students to heal themselves and to encourage and assist them in the development of their work with Reiki or their Reiki practices.

9. Be sensitive to the boundary needs of individual students.

10. Be actively working on your own healing so as to embody and fully express the essence of Reiki in everything that you do.

Reiki Organizations

Many countries now have their own Reiki organizations. In theory, these organizations welcome and support all Reiki branches and are thus nondenominational. They are set up to support Reiki practitioners overall or in certain locations. Due to the "maverick" nature of Reiki, not all Reiki practitioners join these organizations. Use these as a starting point to find accurate information about Reiki where you live. Also check out the later section on "Reiki Branches."

Australia

Australian Reiki Connection: P.O. Box 145, Kalorama, Australia, VIC3766; phone 1-300-130-975; Web site www.australianReikiconnection.com.au/

Canada

Canadian Reiki Association: P.O. Box 74072, Hillcrest RPO, Vancouver, BC, Canada V5V 5C8; phone 1-800-835-7525; Web site www.reiki.ca/

Italy

Centro Internazionale Reiki: Via Lonate 6, 20029, Turbigo (MI); phone +39.0331.891111; Web site www.reiki.it/

New Zealand

Reiki New Zealand Incorporated: P.O. Box 39-416, Howick, Auckland, New Zealand; Web site www.reiki.org.nz/

South Africa

The Reiki Association of Southern Africa: P.O. Box 44207, Linden, 2104, Gauteng, South Africa; Web site www.reikiassociation.co.za/

United Kingdom

The UK Reiki Federation: P.O. Box 1785, Andover, SP11 OWB UK; phone 01264 773774; Web site www.reikifed.co.uk/

United States

The International Association of Reiki Professionals: P.O. Box 6181, Nashua, NH 03063-6182, USA; phone 603-881-8838; Web site www.iarp.org. This is an international organization located in the United States.

Reiki Magazines

When you want up-to-date reading material about Reiki and to connect with other Reiki practitioners around the world, check out these magazines.

- ✔ **Reiki Magazine International:** This 48-page, full-color magazine is published six times a year in English, Dutch, and Italian, and it has a German affiliate also. Reiki Magazine International supports Usui Reiki practitioners and students. Contact: Publishers, Sumatrakade 747.1019 PX Amsterdam, The Netherlands; phone 31-20-419-3755; Web site www.reikimagazine.com/

- ✔ **Reiki News Magazine:** This color magazine is published in English four times a year by Vision Publications and The International Center for Reiki Training (ICRT). It honors all Reiki schools and lineages and provides information about ICRT products and classes. Contact: Vision Publications, 21421 Hilltop St., #28, Southfield, MI 48034; phone 248-948-8112; Web site www.reiki.org/ReikiNewsSubscription/ReikiNewsHomepage.html

Reiki Branches

Reiki in the form that we know it originated with Mikao Usui. After that, each Reiki Master either tried to follow his understanding of Usui Reiki or designed his own version. See the information on Reiki branches in Chapter 3 to give you an idea how these different branches link back to Mikao Usui. Here, I provide you with Web sites for various Reiki branches. Use this list to research different branches, find out more about any particular teacher you are considering (if you know her Reiki branch), and find lists of teachers, in some cases.

Japanese Usui Reiki branches

Here are the major branches of Reiki in Japan that I am aware of and Web site information for them if available. The lineage for each branch starts with Mikao Usui and continues to the current founder or teacher of that branch.

- **Gendai Reiki Ho.** Lineage: Mikao Usui, Kanichi Taketomi, Kimiko Koyama, Hiroshi Doi. Founder: Hiroshi Doi. Web site `www.geocities.jp/g_reiki` or `www.gendai.net` (both in Japanese)

- **Jikiden Reiki.** Lineage: Mikao Usui, Chujiro Hayashi, Chiyoko Yamaguchi, Tadao Yamaguchi. Founders: Chiyoko Yamaguchi and Tadao Yamaguchi. Web site `http://jikidenreiki.org/`

- **Komyo Reiki Kai.** Lineage: Mikao Usui, Chujiro Hayashi, Chiyoko Yamaguchi, Hyakuten Inamoto. Founder: Hyakuten Inamoto. Web site `www.h4.dion.ne.jp/~Reiki` (in Japanese)

- **Usui Reiki Ryoho Gakkai.** Lineage: Mikao Usui, Juzaburo Ushida, Kanichi Taketomi, Yoshiharu Watanabe, Toyoichi Wanami, Kimiko Koyama, Masataki Kondo. Founder: Mikao Usui. This organization seeks to preserve Mikao Usui's teachings, but unfortunately is restrictive in terms of both its membership and the information it gives out.

- **Usui Reiki Ryoho.** Lineage: Mikao Usui, Kanichi Taketomi, Kimiko Koyama, Hiroshi Doi. Founder: Hiroshi Doi. See the Gendai Reiki Ho info earlier in this list.

Japanese-style Usui Reiki

The following two branches were taught by Japanese Reiki practitioners to Western students, who are the founders of these branches:

✔ **Usui-Teate.** Lineage: Mikao Usui, Suzuki san, Chris Marsh. Founder: Chris Marsh. Also called "Method to Achieve Personal Perfection." Web site www.usuireiki.fsnet.co.uk

✔ **Usui-Do.** Lineage: Mikao Usui, Toshishiro Eguchi, Yuji Onuki, Dave King. Founders: Dave King and Melissa Riggall, who presented this system based on Eguchi's work. Web site www.usui-do.org

Western Usui Reiki branches

The main branches of Western Reiki all derive from Hawayo Takata:

✔ **The Radiance Technique (Authentic Reiki).** Lineage: Mikao Usui Chujiro Hayashi, Hawayo Takata, Barbara Weber Ray. Founder: Barbara Weber Ray, who claims that she is the sole successor to Hawayo Takata. Web site www.trtia.org

✔ **Usui Shiki Ryoho.** Lineage: Mikao Usui, Chujiro Hayashi, Hawayo Takata. The Reiki Alliance is a group that formed after Hawayo Takata died. Both the Reiki Alliance and Phyllis Lei Furamoto (who is Hawayo Takata's granddaughter) claim that Furamoto is the true successor to Hawayo Takata. Many independent Reiki Masters (including myself) have studied under this system but are not necessarily part of the Reiki Alliance.

✔ **Usui/Tibetan Reiki.** Lineage: Mikao Usui, Chujiro Hayashi, Hawayo Takata, Phyllis Lei Furumoto, Carrell Ann Farmer, Leah Smith, William Lee Rand. Founder: William Lee Rand (United States). This is my lineage for my Reiki Master training with one of William Rand's students, Kathie Lipinski. Web site www.reiki.org

Additional Reiki branches

In this section you find the Web sites for other branches of Reiki that do not list Mikao Usui as their founder, though the system is derived from Usui Reiki.

✔ **Alchemia Reiki:** www.dovestar.edu

✔ **Angelic RayKey:** www.liteweb.org/raykey/index.html

✔ **Karuna Reiki:** www.reiki.org/KarunaReiki/KarunaHomepage.html

✔ **Karuna-Ki Reiki:** Vincent Amador's original Web site is no longer available. You can still find Karuna Ki practitioners on the Web and can read about this system at http://web.archive.org/web/20040610214800/http://angelreiki.nu/karunaki/.

✔ **Lightarian Reiki:** www lightarian.com

✔ **Mahatma Reiki (Leonie Patrice):** www.mahatmareiki.com

✔ **New Life Reiki (Dr.V.Sukumaran, India):** www.newlifereiki.com

✔ **New Life Reiki Seichim (Margot Deepa Slater, Australia):** www.newlifeReikiseichim.com.au

✔ **Rainbow Reiki (Walter Lubeck):** www.rainbowreiki.net

✔ **Reiki Plus:** www.reikiplus.com

✔ **Seichem:** www.kathleenmilner.com

✔ **Sekhem (Helen Belot):** www.sekhem.org

✔ **Shamballa Multidimensional Healing/Reiki (John Armitage):** www.mahatma.co.uk/ (click Reiki headings)

✔ **SKHM (Patrick Zeigler):** www.skhm.org

✔ **Tera Mai Reiki:** www.kathleenmilner.com

✔ **Wei Chi Tibetan Reiki:** www.weichireiki.com/

Reiki Chat Forums and E-Mail Lists

You can use the Internet as a way to communicate with other folks interested in Reiki. I list a few Reiki chat sites and sources of e-mail groups to get you started.

✔ **www. reiki-4-all.com:** An extensive message board for topics related to Reiki.

✔ **www.reikione.com/msgctr:** A place to read and send messages that is moderated by Reiki teacher Teri A. Moore.

Also check out e-mail lists and groups sponsored by Yahoo, http://groups.yahoo.com/, and MSN, http://groups.msn.com/.

Reiki History and Usage Information

Reiki history has been revised as more information comes from Japan on Mikao Usui and the beginnings of Reiki. If you want to do more research on Reiki history and different Reiki techniques, I suggest you consult some of the following resources.

Books

You may find these books helpful:

- *The Original Reiki Handbook of Dr. Mikao Usui: The Traditional Usui Reiki Ryoho Treatment Positions and Numerous Reiki Techniques for Health and Well-Being* by Mikao Usui and Frank Arjava Petter. Lotus Press, 1999.
- *Reiki Fire* by Frank Arjava Petter. Lotus Press, 1997.
- *The Spirit of Reiki* by Walter Luebeck, Frank Arjeva Petter, and William Lee Rand. Lotus Press, 2001.
- *Hayashi Reiki Manual: Traditional Japanese Healing Techniques* by Frank Arjava Petter, Tadao Yamaguchi, and Chujiro Hayashi. Lotus Press, 2003.
- *Iyashino Gendai Reiki-Ho: Modern Reiki Method for Healing* by Hiroshi Doi. 2000. Fraser Journal Publishing, Canada, 2000.
- *The Reiki Sourcebook* by Bronwen and Frans Stiene. O Books, 2004.

Web sites

Here are some online resources that you may want to refer to:

- **All Energy Therapies Web:** www.aetw.org/. James Deacon, a Master-Level Reiki healer, maintains these pages.
- **Reiki: The New History:** www.usuireiki.fsnet.co.uk/. This is Reiki Master Andy Bowling's Web site.
- **Reiki Threshold:** http://threshold.ca/reiki/index.html. This is Reiki Master Richard Rivard's Web site.
- **Reiki Evolution:** www.Reiki-evolution.co.uk/index9.htm. Taggart King, international Reiki Master/teacher, is in charge of this site.
- **Reiki Ryoho Pages:** www.angelfire.com/az/SpiritMatters/. This is the Web site of Reiki Master Adonea (and Light).

Reiki and medicine

Research continues into the use of Reiki healing for different diseases. Check out these resources to find out the latest studies and their results.

- ✔ *Reiki Energy Medicine: Bringing Healing Touch into Home, Hospital, and Hospice* by Libby Barnett and Maggie Chambers with Susan Davidson. Healing Arts Press, Vermont, 1996. Note: This book has an outdated history of Reiki, but it provides other useful information on using Reiki alongside medicine.

- ✔ *Vibrational Medicine:The #1 Handbook of Subtle-Energy Therapies,* 3rd edition, by Richard Gerber. Bear & Company, Rochester, Vermont, 2001.

- ✔ *Energy Medicine: How to Use Your Body's Energies for Optimum Health and Vitality* by Donna Eden. Piatkus, 1998.

- ✔ *Energy Medicine: The Scientific Basis of Bioenergy Therapies* by James L. Oschman. Churchill Livingstone, 2000.

For online information, check out the Web site Medical Research on Reiki Therapy at www.reikimedresearch.com/.

Clinical trials, using Reiki

Visit www.clinicaltrials.gov and type "Reiki" in the search box. From the results, you can click a button to view information on trials thathave finished recruiting to see all past studies.

Alternative medicine

Check out these sites for more information about alternative therapies you can use in conjunction with Reiki:

- ✔ **National Foundation for Alternative Medicine:** www.nfam.org
- ✔ **National Center for Complementary and Alternative Medicine, National Institutes of Health:** http://nccam.nih.gov/

Energy medicine

If you want to know more about energy medicine, visit the Web site of the International Society for the Study of Subtle Energies and Energy Medicine (ISSSEEM) at www.issseem.org/.

Reiki Schools and Teachers

It would be impossible to list the thousands or even hundreds of thousands of individual Reiki teachers here. As a compromise, I list the most prominent teachers or authors who are either well known or have useful Web sites.

- **The Reiki Alliance:** www.reikialliance.com/. This is the Web site for an international community of Usui system Reiki Masters.

- **International Center for Reiki Training (ICRT):** www.reiki.org. Web site of William Rand, founder of Usui/Tibetan Reiki and Karuna Reiki, and author.

- **International House of Reiki:** www.reiki.net.au. Web site of Bronwen and Frans Steine, authors and Reiki teachers.

- **Reiki Dharma:** www.Reikidharma.com/en/. Web site of Frank Arjeva Petter, Reiki author and researcher.

- **Usui Shiki Ryoho:** www.usuireiki-ogm.com/. The Web site of Phyllis Furomoto and Paul Mitchell.

- **Reiki Center for the Healing Arts:** www.reikifranbrown.com/. Web site of Fran Brown, one of the 22 Reiki Masters trained by Hawayo Takata.

Other Related Information

These books can give you additional information on other topics presented in this book:

- *Crystal Power, Crystal Healing: The Complete Handbook* by Michael Gienger. Blandford, 1998.

- *The Crystal Bible: A Definitive Guide to Crystals* by Judy Hall. Godsfield Press, 2004.

- *Wheels of Life: A User's Guide to the Chakra System* (Llewellyn's New Age Series) by Anodea Judith. Llewelyn, 1987.

- *Anatomy of the Spirit: The Seven Stages of Power and Healing* by Caroline Myss. Three Rivers Press, 1997.

Glossary

Reiki terminology can be a bit confusing and even challenging, so to ease you through some of the more confusing words and terms, I've put together this glossary. Think of it as a sort of short and helpful dictionary to help you get a better handle on the Reiki terms, so you aren't left scratching your head in bewilderment.

Note: Any word printed in *italic and bold type* has its own definition in its own rightful alphabetical place in this glossary.

acupuncture: An ancient Chinese practice that stimulates tiny points of energy along the *meridians.*

Advanced Reiki Training (ART): Part of the third-degree Reiki training that is separated into a separate class by some Reiki branches. You learn the Master symbol, *Dai Ko Myo,* and techniques for healing, but not the methods for teaching.

Antakharana: A nontraditional *Reiki symbol* used by some branches of Reiki (especially Usui/Tibetan branches) as a tool for meditation and healing.

attunement: Initiation process that confers upon the recipient the ability to channel Reiki energy. Attunements are performed by a *Reiki Master* during Reiki training. After you receive a Reiki attunement, you have a lifelong connection to the Reiki energy. Further attunements enhance the levels of energy.

aura: A layer of energy fields around all living beings. The aura is an egg- or oval-shaped energy structure that can go out many feet from the body and be different colors, depending on the person and the situation. Some people can see the aura, and you develop the ability to sense the aura during the practice of Reiki.

beaming: The process of sending Reiki when you are in the same room but standing away from the recipient.

Byosen Reikan Ho: A Japanese technique for scanning the body with the hands to detect regions that are ill or in need of Reiki healing.

chakra: An Indian Sanskrit word that means spinning wheel of energy, vortex, or energy center. The energy centers that convert universal life force energy to a form easily used by the body are called chakras. There are seven main chakras that start at the root and move up to the crown.

channel: Someone who is able to let the Reiki energy flow through them. To channel Reiki, a practitioner takes in Reiki energy for the purpose of letting it emanate from her hands to the Reiki recipient. A channel is like a tube or conduit through which the Reiki energy flows.

channeling: The process of letting Reiki energy flow through you. While the energy passes through, you get to feel the flow of Reiki too.

chi: Chinese word for energy, sometimes spelled qi. This is the same as Japanese *ki.*

Cho Ku Rei: First Usui **Reiki symbol** that means power or focus.

complementary and alternative medicine (CAM): This term is applied to health therapies that can be used in addition to (complementary) or in lieu of (alternative) conventional medical techniques. Reiki is a complementary medicine because it works well alongside other medical treatments. Reiki is not a substitute for conventional medicine.

crown chakra: An energy center associated with the upper brain, pineal gland, and issues of spiritual connection. The crown chakra is the seventh chakra.

crystals: Objects from the earth that have an ordered formation and emit their own healing energy. Can be used alongside Reiki for healing purposes.

Dai Ko Myo: Fourth Usui *Reiki symbol* that means mastership or empowerment.

Double Cho Ku Rei: Nontraditional *Reiki symbol* that is also called Kriya. Two Cho Ku Reis (one in reverse orientation) face each other.

energy medicine: A branch of *complementary and alternative medicine* that treats or diagnoses the body with energy. Reiki is a type of energy medicine that treats the body with subtle energy.

first-degree Reiki: Initial Reiki training level that is also called Reiki I or Shoden. Reiki history, *hand positions,* and self-Reiki are taught in this class.

Gassho: (1) A Japanese hand position with palms facing each other and fingers pointed upward. This is also called the prayer position when the hands are placed in front of the chest. Holding your hands in this position can be used on its own as the basis for a meditation, as a focusing technique before or after a Reiki session, or to open or close other types of meditation. (2) When the hands are in prayer position touching and fingers facing upwards, this is the Gassho hand position. Gassho is also a form of meditation.

Gyosi Ho: A Japanese Reiki method of healing by staring with the eyes.

Halu: Nontraditional symbol used in non-Usui branches of Reiki.

hand positions: *Hawayo Takata* developed a set of standard hand positions that was probably based on *Chujiro Hayashi*'s original hand positions. By following these positions, you cover the entire body and the *meridians* with Reiki energy.

hara: Japanese word for belly or abdomen. Also called tanden.

Harth: Nontraditional symbol used in non-Usui branches of Reiki.

Hatsurei Ho: Japanese Reiki technique that combines *Kenyoku Ho, Joshin Kokyu Ho,* and Seishin Toitsu.

Hayashi, Chujiro: One of *Mikao Usui*'s original students, Hayashi was born in 1880, became a medical doctor, and developed a medical approach to Reiki treatments. He trained *Hawayo Takata,* who brought Reiki to the West.

heart chakra: The fourth *chakra* is associated with the circulatory system, thymus gland, and issues of love and compassion.

Hon Sha Ze Sho Nen: Third Usui *Reiki symbol* that means distance (healing at a distance) or connection.

Hui Yin contraction: An advanced Reiki process in which you hold the energy in a circuit within the body by squeezing the muscles between the genitals and rectum and putting the tongue behind the teeth on the roof of the mouth. Also called the microcosmic orbit.

intention: The goal or hidden purpose behind a thought or action. This is the most important aspect behind giving a *Reiki session.*

intuition: An insight or gut feeling that you know is right. Information that comes from an inner knowing or inspiration.

Jakikiri Joka Ho: A Japanese Reiki method to cleanse inanimate objects, including crystals.

Japanese Reiki: The practice of Reiki in Japan passed through *Mikao Usui*'s Japanese students.

Joshin Kokyu Ho: Japanese breathing meditation that helps focus energy.

Kanji: Chinese characters also used in Japanese language.

Kenyoku Ho: Japanese Reiki technique of dry bathing to purify oneself before or after performing Reiki.

ki: Japanese word for energy, or *chi* in Chinese.

Kirlian photography: A special type of photographic processing that lets you visualize the aura.

Koki Ho: A Japanese Reiki method of healing with the breath.

lineage: The line of teachers going backward to the founder of a *Reiki branch. Mikao Usui* is the founder of Usui Reiki.

mantra: Repetition of sacred words. The names of the *Reiki symbols* can also be considered a mantra and thus chanted to bring forth Reiki energy.

meridian: The set of interconnecting energy pathways that run through the body. Meridians are associated with different organ systems and are also called acupuncture points or acupressure points.

Mount Kurama: Place where *Mikao Usui* spent a 21-day fast and meditation and reached enlightenment and received inspiration about Reiki. The Buddhist Kurama Temple is located on this mountain near Kyoto, Japan.

Nentatsu Ho: Japanese Reiki method for changing habits. Also called the deprogramming technique and used to empower affirmations. Similar to *Seiheki Chiryo Ho.*

Okuden: Japanese Reiki level that corresponds with 2nd-degree Reiki.

om: A Sanskrit symbol used for chanting the "sounds of the universe" that is also used in nontraditional branches of Reiki.

practitioner: Someone who has studied at least the 1st degree of Reiki and has had some training in the ethics of working with others.

Raku: Nontraditional *Reiki symbol* used in the attunement process.

Reiji Ho: A technique to use *Gassho* and intuitively place the hands during a Reiki session.

Reiki: In Japanese, the word Reiki means universal life-force energy. Pronounced *ray-key,* the term Reiki refers to both the energy itself and a system of energy healing developed by *Mikao Usui.*

Reiki branch: A school of Reiki that derives from the original healing system of *Mikao Usui.*

Reiki circle: A group of people coming together to experience the healing power of Reiki. A Reiki circle is usually open to the public and is sometimes called a *Reiki share.* At some point, participants get into a circle for meditation or healing.

Reiki Master: Someone who has studied the first three levels of Reiki training, including the Master's level, or third level, of training. The most important feature of being a Reiki Master is mastering the spiritual growth of oneself.

Reiki Master Teacher: A *Reiki Master* who has training in teaching Reiki and giving *attunements.*

Reiki Principles: Precepts or ideals set forth by *Mikao Usui* that start with the edict "just for today." These principles are guidelines to healthy living and are the basis of meditative practice.

Reiki session: The period of time when a recipient receives Reiki energy that is channeled through a Reiki practitioner. The Reiki session might also be called a Reiki treatment. Each session is unique and involves the placing of the practitioner's hands on or above the body for the purpose of applying Reiki energy.

Reiki share: A group of Reiki practitioners get together to exchange Reiki and information among themselves in a Reiki share, or Reiki exchange. This is also sometimes called a *Reiki circle.*

Reiki symbol: A visual image alongside a spoken name that are used to both elicit Reiki and enhance the channeling of Reiki energy. The image may be a pictogram or a set of Japanese words. There are four traditional Reiki symbols: *Cho Ku Rei, Sei Hei Ki, Hon Sha Ze Sho Nen,* and *Dai Ko Myo.*

root chakra: An energy center associated with excretory systems, spine, adrenal glands, and issues of survival and grounding. The root chakra is the first chakra.

sacral chakra: An energy center associated with the reproductive system, testes and ovaries, and issues of sexuality and creativity. It's also known as the second chakra.

second-degree Reiki: The level of training after 1st degree that is also called Reiki II or **Okuden.** The first three **Reiki symbols** are taught, as are methods for distance healing.

Sei Hei Ki: Second Usui **Reiki symbol** that works at the mental and emotional levels, and also helps with harmony and balance.

Seiheki Chiryo Ho: Japanese Reiki method of changing habits similar to **Nentatsu Ho** except that the Reiki symbols are also used in this method.

self-Reiki: The practice of giving a Reiki treatment to yourself. There are a set of **hand positions** to follow for self-Reiki.

Shinpiden: Japanese Reiki level that corresponds with 3rd-degree or Master/Teacher level.

Shoden: Japanese Reiki level that corresponds with 1st-degree Reiki.

solar plexus chakra: This is the third chakra, associated with the digestive system, the pancreas, and issues of personal power.

subtle energy: Energy systems within and around the body consisting of layers, **chakras,** and **meridians.**

Takata, Hawayo: Born in Hawaii in 1900 to Japanese parents, Takata learned Reiki from **Chujiro Hayashi** and then passed Reiki to 22 **Reiki Masters** in the West. In this way, Reiki spread throughout the world.

third-degree Reiki: A level of Reiki training that's also called Reiki III or Shinpiden. This training involves learning the fourth master's symbol and how to teach Reiki and give **attunements**. Many branches separate the 3rd degree into two levels, Reiki IIIa and IIIb or Advanced Reiki Training and Master Teacher Training.

third-eye chakra: This is the sixth chakra, associated with the lower brain, nervous system, ears, nose, eyes, pituitary gland, and issues about vision or seeing.

throat chakra: This is the fifth chakra, associated with the lungs and vocal apparatus, thyroid and parathyroid glands, and issues of communication.

Tibetan Dai Ko Myo: Nontraditional versions of the master symbol, *Dai Ko Myo.*

Tibetan Fire Serpent: Nontraditional symbol used in the ***attunement*** and healing process.

Usui, Mikao: The founder of Reiki. Born in Japan in 1865 to a Tendai Buddhist family. He developed the system of Reiki energy healing after meditating on ***Mount Kurama*** in Japan and receiving divine inspiration.

Western Reiki: Reiki branches that derived from ***Hawayo Takata*** in Hawaii.

Zonar: Nontraditional symbol used in non-Usui branches of Reiki.

Index

Notes

Notes

BUSINESS, CAREERS & PERSONAL FINANCE

0-7645-5307-0

0-7645-5331-3 *†

Also available:
- Accounting For Dummies †
  0-7645-5314-3
- Business Plans Kit For Dummies †
  0-7645-5365-8
- Cover Letters For Dummies
  0-7645-5224-4
- Frugal Living For Dummies
  0-7645-5403-4
- Leadership For Dummies
  0-7645-5176-0
- Managing For Dummies
  0-7645-1771-6

- Marketing For Dummies
  0-7645-5600-2
- Personal Finance For Dummies *
  0-7645-2590-5
- Project Management For Dummies
  0-7645-5283-X
- Resumes For Dummies †
  0-7645-5471-9
- Selling For Dummies
  0-7645-5363-1
- Small Business Kit For Dummies *†
  0-7645-5093-4

HOME & BUSINESS COMPUTER BASICS

0-7645-4074-2

0-7645-3758-X

Also available:
- ACT! 6 For Dummies
  0-7645-2645-6
- iLife '04 All-in-One Desk Reference
  For Dummies
  0-7645-7347-0
- iPAQ For Dummies
  0-7645-6769-1
- Mac OS X Panther Timesaving
  Techniques For Dummies
  0-7645-5812-9
- Macs For Dummies
  0-7645-5656-8

- Microsoft Money 2004 For Dummies
  0-7645-4195-1
- Office 2003 All-in-One Desk Reference
  For Dummies
  0-7645-3883-7
- Outlook 2003 For Dummies
  0-7645-3759-8
- PCs For Dummies
  0-7645-4074-2
- TiVo For Dummies
  0-7645-6923-6
- Upgrading and Fixing PCs For Dummies
  0-7645-1665-5
- Windows XP Timesaving Techniques
  For Dummies
  0-7645-3748-2

FOOD, HOME, GARDEN, HOBBIES, MUSIC & PETS

0-7645-5295-3

0-7645-5232-5

Also available:
- Bass Guitar For Dummies
  0-7645-2487-9
- Diabetes Cookbook For Dummies
  0-7645-5230-9
- Gardening For Dummies *
  0-7645-5130-2
- Guitar For Dummies
  0-7645-5106-X
- Holiday Decorating For Dummies
  0-7645-2570-0
- Home Improvement All-in-One
  For Dummies
  0-7645-5680-0

- Knitting For Dummies
  0-7645-5395-X
- Piano For Dummies
  0-7645-5105-1
- Puppies For Dummies
  0-7645-5255-4
- Scrapbooking For Dummies
  0-7645-7208-3
- Senior Dogs For Dummies
  0-7645-5818-8
- Singing For Dummies
  0-7645-2475-5
- 30-Minute Meals For Dummies
  0-7645-2589-1

INTERNET & DIGITAL MEDIA

0-7645-1664-7

0-7645-6924-4

Also available:
- 2005 Online Shopping Directory
  For Dummies
  0-7645-7495-7
- CD & DVD Recording For Dummies
  0-7645-5956-7
- eBay For Dummies
  0-7645-5654-1
- Fighting Spam For Dummies
  0-7645-5965-6
- Genealogy Online For Dummies
  0-7645-5964-8
- Google For Dummies
  0-7645-4420-9

- Home Recording For Musicians
  For Dummies
  0-7645-1634-5
- The Internet For Dummies
  0-7645-4173-0
- iPod & iTunes For Dummies
  0-7645-7772-7
- Preventing Identity Theft For Dummies
  0-7645-7336-5
- Pro Tools All-in-One Desk Reference
  For Dummies
  0-7645-5714-9
- Roxio Easy Media Creator For Dummies
  0-7645-7131-1

* Separate Canadian edition also available
† Separate U.K. edition also available

Available wherever books are sold. For more information or to order direct: U.S. customers visit www.dummies.com or call 1-877-762-2974.
U.K. customers visit www.wileyeurope.com or call 0800 243407. Canadian customers visit www.wiley.ca or call 1-800-567-4797.

WILEY

SPORTS, FITNESS, PARENTING, RELIGION & SPIRITUALITY

0-7645-5146-9   0-7645-5418-2

Also available:
- Adoption For Dummies
  0-7645-5488-3
- Basketball For Dummies
  0-7645-5248-1
- The Bible For Dummies
  0-7645-5296-1
- Buddhism For Dummies
  0-7645-5359-3
- Catholicism For Dummies
  0-7645-5391-7
- Hockey For Dummies
  0-7645-5228-7

- Judaism For Dummies
  0-7645-5299-6
- Martial Arts For Dummies
  0-7645-5358-5
- Pilates For Dummies
  0-7645-5397-6
- Religion For Dummies
  0-7645-5264-3
- Teaching Kids to Read For Dummies
  0-7645-4043-2
- Weight Training For Dummies
  0-7645-5168-X
- Yoga For Dummies
  0-7645-5117-5

TRAVEL

0-7645-5438-7   0-7645-5453-0

Also available:
- Alaska For Dummies
  0-7645-1761-9
- Arizona For Dummies
  0-7645-6938-4
- Cancún and the Yucatán For Dummies
  0-7645-2437-2
- Cruise Vacations For Dummies
  0-7645-6941-4
- Europe For Dummies
  0-7645-5456-5
- Ireland For Dummies
  0-7645-5455-7

- Las Vegas For Dummies
  0-7645-5448-4
- London For Dummies
  0-7645-4277-X
- New York City For Dummies
  0-7645-6945-7
- Paris For Dummies
  0-7645-5494-8
- RV Vacations For Dummies
  0-7645-5443-3
- Walt Disney World & Orlando For Dummies
  0-7645-6943-0

GRAPHICS, DESIGN & WEB DEVELOPMENT

0-7645-4345-8   0-7645-5589-8

Also available:
- Adobe Acrobat 6 PDF For Dummies
  0-7645-3760-1
- Building a Web Site For Dummies
  0-7645-7144-3
- Dreamweaver MX 2004 For Dummies
  0-7645-4342-3
- FrontPage 2003 For Dummies
  0-7645-3882-9
- HTML 4 For Dummies
  0-7645-1995-6
- Illustrator CS For Dummies
  0-7645-4084-X

- Macromedia Flash MX 2004 For Dummies
  0-7645-4358-X
- Photoshop 7 All-in-One Desk Reference For Dummies
  0-7645-1667-1
- Photoshop CS Timesaving Techniques For Dummies
  0-7645-6782-9
- PHP 5 For Dummies
  0-7645-4166-8
- PowerPoint 2003 For Dummies
  0-7645-3908-6
- QuarkXPress 6 For Dummies
  0-7645-2593-X

NETWORKING, SECURITY, PROGRAMMING & DATABASES

0-7645-6852-3   0-7645-5784-X

Also available:
- A+ Certification For Dummies
  0-7645-4187-0
- Access 2003 All-in-One Desk Reference For Dummies
  0-7645-3988-4
- Beginning Programming For Dummies
  0-7645-4997-9
- C For Dummies
  0-7645-7068-4
- Firewalls For Dummies
  0-7645-4048-3
- Home Networking For Dummies
  0-7645-42796

- Network Security For Dummies
  0-7645-1679-5
- Networking For Dummies
  0-7645-1677-9
- TCP/IP For Dummies
  0-7645-1760-0
- VBA For Dummies
  0-7645-3989-2
- Wireless All In-One Desk Reference For Dummies
  0-7645-7496-5
- Wireless Home Networking For Dummies
  0-7645-3910-8

HEALTH & SELF-HELP

0-7645-6820-5 *†   0-7645-2566-2

Also available:
- Alzheimer's For Dummies
  0-7645-3899-3
- Asthma For Dummies
  0-7645-4233-8
- Controlling Cholesterol For Dummies
  0-7645-5440-9
- Depression For Dummies
  0-7645-3900-0
- Dieting For Dummies
  0-7645-4149-8
- Fertility For Dummies
  0-7645-2549-2

- Fibromyalgia For Dummies
  0-7645-5441-7
- Improving Your Memory For Dummies
  0-7645-5435-2
- Pregnancy For Dummies †
  0-7645-4483-7
- Quitting Smoking For Dummies
  0-7645-2629-4
- Relationships For Dummies
  0-7645-5384-4
- Thyroid For Dummies
  0-7645-5385-2

EDUCATION, HISTORY, REFERENCE & TEST PREPARATION

0-7645-5194-9   0-7645-4186-2

Also available:
- Algebra For Dummies
  0-7645-5325-9
- British History For Dummies
  0-7645-7021-8
- Calculus For Dummies
  0-7645-2498-4
- English Grammar For Dummies
  0-7645-5322-4
- Forensics For Dummies
  0-7645-5580-4
- The GMAT For Dummies
  0-7645-5251-1
- Inglés Para Dummies
  0-7645-5427-1

- Italian For Dummies
  0-7645-5196-5
- Latin For Dummies
  0-7645-5431-X
- Lewis & Clark For Dummies
  0-7645-2545-X
- Research Papers For Dummies
  0-7645-5426-3
- The SAT I For Dummies
  0-7645-7193-1
- Science Fair Projects For Dummies
  0-7645-5460-3
- U.S. History For Dummies
  0-7645-5249-X

Get smart @ dummies.com®

- **Find a full list of Dummies titles**
- **Look into loads of FREE on-site articles**
- **Sign up for FREE eTips e-mailed to you weekly**
- **See what other products carry the Dummies name**
- **Shop directly from the Dummies bookstore**
- **Enter to win new prizes every month!**

* Separate Canadian edition also available
† Separate U.K. edition also available